A GUIDE TO THE CHURCH OF ENGLAND

Also available from Mowbray / Continuum:

Handbook for Churchwardens, revised edition, Timothy Briden, ISBN 978 08264 8153 5

An ABC for the PCC, 5th edition, John Pitchford, ISBN 978 19062 8607 1

A Guide to the Church of England

Martin Davie

Published by Mowbray, a Continuum imprint

The Tower Building   80 Maiden Lane
11 York Road   Suite 704
London   New York
SE1 7NX   NY 10038

www.continuumbooks.com

First published 2008

British Library Cataloguing-in-Publication Data
A catalogue record for this book is available from the British Library.

ISBN 978 19062 8613 2

Typeset by YHT Ltd, London
Printed and bound by MPG Books Ltd, Bodmin, Cornwall

Contents

List of illustrations

Foreword

A lot of people will be grateful for this handbook. To the vast majority the Church of England is a mysterious organization when set against the globular world in which we now live. This book sets out to achieve a simple task: to take the uninitiated reader with a sure hand through the history, structure, workings and theological stance of what is this country's Established Church. What is striking is how, although the Church remains in terms of spacial allocation and hierarchy essentially as it was in the Middle Ages, that has been overlaid during the last century by a burgeoning bureaucracy. The Church's decision-making processes grow more complicated inversely to the decline in its membership, and this democratization has made it more and not less expensive to run in an age when its financial resources have been steadily dwindling. Both of these factors will present formidable problems for the Church in the present century.

This guide comes at a time when change is in the air. The Prime Minister's role in ecclesiastical appointments has been abdicated, although what exactly is to replace it is by no means clear. What it severs is a direct line which the Church has had for centuries right into the heart of government, making one wonder whether or not the move is a preliminary step towards disestablishment. Already the place of the Anglican bishops in the House of Lords is under consideration as part of the reform of that institution. It clearly cannot be maintained as it is in what is recognized as a multi-faith society. Here the reader will find that the arguments both for and against establishment are well presented, ones which are bound to surface when we enter into a new reign. At that point the ancient rite of coronation, one of the cornerstones defining the nature of the British state, could come under challenge. Its continuance has the support of the other Christian denominations and of the other faith groups who recognized the value of having an Established Church and hence the idea of faith and a higher vision at the heart of the state.

As I write, it is the wider Anglican Communion which seems

most vulnerable with divisions caused by coming to terms with what the modern world has discovered about the nature of human sexuality. Whether the advent of women bishops will cause further disruption it is difficult to speculate. Add to that the realization that the Church must at last come to terms with the demographic changes the country has undergone, and which were there already over a century ago. The Church of England retains the built infrastructure of a rural England which had already vanished by 1900, but has never made the adjustment to the fact. In this century it will be forced to come terms with sorting that out as the present situation, in which rural clergy can be lumbered with up to 15 churches, cannot continue. What is clear is that, no matter what aspect of it one touches, this Church, which assumed its present form four centuries ago in response to a particular politico-religious circumstance, will need to re-position itself – as it did in the Victorian age – in response to an age which is already sometimes labelled post-Christian. I am confident that it will.

Roy Strong
March 2008

Preface

This *Guide to the Church of England* was commissioned by the Church of England's Council for Christian Unity as part of its work of fostering increased understanding between the Church of England and Christians of other traditions. A guide along these lines was originally requested by some of the Church of England's ecumenical partners in Continental Europe who wanted an introduction to the Church of England for those training for ministry, but the Council for Christian Unity felt that such an introduction would also be helpful to those in this country who wanted to learn more about that Church's history, theology and organization.

I am grateful to those at Church House Westminster, Continuum and elsewhere who have read this book through in its draft form and have suggested corrections or improvements. However, responsibility for any remaining errors lies with the author and the opinions that are expressed in this book are likewise the author's and should not be taken to represent the official views of the Council for Christian Unity.

Martin Davie
Church House Westminster

1 When did the Church of England begin?

AN ANCIENT CHURCH

One thing that everyone thinks they know about the Church of England is that Henry VIII created it in the sixteenth century in order to facilitate his divorce from Catherine of Aragon. Like most things that everyone thinks they know, this account of when the Church of England began is mistaken.

Henry VIII did not want a divorce from Catherine of Aragon; he wanted an annulment, a declaration that they had never been properly married in the first place, and by his time the Church of England had been in existence for almost nine hundred years.

The roots of the Church of England go back to the time of the Roman Empire when a Christian church came into existence in what was then the Roman province of Britain. The early Christian writers Tertullian and Origen mention the existence of a British church in the third century AD, and in the fourth century British bishops attended a number of the great councils of the Church such as the Council of Arles in 314 and the Council of Rimini in 359. The first member of the British church whom we know by name is St Alban, who, tradition tells us, was martyred for his faith on the spot where St Albans Abbey in Hertfordshire now stands.

The British church was a missionary church with figures such as St Illtud, St Ninian and St Patrick evangelizing in Wales, Scotland and Ireland, but the invasions by the pagan Angles, Saxons and Jutes in the fifth century seem to have destroyed the organization of the church in much of what is now England, although place names in Lancashire and elsewhere, such as Eccleston and Bisham, may indicate that the ancient British church never entirely died out.

In 597 a mission sent by Pope Gregory the Great and led by St Augustine of Canterbury landed in Kent to begin the work of converting these pagan peoples. What eventually became known as

A medieval picture of the martyrdom of St Alban (courtesy of the Board of Trinity College Dublin)

the Church of England (the *Ecclesia Anglicana* – or the English church) was the result of a combination of three streams of Christianity: the Roman tradition of St Augustine and his successors; the remnants of the old Romano-British church; and the Celtic tradition coming down from Scotland and associated with people like St Aidan and St Cuthbert.

AN ENGLISH CHURCH

These three streams came together as a result of increasing mutual contact and the holding of a number of local synods (councils), of which the Synod of Whitby in 664 has traditionally been seen as the most important. The result was an English church, led by the Archbishops of Canterbury and York, which was fully assimilated into the mainstream of the Christian Church of the West. This meant that it was influenced by the wider development of the Western Christian tradition in matters such as theology, liturgy, church architecture, and the development of monasticism. It also meant that until the Reformation in the sixteenth century the Church of England acknowledged the authority of the Pope.

A REFORMED CHURCH

At the Reformation the Western Church became divided between those who continued to accept Papal authority and the various Protestant churches that repudiated it. The reasons for this division were complex, but they included both the influence of the fresh theological insights offered by the Reformers, the existence of long-standing debates about the relation of the authority of the Pope to other sources of authority, especially that of General Councils and Christian monarchs, and widespread disquiet about the moral corruption of both the Papacy and the institutional Church in general.

The Church of England was affected by these wider European influences and it was among the churches that broke with Rome. The catalyst for this decision was the refusal of the Pope to annul the marriage of Henry VIII and Catherine of Aragon, but underlying this was a Tudor nationalist belief that authority over the English church properly belonged to the English monarchy. During the remainder of Henry's reign the theology and practice of the Church of England remained quite traditional, but in the reign of his son, Edward VI, the Church of England underwent further reformation in a distinctively Protestant direction.

The major architect of this further reformation was the Archbishop of Canterbury, Thomas Cranmer, and the driving force behind it was the conviction that the theology being developed by the theologians of the mainstream Protestant Reformation was more faithful to the teaching of the Bible and the early church than the teaching of those who continued to support the Pope.[1]

In the reign of Mary Tudor, the Church of England once again submitted to Papal authority and was formally reconciled to Rome. However, this policy was reversed when Elizabeth I came to the throne in 1558.

The religious settlement that eventually emerged in the reign of

---

1 There has been debate among historians about whether or not the English Reformation had the support of the English people. The truth seems to be that the English Reformation was not a popular movement but was brought about by the actions of the English monarchs with the assistance and guidance of clergy and politicians who were sympathetic to Protestantism. However, there does seem to have been a fairly large amount of popular support for the Reformation in London, the southeast of England and East Anglia, with opposition in the north and west of England.

A portrait of Archbishop Cranmer (courtesy of Lambeth Palace Library)

Elizabeth gave the Church of England the distinctive identity that it has retained to this day. It resulted in a church that consciously retained a large amount of continuity with the church of the early and medieval periods in terms of its overall structure, its use of the catholic creeds, its pattern of ministry, its buildings and aspects of its liturgy, but that also embodied Protestant insights in its theology and in the overall shape of its liturgical practice. The way that this is often expressed is by saying that the Church of England is both 'catholic and reformed'.

At the end of the sixteenth century Richard Hooker produced the classic defence of the Elizabethan settlement in his *Of the Laws of Ecclesiastical Polity*, a work that sought to defend the Church of England against its Puritan critics who wanted further changes to make the Church of England more like the churches of Geneva or Scotland.

AN ESTABLISHED CHURCH

In the seventeenth century, continuing tensions within the Church of England over bishops and other theological and liturgical issues were among the factors that led to the English Civil War. The Church was associated with the losing Royalist side and, during the period of the Commonwealth from 1645–60, its bishops were abolished and its prayer book, the Book of Common Prayer, was banned. With the restoration of the monarchy in 1660 this situation was reversed and in 1662 those clergy who could not accept this decision were forced to leave their posts. These dissenting clergy and their congregations were then persecuted until 1689 when the Toleration Act gave legal existence to those Protestant groups outside the Church of England who accepted the doctrine of the Trinity.

The settlement of 1689 has remained the basis of the constitutional position of the Church of England ever since, a constitutional position in which the Church of England has remained the established Church with a range of particular legal privileges and responsibilities, but with ever-increasing religious and civil rights being granted to other Christians, those of other faiths and those professing no faith at all.

Until the early nineteenth century, England was still formally a confessional state with a range of public offices and access to the Universities of Oxford and Cambridge being restricted to those who were communicant members of the Church of England. This situation began to change with the repeal of legislation restricting the civic rights of Protestant dissenters and Roman Catholics in 1828 and 1829 respectively, and during the rest of the century the remaining forms of discrimination against those who were not members of the Church of England were gradually abolished, thus reaching the situation described above in which there is an established Church but equality before the law for those of all faiths and none except in relation to the question of who can inherit the throne, an exception which is discussed in chapter five of this book.

As well as being the established Church in England, the Church of England has also become the mother church of the Anglican Communion, a group of separate churches that are in communion with the Archbishop of Canterbury and for whom he is a focus of unity.

A COMPREHENSIVE CHURCH

The history of the Church of England from the eighteenth century onwards has been enriched by the coexistence within it of three broad traditions: the Evangelical, the Catholic and the Liberal.

- The Evangelical tradition has emphasized the significance of the Protestant aspects of the Church of England's identity, stressing the importance of the authority of Scripture, preaching, justification by faith and personal conversion.
- The Catholic tradition, strengthened and reshaped from the 1830s by the Oxford Movement, has emphasized the significance of the continuity between the Church of England and the Church of the early and medieval periods. It has stressed the importance of the visible Church and its sacraments and the belief that the ministry of bishops, priests and deacons is a sign and instrument of the Church of England's catholic and apostolic identity.
- The Liberal tradition has emphasized the importance of the use of reason in theological exploration. It has stressed the need to develop Christian belief and practice in order to respond creatively to wider advances in human knowledge and understanding and the importance of social and political action in forwarding God's kingdom.

It should be noted that these three traditions have not existed in strict isolation. Both in the case of individuals and in the case of the Church as a whole, influences from all three traditions have overlapped in a variety of different ways. It also needs to be noted that since the 1960s a fourth influence, the Charismatic movement, has become increasingly important. This has emphasized the importance of the Church being open to renewal through the work of the Holy Spirit. Its roots lie in Evangelicalism but it has influenced people from a variety of different traditions.

A CHURCH COMMITTED TO MISSION AND UNITY

From the eighteenth century onwards the Church of England has also been faced with a number of challenges that it continues to face today.

- There has been the challenge of responding to social changes in England such as population growth, urbanization and the development of an increasingly multi-cultural and multi-faith society.
- There has been the challenge of engaging in mission in a society that has become increasingly materialist in outlook and in which belief in God or interest in 'spiritual' matters is not seen as being linked to involvement with the life of the Church.
- There has been the challenge of providing sufficient and sufficiently trained clergy and lay ministers to enable the Church of England to carry out its responsibility to provide ministry and pastoral care for every parish in the country.
- There has been the challenge of trying to overcome the divisions of the past by developing closer relationships between the Church of England and other churches and trying to move with them towards the goal of full visible unity.

As this brief account has shown, the changes that have taken place in the Church of England over the centuries have been many and various. What has remained constant, however, has been the Church's commitment to the faith 'uniquely revealed in the Holy Scriptures and set forth in the catholic creeds',[1] its maintenance of the traditional threefold order of ministry, and its determination to bring the grace of God to the whole nation through word and sacrament in the power of the Holy Spirit.

FOR FURTHER READING

Bunting, I. (ed.), *Celebrating the Anglican Way*, London: Hodder & Stoughton, 1996.

Moorman, J., *A History of the Church of England*, Harrisville, PA: Morehouse Publishing, 2003.

Neill, S. C., *Anglicanism*, 4th edn, London: Mowbray, 1993.

Platten, S. (ed.), *Anglicanism and the Western Christian Tradition*, Norwich: Canterbury Press, 2003.

---

1   Canon C15, Preface to the Declaration of Assent.

2 The Organization of the Church of England

The question of how to describe the organization of the Church of England is a controversial one. On the one hand there are those who argue that any description of how the Church of England is organized has to start with the parishes because it is the parishes that are the centre of the life of the Church and all the rest of the Church's organization only has value if it supports the work undertaken at the parochial level. On the other hand, there are those who argue that the basic unit of the Church's organization is the diocese because in terms of Anglican theology the local church consists of the diocesan bishop and the clergy and laity who are in communion with him. From this second perspective the parishes only have existence as part of their diocese and any description of the Church needs to reflect this fact.

This chapter will not attempt to adjudicate in this dispute, but will instead describe the organization of the Church of England in strictly geographical terms, beginning with the largest unit of ecclesiastical organization, the province, and ending with the smallest unit, the parish, before going on to look at two other forms of the Church's life, the cathedrals and what are known as the 'peculiars'.

The fact that parishes come after dioceses is thus not a judgement of value, but merely a reflection of size.

PROVINCES AND DIOCESES

As the early church developed, its organization came to reflect that of the Roman Empire, with dioceses presided over by bishops grouped into provinces, each presided over by a Metropolitan bishop. The *Ecclesia Anglicana* inherited this pattern of organization. The Church of England retained it at the Reformation and has continued to maintain it to the present day. There are currently 44 dioceses in the Church of England and these are grouped into two provinces.

The Province of Canterbury, of which the Archbishop of Canterbury is the Metropolitan, consists of the 29 following dioceses: Bath and Wells; Birmingham; Bristol; Canterbury; Chelmsford; Chichester; Coventry; Derby; Ely; Exeter; Gloucester; Guildford; Hereford; Leicester; Lichfield; Lincoln; London; Norwich; Oxford; Peterborough; Portsmouth; Rochester; St Albans; St Edmundsbury and Ipswich; Salisbury; Southwark; Truro; Winchester; Worcester.

The Diocese of Hereford has a few parishes that are in Wales. The Channel Islands, which are self-governing territories under the British crown, are annexed to the Diocese of Winchester, although they officially remain part of the Diocese of Coutances in Normandy.

The Province of York, of which the Archbishop of York is the Metropolitan, consists of the 14 following dioceses: Blackburn; Bradford; Carlisle; Chester; Durham; Liverpool; Manchester; Newcastle; Ripon and Leeds; Sheffield; Sodor and Man; Southwell and Nottingham; Wakefield; York.

The Diocese of Sodor and Man covers the Isle of Man, which, like the Channel Islands, is not part of England but a self-governing territory under the British crown.

The Diocese in Europe lies entirely outside England and is geographically speaking part of neither province, although for administrative purposes it is deemed to be part of the Province of Canterbury. It is made up of the Church of England churches and chaplaincies in continental Europe, Morocco, Turkey and the Asian countries that were formerly part of the Soviet Union.

The Archbishop of Canterbury is the senior Archbishop and is Primate of All England and Metropolitan. The Archbishop of York is Primate of England and Metropolitan. As Metropolitans the two Archbishops have jurisdiction over the affairs of their respective provinces 'as superintendent of all ecclesiastical matters therein' with the specific responsibility to 'correct and supply the defects of other bishops',[1] should the need arise. The Archbishops have the style The Most Reverend and, because they are

---

1 Canon C17:2 of the Canons of the Church of England.

1. Bath & Wells
2. Birmingham
3. Blackburn
4. Bradford
5. Canterbury
7. Carlisle
8. Chelmsford
9. Chester
10. Chichester
11. Coventry
12. Derby
13. Durham
14. Ely
15. Exeter
16. Gloucester
17. Guildford
18. Hereford
19. Leicester
20. Lichfield
21. Lincoln
22. Liverpool
23. London
24. Manchester
25. Newcastle
26. Norwich
27. Oxford
28. Peterborough
29. Portsmouth
30. Ripon & Leeds
31. Rochester
32. St Albans

33. St Edmundsbury
    & Ipswich
34. Salisbury
35. Sheffield
37. Southwark
38. Southwell
    & Nottingham
39. Truro
40. Wakefield
41. Winchester
42. Worcester
43. York

A map of the dioceses of the Church of England (excluding the Diocese of Europe)
(courtesy of the Church of England)

automatically members of the Privy Council, they are also Right Honourable.[1]

Each of the dioceses has a diocesan bishop, and most dioceses (the exceptions being the dioceses of Leicester, Portsmouth and Sodor and Man) also have one or more suffragan stipendiary assistant bishops to assist the diocesan bishop with his duties. In the diocese of St Albans, for example, the diocesan bishop is the Bishop of St Albans and there are two suffragan bishops, the Bishops of Bedford and Hertford. Bishops have the style The Right Reverend.

There is a historical order of precedence among the diocesan

---

1   The correct form is that the they are The Most Revd and Right Honourable . . .

bishops, with the Bishops of London, Durham and Winchester (in that order) being the most senior bishops after the Archbishops. These five sit automatically in the House of Lords (other diocesan bishops fill the remaining 21 places allocated to Lords Spiritual by chronological seniority; see chapter five). The Bishop of London is also automatically a member of the Privy Council.[1]

Some dioceses operate area schemes in which suffragan bishops have responsibility for particular geographical areas within the diocese delegated to them by the diocesan bishop. In the Diocese of London, for example, the Bishop of London and the Area Bishops of Stepney, Kensington, Edmonton and Willesden have responsibility for specific areas of the capital. In other dioceses, however, the diocesan and suffragan bishops share responsibility for the diocese as a whole.

ARCHDEACONRIES

With the exception of the Diocese of Sodor and Man, every diocese of the Church of England is divided into a number of archdeaconries. For example, the diocese of St Albans is divided into the three Archdeaconries of St Albans, Bedford and Hertford. As its name suggests, an archdeaconry is an area over which an archdeacon exercises authority.

In the early church an archdeacon was the head of the group of deacons who assisted a bishop with his work. In the Church of England, however, the term is now used to refer to a senior priest who has responsibility under the diocesan bishop for the pastoral care of the clergy in his archdeaconry and for ensuring that they are performing their duties correctly. Archdeacons are also responsible for making sure that church buildings and their contents are properly looked after, and they have an important role in the appointment of Church of England clergy to new posts. Archdeacons have the title The Venerable.

In a few cases the archdeacon's role is undertaken by a suffragan bishop. Thus in the Diocese of Hereford the Bishop of Ludlow is also the Archdeacon of Ludlow.

---

1 Hence his full title is The Right Reverend and Right Honourable.

DEANERIES

Each archdeaconry is divided into a number of deaneries. For instance, the Archdeaconry of Hertford in St Albans is divided into the Deaneries of Barnet, Bishop's Stortford, Buntingford, Cheshunt, Welwyn/Hatfield and Hertford and Ware.

Deaneries are small groups of parishes, one of whose parish priests serves as the 'rural' or 'area' dean. These are members of the clergy who provide a link between the bishops and the deanery, conveying information from the bishop to the deanery, and reporting to the bishop 'any matter in any parish within the deanery which it may be necessary for the bishop to know'.[1] They also provide pastoral care for the other clergy within the deanery.

The clergy within each deanery meet together on a regular basis in what is known as the deanery chapter in order to discuss and take action on matters of common interest and concern. The rural or area dean presides over these chapter meetings.

PARISHES

Each deanery is divided into a number of parishes. Thus the author lives in the Parish of St Barnabas, Cray, in the Deanery of Orpington, in the Diocese of Rochester. There are currently 13,150 parishes in the Church of England.

The development of parishes was the way in which the English church of the later Saxon period responded to the challenge of providing pastoral care for all of the inhabitants of England.

When the diocesan system first emerged in the early church the diocese was a small pastoral unit consisting of a town church presided over by the bishop and serving both the town and the surrounding countryside. As the Church grew it became necessary to provide extra churches in each diocese, served by priests and deacons from the bishop's staff and it was these extra churches that came to form the basis of the later parochial system.

In England this system developed in two stages during the Saxon period.

Firstly, there was the creation of a number of 'minster'

---

1   Canon C23:1.

churches. These were mission stations that provided a base for evangelism and pastoral care for a relatively large geographical area. Examples of churches that were originally minsters are York Minster and Beverley Minster in Yorkshire and Southwell Minster in Nottinghamshire.

York Minster (© istock)

Secondly, as both the Church and the general population continued to grow, bishops and, from the tenth century onwards, monasteries and local landowners began to build local churches that served villages or a particular district within a town.

The area served by one of these smaller local churches came to be known as a parish and each of these parishes was served by a priest (who came to be known as the incumbent) who shared with the diocesan bishop the pastoral responsibility for every person living within it.

This is still the situation within England today. The whole country is divided into parishes, each of which is the responsibility of a parish priest (who may be assisted by other priests, deacons or lay ministers) who, together with the bishop, has the pastoral responsibility for the entire area and everyone who lives in it. This pastoral responsibility is reflected in the fact that everyone living in a parish is legally entitled to the services of the parish church and its clergy for baptisms, weddings and funerals.

The area for which an incumbent was responsible came to be known as a benefice. Originally, the term benefice referred to a grant of land given for life as a reward for service. It then came to be used to describe an ecclesiastical office that gave the person holding it the right to certain revenues. Finally, it was used to describe the area for which a parish priest was responsible, for the pastoral care of which he received his income.

In the Church of England today, benefices may cover more than one parish. For example, as its name suggests, the united benefice of Mereworth with West Peckham in the Diocese of Rochester consists of the two parishes of Mereworth and West Peckham. Some benefices in rural areas may consist of quite a large number of parishes. For instance, the benefice of Bildeston, with Wattisham and Lindsey, Whatfield with Semer, Nedging and Naughton in rural Suffolk consists of seven parishes.

In some benefices there is a team ministry. A team ministry consists of a number of churches served by a team of clergy of incumbent status. The senior member of the team will have the title team rector and the others will have the title of team vicar.[1]

The author's former parish in Ipswich, for example, is now part of the South West Ipswich Team Ministry, which includes the churches of St Mary at Stoke, St Peter's Stoke and St Francis, Chantry. It is served by a team rector and two team vicars. In addition to the team rector and the team vicar(s), a team ministry may also be served by other assistant clergy and by lay ministers.

As well as team ministries there are also group ministries. In a group ministry the incumbents in the group assist each other in their ministries. The incumbents involved will meet together on a regular basis and it is their duty to work together in such a way as

---

1 Originally the distinction between rectors and vicars was that the former received the whole income from the parish while the latter received some of the income with the rest being paid to some other person or body. Today this distinction no longer applies and except in the case of team ministries the use of either term simply reflects the history of a particular parish. The word vicar is also incorrectly used as a general term for any member of the clergy.

to provide the most effective pattern of ministry for the group as a whole.

The parochial clergy (and rural and area deans) have the style The Reverend.

CATHEDRALS

A cathedral is the mother church of a diocese and it is so called because it is where the *cathedra*, or official chair, of the diocesan bishop (the symbol of his authority as the chief teacher and pastor of the diocese) is located.

A key feature of the life of cathedrals is the maintenance of a regular cycle of prayer and praise. In most cathedrals this involves the daily celebration of the Eucharist and the holding of daily services of Morning and Evening Prayer. A choir often accompanies the Sunday services and weekday Evening Prayer and many cathedrals are renowned for the excellence of their choral music.

As the mother church of the diocese the cathedral is normally the venue for ordinations and other major diocesan events. In addition, cathedrals often hold major services to mark significant events in the life of the area covered by the diocese.

Like many of the older parish churches, many cathedrals are ancient and architecturally significant buildings that are major tourist attractions as well as centres of pilgrimage.

Each cathedral is served by a team of clergy known as the cathedral chapter. The head of the chapter and the person with overall responsibility for the life of the cathedral is the dean and the other members of the chapter are known as residentiary canons (so called because they normally resided within the cathedral precincts). Each of the residentiary canons will have responsibility for a particular aspect of the life of the cathedral, and the chapter as a whole will be assisted in its work by a team of lay staff.

As well as the residentiary canons, cathedrals also have honorary canons, who may be either clergy or lay people. Honorary canons are appointed by the diocesan bishop, either because they make a particular contribution to the life of the diocese, or because they hold a particular office within it. In some cathedrals such as Exeter the honorary canons are known as prebendaries. Originally the holders of non-residentiary canonries and prebendal stalls received the tithes from particular cathedral estates or prebends (thus St Paul's Cathedral in London has prebendaries of, for example, Reculversland in Essex and Consumpta per Mare – now, as its name suggests, under the sea – where the cathedral once owned land, as well as of the cathedral's London landholdings such as Chiswick and Islington). However, the connection between the canonries and prebendal stalls and the areas from which they used to derive their income is now purely historical and honorary.

The residentiary and honorary canons together form the college of canons. This has an advisory role in the life of the cathedral and has the formal responsibility for electing the diocesan bishop.

The cathedrals at Birmingham, Blackburn, Bradford, Bury St Edmunds, Chelmsford, Derby, Leicester, Manchester, Newcastle, Portsmouth, Ripon, St Albans, Sheffield, Southwark, Southwell and Wakefield were parish churches before being given cathedral status. They retained responsibility for their parishes when they became cathedrals and so they combine the role of a cathedral with that of a parish church. The deans of these parish church cathedrals used to be known as 'provosts', but their title has now been brought into line with that of those holding the same office in the other cathedrals.

Deans have the style The Very Reverend and canons have the style The Reverend Canon.[1]

PECULIARS

A peculiar is a religious institution belonging to the Church of England that is outside the ordinary jurisdiction of the bishop or archbishop in whose diocese or province it is situated. Peculiars developed for a variety of reason from Anglo-Saxon times onwards and, as Paul Welsby notes:

> At one time or another there have been six types of peculiar: Monastic Peculiars, where the great Abbeys and certain Religious Orders were exempt from episcopal jurisdiction; Royal Peculiars, usually where churches were situated on land connected with a Royal castle or palace (e.g. St George's Chapel,

---

1 Lay canons do not have the title The Revd Canon, but are simply styled Canon.

Windsor, and Westminster Abbey); Archiepiscopal peculiars, linked with rights claimed by archbishops to exercise jurisdiction where they had manors or palaces; Episcopal Peculiars, where bishops owned residences in dioceses other than their own; and Cathedral Peculiars, in which Cathedral Chapters had jurisdiction over their property.[1]

The monastic peculiars vanished when the monasteries were abolished at the Reformation and most of the others were abolished between 1836 and 1852. However, a number of peculiars remained in existence and others have been created since.[2]

The best-known of the peculiars that survive today are the Royal Peculiars, which are religious institutions that are outside the jurisdiction of both the dioceses and the provinces in which they are geographically situated; they come under the jurisdiction of the Queen rather than that of the diocesan bishop or the archbishop of the province.

The institutions that come into this category are:

- St George's Chapel, Windsor Castle
- The Chapel Royal, St James's Palace
- The Queen's Chapel, St James's Palace
- The Chapel Royal, Hampton Court
- The Chapel of St John the Evangelist in the Tower of London
- The Chapel of St Peter ad Vincula in the Tower of London
- The Royal Chapel of All Saints, Windsor
- The Queen's Chapel of the Savoy
- The Royal Foundation of St Katharine
- The Chapel of St Edward, King and Martyr, Cambridge
- The Collegiate Church of St Peter, Westminster (Westminster Abbey).

The Chapel Royal was originally a body of priests and choristers rather than a building and it still travels with the monarch as, for example, when the Queen visits one of the cathedrals for the Royal Maundy Service on Maundy Thursday. The Bishop of London is

---

1 P. Welsby, *How the Church of England Works*, London: Church Information Office, 1985, p. 14.
2 For details see P. Barber, 'What is a Peculiar?', in *Ecclesiastical Law Journal*, No. 16, 1995, pp. 304–6.

Westminster Abbey (courtesy of Rosenthal photos)

also Dean of the Chapel Royal (it is in that capacity, rather than in his role as Bishop of London, that he leads the Service of Remembrance at the Cenotaph).

Other institutions with peculiar status include the cathedrals,[1] a number of the college chapels in the Universities of Oxford and Cambridge, such as King's College Cambridge and New College Oxford, and the Temple Church in London. These are part of the

---

1 There is some doubt about the peculiar status of the cathedrals in York, Ripon and Manchester. For the full list of those institutions that are definitely peculiars and those whose peculiar status is possible but disputed see Barber, art. cit., pp. 310–12.

Provinces of Canterbury and York, but are not under the ordinary jurisdiction of the diocesan bishop.

In the case of cathedrals, the right of ordinary jurisdiction rests with the dean and chapter, although the diocesan bishop has rights of 'visitorial jurisdiction' that enable him to supervise the life of the cathedral and, if necessary, to take disciplinary action. In the case of the college chapels, ordinary jurisdiction lies with the college governing bodies, but in their case, too, bishops have rights of visiatorial jurisdiction. New College Oxford, for example, was founded by a former Bishop of Winchester, William of Wykeham, in the Middle Ages, and the Bishop of Winchester is still the college visitor.

CHURCH SCHOOLS, COLLEGES AND UNIVERSITIES

An important part of the life of the Church of England is its network of schools, colleges and universities.

Church schools

Schools of various types have been a feature of the life of the English church from the earliest days of its history. For example, as early as the seventh and eighth centuries there were important monastic schools at Canterbury, York and Wearmouth-Jarrow. During the nineteenth century the Church of England, through the work of the National Society for Promoting the Education of the Poor in the Principles of the Established Church, founded a national educational system in England and Wales, a system that was supplemented by the state from 1870 onwards. Today there are Church of England schools in both the maintained and independent sectors.

(1) Maintained schools
The Education Acts of 1902 and 1944 established a 'dual system' of state education in which Church of England schools (and schools of other religious traditions) were funded by the local authorities alongside schools that did not represent a particular religious tradition. Schools that are funded in this way are known as 'maintained schools'.

Today there are nearly four and a half thousand Church of

England primary schools and just over two hundred Church of England secondary schools in the maintained sector in England.[1] In percentage terms this means that 25.2 per cent of all state primary schools and 5.8 per cent of all state secondary schools are Church of England schools.

Following the recommendations of a commission headed by Lord Dearing, the Church of England is working towards a target of creating a hundred new Church of England secondary schools.

Church schools in the maintained sector are managed by means of a partnership between the Church of England and the Local Authorities. There are three types of school that come into this category.

The first category is *voluntary aided schools*. This type of school is owned by a church-related educational trust[2] and the church appoints a majority of the school governors. Teachers are appointed and employed by the governing body, which is also the admissions authority for the school. The governors are able to appoint head teachers and other teachers who are actively committed to the school's Anglican ethos in terms of their personal faith and religious practice.

The cost of repairs to the school and money for any capital projects is raised by the governing body, with a 90 per cent grant being given by the Department for Children, Schools and Families, the government department responsible for education. Religious education and collective worship are distinctively Anglican.

The second category is *voluntary controlled schools*. This type of school is also owned by a church-related trust and the church appoints governors, but these church appointees do not form a majority of the governing body. The teachers are employed by the Local Education Authority, which also funds repairs and capital projects. Collective worship is Anglican but religious education follows the agreed syllabus drawn up by the Standing Advisory

---

1 The most recent government figures (January 2006) are that there are 4,456 Church of England primary schools and 201 Church of England secondary schools. The latter figure does not include Academies and it is suggested that if these are added in together with other schools opened since January 2006 the true figure is probably now about 220 Church of England secondary schools.

2 This could be the local vicar and church wardens, or a group of self-perpetuating trustees, or a Diocesan Board of Education or Finance.

Committee on Religious Education (SACRE) of the Local Education Authority.

The third category is *foundation schools*. These schools, too, are owned by a church-related educational trust. The church appoints a minority of the governors. The governing body employs the staff and is the admissions authority. Collective worship is Anglican, but religious education follows the SACRE agreed syllabus.

Concern is sometimes expressed that the admissions policy of church schools will exclude children who are not Anglican or Christian, but this is not the case.

Voluntary controlled church schools generally have an admissions policy that is indistinguishable from that of other maintained schools in the area. Voluntary aided church schools welcome children from their local area regardless of whether they or their families are Anglican or Christian, but when there is a shortage of places in a school its admissions policy may give preference to those children who are actively involved in their local church.

Church schools do not see their role as that of seeking to convert children to the Christian faith, but they do seek to bear witness to Christianity through their worship, through religious education, through the moral values they promote and through the way in which the members of the school community relate to each other.

The work of Church of England schools in the maintained sector is supported at the diocesan level by the diocesan Boards of Education, which give advice and support to church schools on matters such as collective worship, religious education and admissions policy and which take part in the inspections of these schools in order to help ensure that their Anglican ethos is maintained. It is supported at the national level by the Church of England's Board of Education and by the work of the National Society, now called the National Society for Promoting Religious Education, which also give advice and support to church schools and which work with the government and other interested parties to help shape national policy with regard to church schools and education in general.

At the moment there are also ten joint Anglican–Roman Catholic state schools, which seek to reflect the ethos of both traditions in terms of the life of the schools as a whole and specifically in terms of their worship, provision for religious education and staff appointments.

In recent years a new category of maintained school has been created. Schools in this category are known as Academies (also known as City Academies). Their trustees, who pay part of the cost of establishing them, own the Academies. The Department for Children, Schools and Families funds them and no fees are charged. In Academies the governors employ the staff and are the admissions authority.

Academies which have either a Church of England foundation or governors appointed to represent the Church of England are designated as Church of England schools. In these Academies the church appoints a minority of the governors and collective worship and religious education are distinctively Anglican.

Thus far there are Church of England Academies in London and Bradford with plans for 25 more currently under discussion. There is also a joint Anglican–Roman Catholic Academy in Liverpool.

(2) Independent schools

Independent schools are schools that receive no funding from either the Local Authorities or central government.

A number of England's leading independent schools such as Eton College, Winchester College, Westminster School and King's School Canterbury were originally church foundations and, until well into the twentieth century, teaching at an independent school was regarded as a normal part of a clerical career. For example, of the eight Archbishops of Canterbury during the twentieth century three were headmasters of independent schools (Frederick Temple was headmaster of Rugby School and William Temple and Geoffrey Fisher were headmasters of Repton School).

Today the links between the Church of England and schools in the independent sector generally remain close. According to the Independent Schools Advisory Service approximately 1,000 out of the 1,300 fee-paying schools in England have a Church of England ethos. A large number of independent schools have Church of England chapels and chaplains who are Church of England clergy and many of the choir schools attached to the Church of England cathedrals are independent Church of England schools.

Independent schools may now be formally designated as having a Church of England character. This means that they provide worship and religious teaching based on the rites, doctrines and practices of the Church of England. As in the case of voluntary aided schools in the maintained sector, it also means that the governors are able to appoint head teachers and other teachers who are actively committed to the school's Anglican ethos.

Church colleges and universities

(1) The ancient universities
The two ancient English Universities of Oxford and Cambridge were traditionally part of the Church of England, with teaching positions restricted to Church of England clergy and with students having to subscribe to the doctrines of the Church of England and attend Church of England chapel services. When originally founded in the early nineteenth century, King's College London and the University of Durham were likewise explicitly Anglican. The original college of Durham University (University College) was established in what had been the Bishop of Durham's residence at Durham Castle, a residence which he gave to establish the university.

Most aspects of the distinctively Church of England character of these institutions were abolished during the nineteenth and twentieth centuries. For example, the requirement that those wishing to graduate from Oxford, Cambridge or Durham had to subscribe to the doctrines of the Church of England was abolished in 1871 and the requirement for compulsory college chapel vanished during the twentieth century.

However, aspects of their Anglican character remain, such as the Anglican nature of many of the college chapels and the continuing restriction of some professorships in theology and Hebrew to ordained Anglicans.

(2) Church colleges and universities
Although the institutions just mentioned are no longer part of the Church of England, there is now a network of 11 church colleges of higher education and universities, all of which provide degree and other higher education courses for over 70,000 students. These colleges and universities are: Bishop Grosseteste University College, Lincoln; Canterbury Christ Church University; The University of Chester; The University of Chichester; The University of Gloucestershire; Liverpool Hope University (a joint Anglican–Roman Catholic University); the University College of St Mark and St John, Plymouth; the University of Chester); the

University of Gloucestershire; Whitelands College, Roehampton University; the University of Winchester; York St John University.

These institutions began life as teacher training colleges, and this remains an important part of what they offer. However, they now also offer a wide range of different courses. For example, the University of Gloucestershire offers courses in business studies and it and the University of Chester and St Martin's College offer courses in health and social care.

As these institutions have grown and diversified they have tended to become less specifically Anglican in character and this raises the question, which is addressed in a new report on them by the Church of England's Board of Education, about '. . . the distinctive identity of this group of higher education institutions and how their identity as Church Colleges can and should be preserved and enhanced'.[1]

This report rejects the view that the Church of England '. . . should now quietly withdraw from any more active engagement with these institutions than it has with the ancient universities and hospitals founded in the great ages of faith'.[2] It argues that:

> . . . the Church has rich gifts to offer the church colleges and universities and the church colleges and universities have rich gifts to offer the Church. The relationship stands as a sign of a common mission to the nation and to communities. It also serves the partners' mutual benefit, helping each other fulfil their particular mission, especially in relation to the education of teachers, of health and social care professionals, and of those engaged in the Church's ministry lay and ordained.[3]

In order to help develop the relationship between the Church and these colleges and universities, the report lists in detail what it thinks the Church can offer them and what they can offer the Church. These lists can be found in Appendix 1 at the end of this chapter.

A particular focus of discussion at the moment is what these bodies might have to offer to the training of lay and ordained

---

1 *Mutual Expectations – The Church of England and Church Colleges/Universities*, London: The Board of Education, 2006, p. 5.
2 Ibid., p. 5.
3 Ibid., p. 5.

ministers in the Church of England and how their theology and religious studies departments might assist in 'education for discipleship' by equipping the people of God as a whole '. . . with a deeper and wider knowledge and understanding of God's mission to his creation and his people, as expressed through the life, death and resurrection of the Son and the continuing work of the Holy Spirit'.[1]

(3) Theological colleges and courses
The Church of England also has a network of theological colleges and courses that offer courses of study in theology and religious studies to degree level. The primary purpose of these colleges and courses is to train people for lay and ordained ministry in the Church of England. More details about these colleges and courses can be found in chapter eight in this guide, which deals with Ministry in the Church of England.

FOR FURTHER READING

The Board of Education, *Mutual Expectations – The Church of England and Church Colleges/Universities*, London: Board of Education, 2006.

The Board of Education, *The Way Ahead: Church of England Schools in the New Millennium*, London: Church House Publishing, 2001.

Podmore, C., *Aspects of Anglican Identity*, London: Church House Publishing, 2005.

Welsby, P., *How the Church of England Works*, London: Church Information Office, 1985, Chs II–VII.

Details of the provincial and diocesan structure of the Church of England and of its involvement in education can also be found in the current edition of the *Church of England Year Book*, published annually by Church House Publishing.

---

1   Ibid., p. 10.

APPENDIX 1

What the Church of England and the church universities/colleges can offer each other.

What can the Church offer the partnership with the church universities/colleges?

(1) Actively to support the HEIs (Higher Education Institutions) by prayer.

(2) To encourage and promote, in partnership with the HEIs, the Christian vocations of teaching and of ordained ministry and of lifelong learning and discipleship.

(3) To learn from the experience of the HEIs in developing networks of influence and support and to see them as partners in the work of transforming society.

(4) To provide priests and others for chaplaincy and to give them practical and pastoral support.

(5) To engage with the HEIs and their staff as key resources for the Church's mission.

(6) To involve the Vice Chancellor/Principal and institutional leadership in developing the Church's mission nationally and in the local dioceses.

(7) To encourage suitable church members to undertake the work of governance.

(8) To support and encourage the HEIs in the recruitment of students through the churches.

(9) To share the insights and commitment of the HEIs, for example in the promotion of the inclusion of people who are socially disadvantaged and of international students.

(10) To provide advocacy for the HEIs and to include them in national and diocesan strategic planning.

What can the church colleges/universities offer the partnership with the Church?

(1) To be communities of learning teaching and scholarship.

(2) To offer the highest possible quality of education to students.

(3) To be excellent employers.

(4) To recruit and retain staff with appropriate experience for

their responsibilities with a church Higher Education Institution (HEI).

(5) To be actively involved in the development of local, regional, national and international communities, with a continuing regard for sustainability.

(6) To have a particular care for overcoming disadvantage and promoting inclusion.

(7) In association with local dioceses, to serve the Church of England, the Anglican Communion and the wider Christian Church.

(8) To maintain at the heart of the Institution a chapel and chaplaincy nourished by the Anglican tradition.

(9) Through active dialogue and cooperation with those of other faith traditions, to promote the spiritual and religious development of individuals and communities.

(10) To foster the moral and human integrity of individuals and the communities to which they contribute.[1]

---

1 Ibid., p. 7.

3 The Government of the Church of England at the National Level

THE CONCILIAR SYSTEM

From very early in the history of the English church, important decisions were taken by councils in which bishops met together to discuss matters of mutual concern.

According to the Saxon church historian Bede, the first of these meetings was the Synod of Hertford in 673. This was summoned by the Archbishop of Canterbury, Theodore of Tarsus, and was also attended by Bisi, Bishop of the East Angles, Putta, Bishop of Rochester, Leutherius, Bishop of the West Saxons, Wynfrid, Bishop of the Province of the Mercians, and the representatives of Wilfrid, Bishop of the Northumbrian people. At this synod the bishops agreed to abide by ten church laws, or 'canons', that declared, for example: 'That we all unite in observing the holy day of Easter on the Sunday after the fourteenth day of the moon of the first month' and 'That monks shall not wander from place to place, that is, from monastery to monastery, except with letters dimissory from their own abbot; and that they keep the promise of obedience which they made at the time of their profession.'[1]

The Convocations

During the later Middle Ages other members of the clergy also came to take part in the councils of the English church alongside the bishops. Initially these were senior clergy such as abbots,

---

1 'Canons of the Council of Hertford', in Bede, *A History of the English Church and People*, Bk IV, chapter 5. Text in L. Sherley-Price, *Bede: A History of the English Church and People*, Harmondsworth: Penguin, 1977, p. 215.

priors, deans and archdeacons, but by the fourteenth century representatives of the ordinary parochial clergy were included as well. By the fifteenth century these arrangements had become formalized into a system in which each of the two Provinces of Canterbury and York had a Convocation consisting of an Upper House (the bishops) and a Lower House (the other members of the clergy).

Under the Convocation system the Upper House had greater authority than the Lower House, but the Lower House had the power to withhold consent from what the Upper House proposed. The Convocations were responsible not only for decision making, but also for the taxation of the clergy.

At the Reformation the system of Convocations was retained, but a number of changes were introduced to it. Firstly, with the dissolution of the monasteries, the abbots and priors disappeared from the Lower House. Secondly, from then on, the Convocations could only meet when summoned by a writ from the monarch, they could only make canons with a royal licence and those canons could only have legal authority when given royal assent. Thirdly, canons that conflicted with the royal prerogative, or with English custom or laws, or with statute law could not be put into effect.

The result of the second and third of these changes was to subordinate the authority of the Convocations to the authority of the Crown and Parliament. This was an expression of the idea of royal supremacy but it was also an expression of the idea that the voice of the laity, as expressed through Parliament, should carry equal weight in the affairs of the Church alongside the voice of the clergy, as expressed through the Convocations.

In the seventeenth century the right of clergy to tax themselves through the Convocations was given up and in the early eighteenth century internal conflicts between the Houses of the Convocations and fear that the Convocations would become a focus of opposition to the government led to the Convocations not being summoned to transact business from 1717 onwards (with exception of a solitary meeting in 1741).

During the nineteenth century the gradual admission of non-Anglicans and non-Christians to Parliament led to a growing view within the Church of England that Parliament was no longer a suitable body to exercise sole authority over the Church. In response to this belief, the Convocation of Canterbury began to meet again from 1852 and the Convocation of York from 1861. In addition, because Parliament could no longer be seen as expressing the voice of the laity of the Church of England, advisory Houses of Laity were established by the Convocations of Canterbury and York in 1886 and 1892 respectively.

THE CHURCH ASSEMBLY

In 1902 a Representative Church Council consisting of the two Convocations and the two Houses of Laity was formed. This Council was then superseded by the Church Assembly, which was established by Act of Parliament in 1919.

The Church Assembly consisted of a joint meeting of the two Convocations and a House of Laity representing both Provinces. Under the Enabling Act of 1919 it was given the power to pass Measures that had the force of law once they were agreed by Parliament and given the royal assent and that could amend existing Acts of Parliament. A situation under which the law affecting the Church could only be changed by an Act of Parliament was thus ended.

Although it was an improvement on the situation that had gone before, the Church Assembly suffered from a number of weaknesses.

- Firstly, the fact that the Convocations continued to meet separately as well as being part of the Church Assembly meant that the new system was time consuming for the members of the Convocations.
- Secondly, because it was made up of 750 members, the Church Assembly was too big to allow for satisfactory debate.
- Thirdly, there was a considerable overlapping of responsibility between the Convocations and the Church Assembly so that some business was transacted in both Convocations and the Assembly.
- Fourthly, while the right to legislate for the Church of England by means of Measures was given to the Church Assembly, the power to legislate by means of Canons was reserved to the Convocations and there was no procedure by which the House of Laity and the Convocations could discuss proposed changes to the Canons together. This was exposed as a major weakness when the Canons of the Church of England were completely revised between 1947 and 1969.

- Fifthly, matters of worship and doctrine were also reserved to the Convocations, thus preventing the laity from having a role in discussing and debating them.
- Sixthly, the Church Assembly was seen as being too remote from the dioceses and parishes.

THE GENERAL SYNOD

In order to counteract these weaknesses and to give more effective expression to the idea that the whole people of God (laity as well as clergy) should have full responsibility for decision making by the Church, the Church Assembly was in turn superseded by General Synod in 1970 and the synodical system is the one that still exists today.

Under this system the Convocations remain in existence but they do not meet regularly. Most business is conducted by General Synod meeting as a single body consisting of a House of Bishops made up of the combined Upper Houses of the Convocations, a House of Clergy made up of the combined Lower Houses of the Convocations[1] and a House of Laity drawn from both Provinces as under the Church Assembly system.

The House of Bishops is made up of the forty-four diocesan bishops together with seven elected suffragan bishops and the suffragan Bishop of Dover, who is an ex officio member of Synod as the bishop with day-to-day responsibility for the Diocese of Canterbury.

The House of Clergy is made up of five cathedral deans, the Dean of Jersey or Guernsey, six representatives of the Universities, two representatives of the religious communities, three chaplains from the armed forces and the Chaplain General of the Prison Service, one hundred and eighty-three other representatives of the clergy and up to five co-opted members.

The House of Laity is made up of two representatives of religious communities, three lay members of the armed services, the First and Second Church Estates Commissioners, 195 other lay representatives and up to five co-opted members.

---

1 Members of the House of Clergy are technically members of Synod because they have been elected to the Convocations.

In addition there are 11 other ex-officio members of General Synod[1] (who may be members of any of the three Houses) and representatives of other churches, the Church of England Youth Council and Deaf Anglicans Together are invited to attend General Synod and to speak at its meeting, but do not have voting rights.

The Convocations remain in existence and meet on occasion to consider matters of specific concern to the clergy. For example, they met in relation to the debates on the ordination of women to the priesthood in the early 1990s.

The synodical system is designed to avoid the weaknesses of the Church Assembly.

- Firstly, the fact that Synod normally meets as one body means that the synodical system is less time consuming than its predecessor and that the issue of the overlapping of responsibilities between different representative bodies no longer exists.
- Secondly, the fact that matters of doctrine and worship are now the responsibility of General Synod rather than the Convocations alone means that the laity have responsibility for them as well as the clergy.
- The importance of the joint agreement of the bishops, clergy and laity is also shown by the fact that under Article 5 of the General Synod constitution provision is made for matters to be decided by a vote in which a majority in each of the three Houses is required. This includes any motion for the final approval of a Measure or Canon. A vote taken in this way is known as a 'vote by Houses'.
- Thirdly, the fact that General Synod is now made up of 476 members[2] rather than 750 makes it a more suitable forum for debate.
- Fourthly, there is now a closer link between the General Synod and the dioceses and parishes than was the case with the Church Assembly. This is because the House of Laity is now elected at a deanery level rather than at a Diocesan Conference.

---

1   The Dean of the Arches, the two Vicars General, the Third Church Estates Commissioner, the Chairman of the Pensions Board and six appointed members of the Archbishops' Council.

2   The membership was originally 581. It was reduced to the current level in 2005.

It is also because under Article 8 of the General Synod constitution certain Measures or Canons (relating to the sacraments, the ministry or ecumenical relationships) have to be
approved by Diocesan Synods before being given final approval
by General Synod[1] and on other issues the dioceses are consulted. When matters are referred to the dioceses in this way
they are often passed down to Deanery Synods in order that
these can consider them as well.

*Archbishop Joseph Marona of the Sudan addressing General Synod (courtesy of the
Church of England)*

---

1   'A Measure or Canon providing for permanent changes in the Services of
    Baptism or Holy Communion or in the Ordinal, or a scheme for a con-
    stitutional union or a permanent and substantial change of relationship
    between the Church of England and another Christian body a substantial
    number of whose members reside in Great Britain, shall not be finally
    approved by the General Synod unless, at a stage determined by the
    Archbishop, the Measure or Canon or scheme, or the substance of the
    proposals embodied therein, has been approved by majority of dioceses at
    the meetings of their Diocesan Synods, or, in the case of the Diocese in
    Europe, of the Bishop's Council and standing Committee of that diocese'
    (*Constitution of the General Synod* 8 (1)).

The role of the General Synod in the life of the Church of England can be summarized as follows.

First, it has a *legislative* role. General Synod has the legislative authority previously exercised separately by the Church Assembly and the Convocations and therefore it has the power to regulate the internal life of the Church of England and its ecumenical relationships by means of Measures, Canons, Acts of Synod and other legal instruments.

Second, it has a *financial* role. The General Synod has the responsibility for approving the annual budget for the work of the Church of England as a national body and for approving any additional expenditure during the course of the year.

Third, it has a *deliberative* role. In the words of Paul Welsby, the General Synod acts as a forum for 'expressing Christian views and insights on major public issues, political, economic, social or moral'.[1]

THE HOUSE OF BISHOPS

The House of Bishops has two particular areas of responsibility.

The first of these areas is the doctrine, liturgy and the administration of the sacraments. Under Article 7(1) of the constitution of the General Synod, matters to do with the doctrine and liturgy of the Church of England or the administration of the sacraments have to be referred to the House of Bishops and can only be given final approval in a form proposed by the House of Bishops.[2]

The second area is that of ministry. The House of Bishops has a particular responsibility for the selection and training of the clergy and nationally authorized lay ministers. This responsibility is exercised through the work of the Bishops Committee for Ministry, which oversees the work of the Church of England's Ministry Division.

1   P. A. Welsby, *How the Church of England Works*, London: CIO Publishing, 1985, p. 52.
2   'A provision touching doctrinal formulae or the services or ceremonies of the Church of England or the administration of the Sacraments or sacred rites thereof shall, before it is finally approved by General Synod, be referred to the House of Bishops, and shall be submitted for such final approval in terms proposed by the House of Bishops and not otherwise' (*Constitution of the General Synod* 7(1)).

In addition to meeting as part of the General Synod, the House of Bishops also meets separately three times a year to consider issues relating to these two areas of responsibility and any other issues relevant to the role of the bishops in providing oversight and leadership to the Church of England.

The Archbishops' Council

The Archbishops' Council was established in 1999 with the aim of giving more coherence and coordination to the working of the central structures of the Church of England.

It consists of the Archbishops of Canterbury and York (who are its joint presidents), the prolocutors (chairmen) of the lower houses of the two Convocations, the chairman and vice chairman of the House of Laity, two members elected by the House of Bishops, two members elected by the House of Clergy, two members elected by the House of Laity, a Church Estates Commissioner and six people appointed by the Archbishops.

Under the terms of the National Institutions Measure 1998, the overall task of the Archbishops' Council is to '. . . co-ordinate, promote, aid and further the work and mission of the Church of England'. It seeks to fulfil this task by:

- giving a clear strategic sense of direction to the national work of the Church of England within an overall vision set by the House of Bishops and informed by an understanding of the Church's opportunities, needs and resources;
- encouraging and resourcing the Church in parishes and dioceses;
- promoting close collaborative working between the Church's national bodies, including through the management of a number of common services (Communications, Human Resources, IT etc.);
- supporting the Archbishops with their diverse ministries and responsibilities; and
- engaging confidently with Government and other bodies.[1]

The Archbishops' Council is also the Central Board of Finance for

---

1 *The Church of England Year Book 2006*, London: Church House Publishing, 2005, p. 14.

the Church of England, which means that it is responsible for proposing and managing the budget for the central work of the Church agreed by General Synod.

THE NATIONAL CHURCH INSTITUTIONS

The policies agreed by the General Synod and the Archbishops' Council are implemented at the national level by a number of boards, councils and divisions that are known collectively as the National Church Institutions and that are staffed by the employees of the Archbishops' Council. The constitution of each of these bodies varies but each is answerable in some way to the Archbishops' Council and to the General Synod.

- *The Board of Education*: In partnership with the National Society (a Church of England voluntary society working in the field of education), the Board of Education seeks to be a voice for the Church of England on education matters, and provides support and resources for work in schools and institutions of further and higher education (including the Church of England's own schools, colleges and universities), work with children and young people, lifelong learning and adult lay training.
- *The Cathedrals and Church Buildings Division*: The Cathedral and Church Buildings Division, which includes the Council for the Care of Churches and the Cathedrals Fabric Commission, provides advice and support relating to the use and maintenance of the Church of England's 16,000 parish churches and 41 cathedrals.
- *The Central Secretariat*: The Central Secretariat provides the secretariat for the General Synod, the House of Bishops and the Archbishops' Council. It also includes the Council for Christian Unity (CCU) (which is responsible for the development and implementation of the Church of England's ecumenical relationships and which is the parent body for the Faith and Order Advisory Group, the group that is responsible for considering Faith and Order matters on behalf of the Church of England) and Research and Statistics (which, as its name suggests, provides the Church of England with research and statistical data).
- *The Communications Unit*: The Communications Unit handles

the relations between the Church of England and the media at the national level. It also provides communications training for people across the Church, maintains the Church of England's website and incorporates the Church's Enquiry Centre which handles enquiries about the Church of England and the Christian faith from around the world.

- *The Financial Policy Unit*: This exists to support the Archbishops' Council in '. . . the development of its financial policy and in the monitoring and management of its finances'.[1] The Christian Stewardship Committee, which promotes '. . . the principle and practice of Christian stewardship as a part of discipleship',[2] comes under the Financial Policy Unit.
- *The Common Services Division*: This consists of a number of bodies providing a variety of services for the National Church Institutions and the wider Church of England. These bodies are Accounts, the Internal Audit Department, Church House Publishing (the official publishing arm of the Church of England), Information Technology and Office Services.
- *The Human Resources Division*: The Human Resources Division provides HR support for the staff of the National Church Institutions.
- *The Legal Office*: The Legal Office provides legal advice and other legal services for the General Synod, the Archbishops' Council and the National Church Institutions.
- *The Ministry Division*: The Ministry Division has responsibility, on behalf of the House of Bishops, for the selection, recruitment, training, deployment and remuneration of the Church of England's ordained ministers. It consists of four main committees: Vocation, Recruitment and Selection; Theological Education and Training; Deployment, Remuneration and Conditions of Service; and Ministry of and among Deaf and Disabled People. The Central Readers Council, which oversees the work of over 10,000 lay ministers in the Church of England, works in cooperation with the Ministry Division, which moderates and coordinates the training of readers.
- *The Mission and Public Affairs Division*: The work of the Mission and Public Affairs Division covers four main areas. These are: the Church's response to political, social and ethical issues

1 Ibid., p. 36.
2 Ibid., p. 36.

(here it continues the work of the former Board for Social Responsibility); issues facing ethnic minorities in the Church and wider society; mission and evangelism; and interfaith relations (here it continues the work of the former Board of Mission) and hospital chaplaincy. Its responsibilities in the fourth area are exercised through the work of the Hospital Chaplaincies Council.

- *The Records Centre*: The Church of England Record Office in Bermondsey houses the non-current records of the central bodies of the Church of England, the National Society and some ecumenical bodies. Its main function is to house the business records of the Church of England's central bodies, but it also provides advice for general queries concerning the archives of the Church of England. Some of these archives are also held in the library at Lambeth Palace, the official London residence of the Archbishop of Canterbury.

CENTRAL CHURCH COMMISSIONS

As well as the National Church Institutions just mentioned, there are also a number of commissions that undertake specific tasks, mostly of an advisory nature, for the Church of England at the national level.

The principal commissions are as follows:

- *The Clergy Discipline Commission*: This gives legal advice in relation to the working of the Clergy Discipline Measure of 2003, the new framework for taking disciplinary action against members of the clergy.
- *The Crown Nominations Commission*: This plays a key role in the appointment of diocesan bishops. When there is a vacancy for a diocesan bishop the Crown Nominations Commission agrees on two names (which may be in order of preference) that are submitted to the Prime Minister. The Prime Minister may then submit either of the two names to the Queen for her approval or may ask for other names to be proposed.[1]

---

1 As is noted in Chapter 5 below, the practice of submitting two names to the Queen via the Prime Minister is currently under review and it may change.

- *The Dioceses Commission*: This gives advice on matters relating to the diocesan structure of the Church of England. Such matters would include, for instance, changes in diocesan boundaries, the creation of new suffragan bishoprics, and the delegation of episcopal functions to a suffragan bishop by a diocesan bishop.
- *The Doctrine Commission*: This is a panel of theologians that gives advice on doctrinal issues referred to it by the House of Bishops and suggests to the House of Bishops matters that are of doctrinal concern to the Church of England. It has traditionally carried out this role by the production of scholarly reports, the most recent of which was the 2003 report on Christian anthropology entitled *Being Human*. The Doctrine Commission is currently in abeyance.
- *The Fees Advisory Commission*: This gives advice to General Synod on certain fees to be paid to ecclesiastical judges, legal officers and others.
- *The Legal Advisory Commission*: This gives advice on legal matters of general interest to the Church that are referred to it by national church bodies or by diocesan officials.
- *The Legal Aid Commission*: This administers the legal aid fund, which provides assistance with the legal costs of those appearing before Church of England courts or tribunals.
- *The Liturgical Commission*: This promotes the development and understanding of liturgy in the Church of England, exchanges liturgical information and advice with other churches, and develops new forms of liturgy for use in the Church of England such as the *Common Worship* services.

THE CHURCH COMMISSIONERS AND THE CHURCH OF ENGLAND PENSIONS BOARD

Two other important institutions that serve the Church of England nationally are the Church Commissioners and the Church of England Pensions Board.

The Church Commissioners for England, who are responsible to both the Church and Parliament, were created in 1948 by a merger between two existing bodies: Queen Anne's Bounty, and the Ecclesiastical Commissioners.

Queen Anne established the former in 1704 in order to provide money 'for the augmentation of the maintenance of the poor clergy'. The money for this came from the restoration to the Church of payments by the clergy that had gone to the Pope prior to the Reformation, but which had subsequently gone to the Crown.

The latter were established by Parliament in 1836 as part of an attempt to organize the finances of the Church of England on a more rational basis. To quote Welsby once again, it became their task:

> . . . to carry out a great scheme of rearrangement of dioceses, to re-apportion bishops' incomes, and to re-model cathedral establishments. The large funds and properties which, as a result of these reforms, were diverted to the Commissioners were to be used to make additional provision for the cure of souls where most required. This came to include the augmentation of the incomes of poor benefices, and the provision of parsonage houses and stipends for assistant curates. The Commissioners did their work most efficiently and in the years that followed their creation they had laid upon them additional responsibilities, so that their office became a clearing house for most of the administrative problems of the Church, and particularly those concerned with 'the cure of souls'.[1]

There are 33 Church Commissioners, consisting of the two Archbishops, the First, Second and Third Church Estates Commissioners, eleven people elected by General Synod (four bishops, three clergy, three lay people), two deans or provosts, nine people appointed by the Crown and the Archbishops (including three appointed by the Archbishops after consultation with others including the Lord Mayors of London and York and the Chancellors of Oxford and Cambridge) and six *ex-officio* members (the Prime Minister, the Lord President of the Council, the Home Secretary, the Secretary of State for Culture, Media and Sport, the Speaker of the House of Lords and the Speaker of the House of Commons).

The First and Third Church Commissioners represent the Church Commissioners in the General Synod. They are part-time

---

1 Welsby, op. cit., p. 64.

salaried appointments and are responsible for the management and control of the Commissioners' day-to-day business. The Second Estates Commissioner is an MP who is unpaid and represents the Commissioners in the House of Commons.

The main function of the Church Commissioners is to manage the historic assets of the Church of England in order to provide support for the Church's ministry.

Its responsibilities in support of the Church's ministry include paying pensions for service before 1998, providing financial support for parishes in areas of 'need and opportunity', providing assistance to cathedrals to help with the cost of clergy and lay staff, paying the stipends and working expenses of bishops, and maintaining diocesan bishops' houses.

The Church Commissioners also have administrative responsibilities in relation to schemes for pastoral reorganization involving the combination of parishes in new benefices or in team or group ministries. In addition, they are involved with the procedures for declaring church buildings redundant and with certain other matters to do with church property.

Finally, the Church Commissioners are the channel through which clergy stipends and church pensions are paid.

As its name suggests, the Church of England Pensions Board, which was established in 1926, is responsible for providing pensions for Church of England clergy and lay workers.

FOR FURTHER READING

'Archbishops' Council', www.cofe.anglican.org/about/archbishopscouncil.
'The Church Commissioners', www.cofe.anglican.org/about/churchcommissioners.
The Church of England Year Book, London: Church House Publishing, published annually.
'General Synod', www.cofe.anglican.org/about/gensynod.
Podmore, C., *Aspects of Anglican Identity*, London: Church House Publishing, 2005, Ch. 7.
Welsby, P., *How the Church of England Works*, London: Church Information Office, 1985, Chs XI–XII (some of the details in this are now out of date).

4 The Government of the Church of England at the Diocesan, Deanery and Parochial Levels

THE DIOCESE

Diocesan synods

Diocesan synods were an important feature of the life of the Church of England in the pre-Reformation period. They ceased to exist after the end of the seventeenth century, but the practice of holding some form of representative diocesan assemblies of clergy and lay people became universal during the second half of the nineteenth century. When the Church Assembly was established, its counterpart in the diocese became the diocesan conference. Because these conferences had an average membership of between 500 and 900 people they were too large to operate effectively and when the General Synod was established in 1970 these conferences were replaced with the smaller diocesan synods that exist today.

These diocesan synods, which meet at least twice a year, normally have between 120 and 270 members made up of approximately equal numbers of clergy and laity. Like General Synod, they are made up of three houses. There is a House of Bishops (consisting of the diocesan bishop, the suffragan bishops of the diocese (if any) and other assistant bishops nominated by the diocesan bishop with the agreement of the archbishop of the province), a House of Clergy and a House of Laity. The president of the synod is the diocesan bishop and there are two vice-presidents, one clerical and one lay, elected by their respective Houses.

The functions of the diocesan synods are the following:

(a) to consider matters concerning the Church of England and to make provision for such matters in relation to their diocese, and to express their opinion on any other matters of religious and public concern;

(b) to advise the bishop on any matters on which he may consult the synod;

(c) to consider and express their opinion on any matters referred to them by the General Synod, and in particular to approve or disapprove provisions referred to them by the General Synod under Article 8 of the Constitution;

(d) to consider proposals for the annual budget and to approve or disapprove them;

(e) to consider the annual accounts of the diocesan board of finance of the diocese.

Provided that the functions referred to in paragraph (a) hereof shall not include the issue of any statement purporting to declare the doctrine of the Church on any question.[1]

Diocesan synods normally vote as a single body, but either the diocesan bishop or ten members of the synod can require a vote by Houses and the Church Representation Rules state that 'nothing shall be deemed to have the assent of the diocesan synod unless the three houses which constitute the synod have assented thereto'.[2] In addition the rules further state that 'if . . . the diocesan bishop . . . so directs, the question shall be deemed to have the assent of the house of bishops only if the majority of the members of that house who assent thereto includes the diocesan bishop'.[3]

These rules give the diocesan bishop an effective veto over the decisions of his diocesan synod. This is intentional and reflects a

---

1 Synodical Government Measure 1969, section 4(2) as amended by the Synodical Government (Amendment) Measure 2003.

2 Church Representation Rules 34:1 (e).

3 Ibid. As Colin Podmore notes: 'These provisions do not apply to references under Article 8 of the General Synod's constitution, since the diocesan bishop will have the right to vote on the same matter as a member of the House of Bishops of the General Synod at the final approval stage. A matter referred under Article 8 is deemed to have been approved by the diocesan synod if the House of Clergy and House of Laity voting separately have approved it' (C. Podmore, *Aspects of Anglican Identity*, London: Church House Publishing, 2005, p. 180).

conviction that the diocesan bishop carries the ultimate responsibility for the well-being of the diocese and that in the last resort it is therefore his duty to block any decision that he believes to be detrimental to this. On the other hand, Canon C18 also expresses the conviction that this power of veto should not be used lightly: 'Where the assent of the bishop is required to a resolution of the diocesan synod it shall not lightly nor without good cause be withheld.'

The Bishop's Council

Each diocese is also required to have a Bishop's Council, which is also the standing committee of the diocesan synod. This body consists of members of the diocesan synod and its function is to perform the advisory and consultative functions of the diocesan synod between synod meetings, with the proviso that either the diocesan bishop or the Bishop's Council may require any matter to be referred to the synod itself.

In the Diocese of London, which is divided into five Episcopal Areas, there are Area Councils. The function of these Area Councils is:

- to provide support and advice to the Area Bishop on the whole mission, ministry and administration of the Church in the Area and to consider such matters about which the Area Bishop may choose to consult it;
- to decide on such matters of Area concern as the diocesan synod, or other competent authority within the diocese designated by it under the terms of the London Area Scheme, may from time to time delegate to it, subject to policy agreed by the Diocesan Synod or other designated body.

Diocesan boards and committees

The diocesan synod and the Bishop's Council determine the overall policy of a diocese, but policy in more specific matters is decided by a series of diocesan boards and committees. The way these are organized varies from diocese to diocese, but in the Diocese of St Albans, for example, the main boards and committees are:

- The Diocesan Board of Finance
- The Diocesan Pastoral Committee
- The Redundant Churches Uses Committee
- The Diocesan Board of Education
- The Diocesan Board for Christian Development
- The Diocesan Board for Church and Society
- The Diocesan Advisory Committee for the Care of Churches
- The Diocesan Board of Patronage
- The Liturgical Committee

Only the Diocesan Board of Finance, the Diocesan Pastoral Committee and the Board of Education are required by law to exist and there is an increasing tendency for dioceses to have fewer boards and committees than are on the current St Albans list. There is also an increasing tendency for dioceses to integrate the Bishop's Council with the Diocesan Pastoral Committee and/or the Board of Finance.

In addition to such boards and committees each diocese also has a number of bodies made up of full- or part-time staff that exist to implement at the diocesan level policies agreed by the diocese and by the Church of England nationally.

What these bodies are called and how they are organized varies from diocese to diocese, but the Diocese of St Albans, for instance, calls these bodies 'teams' and it currently has an Administration Team, an Education Team, a Ministry Development Team, a Parish Development Team, a Vocations Team and a Church and Society Team. In addition, the diocese also has its own legal officers.

THE DEANERY

From 1919 to 1969 most dioceses in the Church of England had not only diocesan conferences but also ruridecanal conferences in which clergy of the deaneries were joined by lay representatives.

With the introduction of the General Synod and diocesan synods in 1970, these ruridecanal conferences were replaced by a system of deanery synods.

Deanery synods have a minimum of 50 members and a maximum of 150. They consist of a House of Clergy and a House of Laity. All the beneficed and licensed clergy in the deanery are automatically members of the House of Clergy. Although each parish has at least one representative in the House of Laity, the number of lay representatives it has varies according to its size. The joint chairs of a deanery synod are the rural dean and an elected member of the House of Laity.

The functions of the deanery synods are the following:

(a) to consider matters concerning the Church of England and to make provision for such matters in relation to their deanery, and to consider and express their opinion on any other matters of religious and public interest;

(b) to bring together the views of the parishes of the deanery on common problems, to discuss and formulate common policies on these problems, to foster a sense of community and interdependence among those parishes, and generally to promote in the deanery the whole mission of the Church, pastoral, evangelistic, social and ecumenical;

(c) to make known and so far as appropriate to put into effect any provision made by the diocesan synod;

(d) to consider the business of the diocesan synod, and particularly any matters referred to that synod by the General Synod, and to sound parochial opinion whenever they are required or consider it appropriate to do so;

(e) to raise such matters as the deanery synod considers appropriate with the diocesan synod.

Provided that the functions referred to in paragraph (a) hereof shall not include the issue of any statement purporting to declare the doctrine of the Church on any question.[1]

In addition to these statutory functions, diocesan synods may also delegate other functions to deanery synods, including the setting of the parish 'quota' or 'share' – the amount of money to be paid by each parish to finance diocesan expenditure. Increasingly dioceses are asking deaneries to decide on the deployment of paid ('stipendiary') clergy within the deanery as part of a coherent diocesan mission strategy.

Finally, deanery synods also act as the electoral college for most

---

1   The Synodical Government Measure 1969, 5 (3).

of the clerical and almost all of the lay members of both the diocesan synod and General Synod.

In the Diocese in Europe there are either archdeaconry synods or one or more deanery synods in each archdeaconry. This provision reflects the varying sizes of the archdeaconries of the Diocese in Europe, some of which are not big enough to make it sensible to have separate deanery synods.

THE PARISH

Parochial church councils

In England, from the sixteenth century onwards, the body responsible for the government of a parish was the vestry. The vestry was responsible for both the ecclesiastical affairs of the parish and also for other matters relating to the government of the parish such as the administration of the Poor Law.

In 1894 the civil functions of the vestries were taken over by a system of parish councils and in 1919 parochial church councils (PCCs) were established as part of the new Church Assembly system to give the laity a share in the government of the Church of England at the parochial level.[1]

Under the terms of the Synodical Government Measure the functions of the parochial church councils are defined as including:

(a) cooperation with the incumbent in promoting in the parish the whole mission of the Church, pastoral, evangelistic, social and ecumenical;

(b) the consideration and discussion of matters concerning the Church of England or any other matters of religious or public interest, but not the declaration of the doctrine of the Church on any question;

(c) making known and putting into effect any provision made by the diocesan synod or the deanery synod, but without

---

1   It is important to note the distinction between parish councils and parochial church councils because the two are still frequently confused. The popular BBC comedy series *The Vicar of Dibley*, for example, depicts the vicar as attending meetings of the parish council at which the affairs of the local church are discussed.

prejudice to the powers of the council on any particular matter;

(d) giving advice to the diocesan synod and the deanery synod on any matter referred to the council;

(e) raising such matters as the council consider appropriate with the diocesan synod or deanery synod.[1]

In addition to these general responsibilities, parochial church councils also have a number of specific rights and responsibilities.

- They have the right to be consulted about the appointment of a new incumbent and about any proposal for parochial reorganization or any proposal for the sale or demolition of the 'parsonage house'.[2]
- They have an important voice in deciding which forms of liturgy shall be used in the church.
- They are responsible for the financial affairs of the church.
- They are responsible for the maintenance of the church building[3] and the churchyard, and for the maintenance and administration of any other property that the church owns.
- They are the employers of anyone employed to work for the church such as, for instance, vergers, youth workers or organists.

The membership of a parochial church council is made up of the parochial clergy,[4] any deaconesses, lay workers or readers licensed to work in the parish, the churchwardens, the deputy churchwardens (if any), any lay General Synod, diocesan synod or deanery synod members from the parish, elected lay representatives and any co-opted members. The chairman of the parochial church council is always the incumbent or priest-in-charge of the parish and there is also a vice-chairman, who is a member of the laity.

Elections to the parochial church council take place at the

---

1 The Synodical Government Measure 1969, 6:2 (2).

2 'Parsonage house' is the technical term for the house provided for the incumbent of the parish. It is more normally known as the 'rectory' or the 'vicarage'.

3 Or church buildings if, as sometimes happens, there is more than one church building in a parish.

4 'All clerks in Holy Orders beneficed in or licensed to the parish' – Church Representation Rules 2006, 14(1) (a).

Annual Parochial Church Meeting (the APCM) and the electors are those who are on the Church Electoral Roll. This consists of those aged 16 or above who are baptized and who have declared themselves:

(a) to be a member of the Church of England or of a Church in communion therewith resident in the parish; or

(b) to be such a member and, not being resident in the parish, to have habitually attended public worship in the parish during a period of six months prior to the enrolment; or

(c) to be a member in good standing of a Church which subscribes to the doctrine of the Holy Trinity (not being a Church in communion with the Church of England) and also prepared to declare himself to be a member of the Church of England having habitually attended public worship in the parish during a period of six months prior to the enrolment.[1]

The Parochial Church Council of St-Martin-in-the-Fields, in London (courtesy of St-Martin-in-the-Fields)

It should be noted that the older vestry system still has a residual existence in the sense that churchwardens are chosen at an annual parish meeting, known also as a meeting of the parishioners or the Easter vestry meeting. Although this is normally held at the same

---

1 Church Representation Rules 1(2).

time as the APCM, it is a separate meeting at which anyone living in the parish whose name is on the local government register of electors is entitled to vote, as well as anyone on the Church Electoral Roll even if they do not live in the parish.

Other local church councils

In parishes where there is more than one church building there are often district church councils (DCCs) that are responsible under the authority of the parochial church council for matters relating to that building, to the services and other activities taking place there, and to that part of the parish.

Where two or more parishes form part of one benefice, or where the same incumbent is responsible for two or more parishes separately, provision is made for the setting up of a joint parochial church council to exist alongside the PCCs for the purpose of considering matters of common concern to the parishes involved. Where there are team or group ministries, team or group councils responsible for the affairs of that team or group may also be established.

In the Diocese in Europe, where there are chaplaincies rather than parishes, there are chaplaincy councils that have the same functions as PCCs, and in cathedrals there are congregational councils that have responsibility for various matters relating to the life of the regular cathedral congregation. These latter are not, however, responsible for the fabric of the cathedral or its overall finances. These are a matter for the dean and chapter.

PRINCIPLES OF CHURCH GOVERNMENT IN THE CHURCH OF ENGLAND

There are a number of key principles that underlie the way that the Church of England is governed.

The first of these is that the government of the Church of England is something that takes place before God and under His authority. It is in acknowledgement of this fact that meetings of synodical bodies at all levels in the Church take place in an atmosphere of prayer and worship and are often accompanied by the celebration of the Eucharist. It is as God's worshipping people that the members of synodical bodies meet to take decisions for the well-being of His Church and for the furtherance of His mission in the world.

The common practice of pausing for prayer before any particularly difficult decision is made also indicates an awareness of the fact that the government of the Church of England is not meant to be an exercise in human autonomy, but something that is guided by God.

The second principle is that the government of the Church of England is undertaken with royal authority and is part of the government of the country. General Synod meets in accordance with a writ issued by the Queen and its five yearly sessions are opened by the Queen in person. Measures and Canons passed by General Synod, having received the royal assent, are part of the law of the land just as much as a law passed by Parliament.

It is also important to note that the other side of this is that General Synod cannot meet without royal authority and that it cannot legislate for itself without royal assent, both limitations put in place by Henry VIII at the Reformation. The power of the Church of England to govern itself is thus both upheld and limited by its relationship with royal authority, an issue which we shall look at in more detail when we come to look at the establishment of the Church of England in the next chapter.

The third principle is that the Church of England is a single national church.[1] It is often believed by people in the Church of England that the Church of England is a federation of parish churches or alternatively that it is a federation of dioceses, each of which, led by its diocesan bishop, constitutes a church in its own right. However, from Saxon times onwards the *Ecclesia Anglicana* was seen as a single national body and this principle was upheld at the Reformation and continues to be upheld today. In the words of Colin Podmore:

> The Church of England has a corporate identity at the national level. Its bishops attend meetings of the General Synod not just at the head of the representatives of their own dioceses but also

---

1 When it is said that the Church of England is a 'national church' what this means is that it is in a particular way the church of and for the people of England, even though it now operates over a far wider geographical area. For more on this issue see chapter 5, 'The Establishment of the Church of England'.

as members of the Church of England's corporate episcopal leadership at the national level. The importance of this is symbolized by the fact that the bishops mainly sit together, rather than sitting with the members of their own dioceses. The General Synod is not a federal conference at which largely autonomous dioceses are represented by delegations casting 'block votes'. Each member speaks and votes as an individual member of the whole Synod (or of his or her house within the Synod), and exercises those responsibilities on behalf of the whole church at the national level.[1]

The existence of the Church of England as one church at both the national and the local levels is reflected in the way in which matters concerning the faith and worship of the Church of England are determined for the whole Church at the national level by General Synod. Diocesan and deanery synods and parochial church councils are specifically precluded from making their own decisions on such matters.

On the other hand the fact that the Church of England exists as one church at both the national and local levels is shown by the fact that under Article 8 of the General Synod matters to do with the sacraments, the ministry of the Church and certain schemes for church unity have to be referred to the dioceses for discussion and agreement before General Synod can give them final approval. On these key matters affecting the fundamental identity of the Church of England, General Synod can only proceed after the Church at the local level has been properly consulted. It is also shown by the fact that it is possible for matters of concern raised at the local level to be passed on from parochial level via the deanery and diocesan synods for discussion and action at General Synod.

The government of the Church of England is thus neither a 'top down' nor a 'bottom up' system, but both. It is a system of interdependence, reflecting the interdependence of the members of the one body of Christ outlined by St Paul in 1 Corinthians 12:12–31 and Ephesians 4:1–16.

The fourth principle is that in the government of the Church, bishops, clergy and laity all need to work together. To quote Podmore again: 'A synod is a representative gathering of the whole

---

1 Podmore, op. cit, p. 121.

Church at the level concerned, and thus necessarily involves representatives of the clergy and of the laity as full members.'[1] Although parochial church councils are not called synods they are in reality an extension of the synodical system to the parochial level and thus the synodical principle applies in their case as well.

Despite the fact that the synodical system is a representative system of government, as Podmore further notes, it is not a straightforwardly democratic one. Referring to the synodical system at deanery level and above, he writes that:

> Synods do not . . . simply represent the members of the Church in numerical proportion (which would result in a huge majority of lay members); instead the partnership between clergy and laity is expressed by the clergy and the laity having approximately equal numbers of members. Furthermore, important or controversial proposals need the support of all three houses (bishops, clergy and laity voting separately).[2]

The fifth and final principle is that the bishops have a particular role in the government of the Church of England because it is an episcopal church in which the bishops are the guardians of its faith and those with overall pastoral responsibility for their dioceses. As we have seen, this principle is expressed in the fact that in the General Synod the bishops have a specific responsibility for matters to do with worship and doctrine and that in diocesan synods a resolution cannot be passed without the agreement of the diocesan bishop.

The central place that the bishops have in the government of the Church of England also finds expression in the fact that the bishops sit at the centre of the assembly chamber at Church House, Westminster with the rest of the Synod gathered around them, by the fact that the Archbishops of Canterbury and York are the presidents of the General Synod and of the Archbishops' Council, and by the fact that the diocesan bishop is the president of the diocesan synod and of the bishop's council.

---

1 Ibid., p. 120.
2 Ibid., p. 120.

HOW THE CHURCH OF ENGLAND IS FUNDED

The activities of the Church of England at all levels of its life have to be paid for. Many people still believe that the Church of England receives money directly from the state, but this is not the case. In addition, there is no church tax or membership fee as there is in some other European countries.

Traditionally the Church of England was financed in four ways.

- The Church owned land and property and this brought in income.
- There were tithes, which were a percentage of agricultural production paid to the Church.
- There were fees payable for some of the services of the Church such as weddings or funerals.
- There was voluntary giving by the faithful.

Although this way of financing the Church lasted for over a thousand years, by the nineteenth and twentieth centuries there were seen to be two large problems with it.

Firstly, farmers became increasingly unwilling to pay tithes, both because in many cases they were themselves struggling to survive financially and also because those farmers who were not Anglicans felt that they should not have to pay for a church to which they did not belong. Tithes were finally abolished in 1936.

Secondly, the resources of the Church of England were unevenly spread across the country, which meant that while some parishes and dioceses were extremely wealthy others were extremely poor.[1] This was felt to be something that needed to be addressed, both in order to express more clearly the truth of the mutual interdependence of the body of Christ and in order that the mission of the Church to the whole nation might be carried out more effectively.

In response to these two problems, the system of financing the Church of England that we have today developed instead.

The parishes have five sources of income:

---

1 This affected not only how much money the serving clergy received but also the size of pensions for retired clergy since the pensions of the clergy were paid by their successors out of the income they received from the parish.

- voluntary giving by the faithful (this has become increasingly important and now accounts for three-quarters of the Church's income);
- the payment of fees (fees for baptism certificates, weddings, funerals, memorials in churchyards and searches in church registers are used to cover the cost of using church buildings, to pay those taking part in services – such as organists, choir members and bell ringers – and also to provide a source of income to the parish);
- reserve funds (as the name suggests, these are sums of money that are not required for immediate expenditure and are kept in reserve to be called on in case of need);
- historic assets (some parishes have assets in terms of land, property or investments that have been inherited from the past and still produce income today. For example, the author once knew a rural parish in Devon that owned a field and used it to raise sheep that were sold to raise money for the Church);
- fund-raising activities (these take a wide variety of forms, ranging from asking for donations from, and selling souvenirs to, visitors to historic churches, through sales of recordings of church choirs, to hiring out church halls for use by community groups).

Parishes use the money that they raise to pay for the working expenses of their clergy, to pay for any locally employed staff (for example parish administrators, youth workers or community workers), to pay for other parochial activities and to pay for the upkeep of the church building and any other property the parish owns as well as any new building projects the parish wishes to undertake. As we have previously indicated, a proportion of the parish's income, known as the 'quota' or 'share', is also paid to the diocese to finance diocesan expenditure. The amount paid by each parish to the diocese depends on its size and its ability to pay. Finally, most parishes give away part of their income to support national and international mission and charitable work at home and overseas.

The dioceses have four sources of income:

- money from the parishes via the parish share (this provides the bulk of diocesan income);
- reserve funds;

- historic assets;
- money from the Church Commissioners (the Church Commissioners pay the stipends and working expenses of both diocesan and suffragan bishops and for the housing of diocesan bishops. They pay the stipends of the dean and two residentiary canons in each cathedral and give grants to cathedrals, mostly for the salaries of other staff. They also provide funds to help pay for parochial ministry in areas of particular need or mission opportunity).

Dioceses use most of their money (around 90 per cent) to pay for the stipends, housing, National Insurance contributions, Council Tax, pensions and training expenses of the stipendiary clergy.[1] Most of the remaining money is used to pay for diocesan staff and activities, but some of it is paid to the Church of England nationally, this latter amount depending on the size of the diocese and its ability to pay.

The Church of England nationally has three sources of income:

- money from the dioceses;
- reserve funds;
- the historic assets managed by the Church Commissioners.

This money is spent in five main ways:

- to pay for the selection, training and ordination of the clergy;
- to pay for the General Synod, the Archbishops' Council and the National Church Institutions;
- to pay grants to ecumenical and other bodies such as the World Council of Churches, the Conference of European Churches and Churches Together in England;
- to pay the pension contributions of Church of England clergy working for mission agencies;
- to subsidize and pay for the administration of the scheme that provides retirement housing for the clergy.

In addition, the Archbishops' Council disperses two types of funds from the Church Commissioners. There is the 'selective

---

1   This money is collected together and paid out on a national basis through the Church Commissioners and the Church of England Pensions Board.

allocation', which is given to the least-well-off dioceses to help pay for the stipends and housing of the clergy, and the 'parish mission fund', which is given to all dioceses to support mission initiatives, but which can also be used to help pay for stipends.

Inequalities of income between parishes and dioceses are still a feature of the life of the Church of England. It is still the case that some parishes and dioceses are much wealthier than others. However, the current system of financing the Church of England has helped to lessen these inequalities and ensures that although there is some variation of stipends between dioceses, there is a national minimum stipend that all clergy receive no matter in which diocese or parish they are serving.

Overall, the Church of England is a financially robust institution, but it faces three financial challenges.

The first challenge is to persuade parishioners that regular financial support to the Church of England at a realistic level is an integral part of their Christian discipleship. Because of the misperception that the Church of England is supported by the state or has a lot of central funds it has taken a long time to get the message across that the Church is dependent on voluntary giving in the parishes for the bulk of its income and that in order to sustain its mission to the nation this giving needs to increase.

The second challenge is to pay for pensions. Like most institutions across the Western world the Church of England is facing an increasing pensions bill because its pensioners are living longer.

The third challenge is to pay for upkeep of the Church's cathedrals and parish churches. Unlike in some other countries, such as France in which the maintenance of all church buildings built prior to 1904 is the responsibility of the local municipalities, the upkeep of cathedrals and parish churches, many of which are among the country's most ancient and beautiful buildings, is paid for entirely by the Church and this is enormously expensive.

FOR FURTHER READING

Behrens, J., *Practical Church Management*, Leominster: Gracewing, 2005, Part I.

The Church of England Year Book, London: Church House Publishing, published annually.

Church Representation Rules 2006, London: Church House Publishing, 2006.

'Funding the Church of England', www.cofe.anglican.org/info/funding.

Podmore, C., *Aspects of Anglican Identity*, Ch. 7.
Welsby, P., *How the Church of England Works*, London: Church Information
Office, 1985, Chs III–VII (some of the details in this are now out of date).

5 The Establishment of the Church of England

THE MEANING OF 'ESTABLISHMENT'

At his or her coronation the British monarch takes an oath to uphold 'the Protestant reformed religion established by law' and 'to maintain and preserve inviolably the settlement of the Church of England, and the doctrine, worship, discipline and government thereof, as by law established in England'.

There can therefore be no doubt that the Church of England is officially regarded as an 'established' church. However, there is no official definition of precisely what the establishment of the Church of England involves. As Paul Welsby points out: 'one will search in vain for any act of Parliament or Deed of Trust formally establishing it in the same way that other Churches have been legally recognized since the Toleration Act of 1689'.[1] Furthermore, as Paul Avis notes, the term 'establishment' is one that has a number of different meanings.[2]

In fact, describing the Church of England as the 'established Church' in England is shorthand for saying that over the centuries the Church of England has developed a relationship with the state that is reflected in a whole series of laws. This relationship is different from that enjoyed by any other church and, in spite of the gradual loosening of the ties between church and state referred to in chapter one, it continues to give the Church of England a particular place in the life of the English nation.

---

[1] Welsby, op. cit., p. 45.
[2] Paul Avis, *Church, State and Establishment*, London: SPCK, 2001, Ch 3: 'The Meanings of Establishment'.

THE KEY FEATURES OF ESTABLISHMENT

The key features of the relationship that the Church of England has with the state are as follows:

(1) Being the Church 'of England' means that it has spiritual responsibility for every place and to every person in England. That is why the Church of England could never decide simply to walk away from any parish in England by, for example, giving up its ministry to rural areas or to the inner urban areas on the grounds that it was too difficult or too costly to go on ministering there.

This spiritual responsibility for every person and place in England means that parish priests have the legal obligation to baptize, marry[1] and to inter the body or ashes of those resident in their parishes when requested to do so. In the case of marriages, clergy act as registrars for the state and thereby make the marriage legal.

(2) The monarch must be in a position to receive communion within the Church of England.

(3) The Archbishop of Canterbury is the person who crowns the monarch.

(4) Representatives of the Church of England have: 'precedence in all religious services associated with events of importance in the national life'.[2]

(5) Bishops of the Church of England sit in the House of Lords by virtue of their office and a bishop says prayers in the House each day at the beginning of the day's sitting.

There are 26 bishops in the House of Lords at any one time, consisting of the two Archbishops, the Bishops of London, Durham and Winchester and the 21 other longest-serving diocesan bishops, with the exceptions of the Bishop of Sodor and Man, who sits in the Tynwald (the Manx Parliament), and the Bishop of Gibraltar in Europe.

(6) All bishops, both diocesan and suffragan, except the Bishop of Gibraltar in Europe and his suffragan, are appointed by

---

1 Except in the cases of divorced people whose former spouse is still living, who clergy may decline to marry.
2 *Church and State: Being the Report of a Commission Appointed by the Church Assembly*, London, 1952, p. 7.

Elizabeth II at her Coronation in Westminster Abbey in 1953 supported by the Bishop of Durham (Michael Ramsey) and the Bishop of Bath and Wells (Harold Bradfield) (Milton Archive, Getty Images)

the crown on the advice of the Prime Minister who in turn has names presented to him or her by the Church.

As previously noted, in the case of diocesan bishops names are presented to the Prime Minister by the Crown Nominations Commission. In the case of a suffragan bishop a name is presented to the Prime Minister by the diocesan bishop of the diocese in which the suffragan is to serve.

(7) The Crown also appoints some deans of cathedrals, some residentiary canons, and a large number of parish priests. This is also on the advice of the Prime Minister.

It is important to note that although the Crown appoints people to act as bishops and priests in particular places, it does not make them bishops or priests. People become bishops or priests by an act of God through the Church at their ordination and not by an act of the Crown. As a member of the laity the monarch cannot and does not ordain.

The role of the Prime Minister in Crown appointments is currently under review in response to the Church of England report *Talent and Calling*,[1] which looked at the appointment of suffragan bishops, deans, archdeacons and residentiary canons, and in the light of the recent Government paper *The Governance of Britain*.[2] However, at the moment the system just described still remains in force.

(8) All clergy who are British subjects have to take an oath of allegiance to the Crown before they can take office.

(9) The office of Chaplain to the Speaker of the House of Commons and certain professorships and chaplaincies in the Universities or Oxford, Cambridge and Durham are legally restricted to Anglican clergy.

(10) The Convocations and hence General Synod can only meet when a writ for them to do so has been issued by the Crown and the Queen opens each five-yearly session (Quinquennium) of the Synod.

(11) Canons and Measures agreed by General Synod are, as has been noted, laws of the land. However, as has also been noted, they have to receive the royal assent in order to become laws, and, in the case of Measures, they have to be agreed by Parliament.

(12) Church courts are part of the country's legal system and their verdicts are enforceable by the state. In addition, except in cases concerning worship and doctrine and those brought under the new Clergy Discipline Measure, the final court of appeal in ecclesiastical cases is a secular court, the Judicial Committee of the Privy Council (usually sitting with ecclesiastical assessors).

(13) The Church of England cannot discontinue using the Book of Common Prayer unless Parliament gives its agreement to a Measure specifically allowing it to do so.

---

1 *Talent and Calling*, London: Church House Publishing, 2007.
2 *The Governance of Britain*, CM 7170, July 2007, paragraphs 57ff.

THE THEOLOGY OF ESTABLISHMENT

The theological starting point for considering the issue of establishment is the recognition that both the Christian Church and the authority of the state are ordained by God for the well-being of humankind (Mt. 16:18; 1 Pet. 2:9–10; Rom. 13:1–7; 1 Pet. 2:13–14).

As Paul Avis explains, what follows from this starting point is that:

> As twin divinely ordained institutions – two channels through which God works for the well-being of God's human creatures – Church and State must necessarily relate to each other. They cannot ignore each other's existence. This can be put more positively by saying that they have mutual obligations and must, therefore, reach an arrangement that respects the calling and integrity of the other. The Church should not attempt to usurp the role of the State, legislating for the temporal aspects of society. The State should not attempt to dominate or control the Church or to usurp its spiritual authority. But that cannot mean that there is no interaction between them. In cognizance of its moral and spiritual obligations, the State may give formal recognition, in law and in the constitution, to the Christian religion and to one or more particular churches. This acknowledgement provides the Church with pastoral and prophetic opportunities that it cannot renounce without betraying its mission. It is helped to bring its ministry to bear on the life of the nation in every level: in local communities; in the numerous institutions that make up civil society; and nationally, in terms of public doctrine. It will not always be heeded, but to speak and sometimes to be ignored is better than to be structurally marginalized and socially invisible.[1]

The establishment of the Church of England as it exists today came into existence at the English Reformation on the basis of this idea of the distinct but related responsibilities of the Church and the state.

---

1 Avis, op. cit, p. 62.

We can see this if we consider two classic quotations from the Reformation period.

The first is the statement of royal authority contained in Article XXXVII of the Thirty-Nine Articles:

> The Queen's Majesty hath the chief power in this realm of England and her other dominions, unto whom the chief government of all estates of this realm, whether they be ecclesiastical or civil, in all causes doth appertain, and is not nor ought to be subject to any foreign jurisdiction.
>
> Where we attribute to the Queen's Majesty the chief government, by which titles we understand the minds of some slanderous folks to be offended, we give not to our princes the ministering either of God's word or of sacraments, the which thing the Injunctions also lately set forth by Elizabeth our Queen doth most plainly testify: but that only prerogative which we see to have been given always to all godly princes in Holy Scriptures by God himself, that is, that they should rule all estates and degrees committed to their charge by God, whether they be ecclesiastical or temporal, and restrain with the civil sword the stubborn and evil-doers.

The context for this statement is the disputes about the relationship between the Church, and more specifically the Papacy, and secular authorities that took place throughout the Middle Ages. The point that the statement makes is that there are two distinct spheres of authority. First of all, there is the political sphere and in this sphere the head of state, in this case the Queen, has supreme and God-given authority under the law over every sector of society, including the Church. In the words of Canon A7: 'We acknowledge that the Queen's excellent Majesty, acting according to the laws of the realm, is the highest power under God in this kingdom, and has supreme authority in all causes, as well ecclesiastical as civil.'

Secondly, there is the spiritual sphere and in this sphere authority belongs to the Church and to its properly appointed ministers. It is these ministers, and not the Queen, who have the authority to preach the word and celebrate the sacraments, the two defining activities that make the Church the Church.

The place of bishops in the House of Lords is often a factor in the debate about the relationship between Church and state. Their presence there has to be understood in relation to the authority of the bishops in the spiral sphere. This is because, although bishops are able to contribute to the business of the Lords as regional figures who are in close touch with a local constituency in any particular part of the country and to speak on behalf of the Church as an institution, these are not the primary reasons for their presence. Instead they are there primarily to lead the House in prayer at the start of each day's business (which they do on a rota basis), and to ensure that God's voice is heard when the business of the nation is being discussed (notably, for example, when major ethical issues are debated). Their work as members of the House of Lords is thus, from a theological perspective, a specific form of their general vocation as bishops to preach God's word and to lead people in prayer.

The second quotation is from Book VIII of the *Laws of Ecclesiastical Polity* by Richard Hooker, the classic apology for the sixteenth-century English settlement of religion. Responding to those who argued that the monarch had no right to exercise authority in matters to do with the Church, Hooker states:

> A gross error it is, to think that regal power ought to serve for the good of the body, and not of the soul; for men's temporal peace, and not for their eternal safety: as if God had ordained kings for no other end and purpose but only to fat up men like hogs, and to see that they have their mast. Indeed, to lead men unto salvation by the hand of secret, invisible and ghostly regiment, or by the external administration of things belonging unto priestly order, (such as the word and sacraments are,) this is denied unto Christian kings: no cause in the world to think them uncapable of supreme authority in the outward government which disposeth the affairs of religion so far as the same are disposable by human authority, and to think them uncapable thereof, only for that the said religion is everlastingly beneficial to them that faithfully continue in it.[1]

Like Article XXXVII, Hooker is clear that the monarch does not have authority in spiritual matters. However, again like the Article,

---

1   R. Hooker, *The Laws of Ecclesiastical Polity*, Bk VIII: iii.3.

he does hold that the monarch has rightful authority in matters to do with the 'outward government' of the Church; that is to say, how it functions as a human institution. What is distinctive though about Hooker is that he explains *why* it is that Christian kings should exercise authority in matters to do with the Church.

The point he makes is that human beings have souls as well as bodies. They are not purely material beings that can find their true end in life if their material needs are taken care of. They are also spiritual beings who can only find their true fulfilment in a right relationship with God. As the person with responsibility for the welfare of his subjects, it is consequently the monarch's job to see that the Church as an institution is in a state in which it can perform its spiritual tasks properly so that this right relationship with God is made possible.

As another writer has put it, the royal supremacy in regard to the Church is '. . . in its essence the right of supervision over the administration of the Church, vested in the Crown as the champion of the Church, in order that the religious welfare of its subjects may be duly provided for'.[1] It was this understanding of the role of the monarch that underlay the Reformation settlement in England and, although this fact is not always understood, it is this same understanding of the role of the monarch that underlies the role of the Queen in relation to the Church of England today. The role of the Queen, acting with the advice and consent of Parliament and in fulfilment of her coronation oath, is in relation to the legal framework within which the Church of England operates, and her ability to give or withhold assent to the Church's legislation and the appointment of its senior leaders means that, in the last resort, the Church could be forced to think again if it made decisions that compromised its ability to carry out its mission to the nation.

When the Queen is described as the 'Supreme Governor' of the Church of England, it is her right to exercise the role just described that is meant. What is being referred to is the outworking in relation to the Church of England of her role as head of state within Britain's constitutional monarchy. It is perhaps worth noting that all the churches in Great Britain are subject to the

---

1 Wakeman, *Introduction to the History of the Church of England*, quoted in E. C. S. Gibson, *The Thirty-Nine Articles of the Church of England*, 6th edn, London: Methuen, 1908, p. 771.

authority of the Queen as head of state. What is different in the case of the Church of England is the details of the relationship.

Under the Act of Supremacy of 1534 Henry VIII was described as the 'Supreme Head of the Church of England'. When Elizabeth I came to the throne the title was changed to that of 'Supreme Governor', which has been used ever since, in order to make it clear that the headship of Christ over the Church was not being challenged and that what was meant was the monarch's governmental role in relation to the Church resulting from him or her being the civil ruler of the country.

OBJECTIONS TO THE ESTABLISHMENT OF THE CHURCH OF ENGLAND

There are three objections to the establishment of the Church of England that are often raised today.

Objection 1

The first objection is that in an ecumenical age and in a pluralist society it is wrong for a particular Church and a particular religion to be given a special place in the life of the state. Three points are made in response to this objection.

The first response is to note that in a divided Church the establishment of the Christian religion necessarily involves the establishment of a particular form or forms of the Christian religion which in this country, for historical reasons, is the Church of England.

Furthermore, aware of its ecumenical obligations, the Church of England seek to ensure that it undertakes its established role in a way that supports other Christian churches; and in fact the leaders of the other churches often acknowledge that the established status of the Church of England is helpful in lending Christianity a degree of visibility in the public arena that it might not otherwise possess.

The second response is to say that England has historically been a Christian nation and that a large majority of people in this country who are not necessarily regular church attenders nevertheless still see themselves as having an inherited Christian identity. It therefore makes sense for the importance of religion in the life of the nation to be marked by a Christian establishment (in this case, for reasons already noted, the establishment of the Church of England).

In relation to this second response it is important to note that, just as the Church of England exercises its established role on behalf of other churches, it also exercises it on behalf of members of other religions by acting in a way that is helpful to the interests of religion in general as well as Christianity in particular. This is something that is acknowledged by the leaders of other religions who see the establishment of the Church of England as acting as a bulwark against the advent of a secular society in which the importance of religion is no longer given public recognition.

A further response, which is made by some (although not all) of the supporters of establishment, is to say that the recognition offered to Christianity by the state through the establishment of the Church of England is appropriate not simply because Christianity is the historical religion of this country or because most people would still identify themselves as being Christian in some way, but because Jesus Christ is the full and final revelation of God and eternal life is received only through Him.[1] As Anglican theologians such as Hooker have argued, it follows that a state that truly wishes to promote the welfare of its people will give its support to the Christian religion by making provision for the Christian religion to be proclaimed and promoted so that its truth is publicly acknowledged and people come to faith and baptism.

Objection 2

The second objection to establishment is that it is unjust and discriminatory to exclude Roman Catholics from inheriting the throne. The Act of Settlement of 1701, which still determines the matter, declares that:

> . . . all and every person and persons that then were, or afterwards should be reconciled to, or shall hold communion with the see or Church of Rome, or should profess the popish religion, or marry a papist, should be excluded, and are by that Act made for ever incapable to inherit, possess, or enjoy the Crown

---

1 For this point see the Church of England Doctrine Commission's report *The Mystery of Salvation* (London: Church House Publishing, 1995).

and government of this realm, and Ireland, and the dominions thereunto belonging . . .

In response, the point that needs to be understood is that while the fear of persecution of Protestants by a Roman Catholic monarch that lies behind this Act[1] is now happily a thing of the past, the relationship between a Roman Catholic sovereign and the established Church would still face a number of serious difficulties.

In spite of the significant improvement in the relations between the Roman Catholic and Anglican traditions in recent decades, it remains the case that the Roman Catholic Church still does not officially recognize the Church of England as being a church or its ministers as validly ordained. Because this is the case, the Canon Law of the Roman Catholic Church prevents Roman Catholics from receiving the Eucharist in Church of England churches. This in turn means that a Roman Catholic monarch would not be in a position to fulfil the requirement of being able to receive communion within the Church of England.

In addition the fact that the Roman Catholic Church does not officially recognize the Church of England as being a church or its ministers as validly ordained would make it difficult for a Roman Catholic to accept the role of supreme governor, to accept coronation by the Archbishop of Canterbury or to take the coronation oath to 'maintain in the United Kingdom the Protestant Reformed Religion established by law'.

Furthermore, given the hereditary nature of the monarchy and given the expectation of the Roman Catholic Church that children of mixed marriages should be brought up as Roman Catholics, it follows that for the monarch to be married to a Roman Catholic would be liable to cause the problems outlined in the previous paragraphs to recur in future generations.

Abolishing the Act of Settlement would thus run the danger of calling key aspects of the establishment of the Church of England into question. A better way of tackling the current situation is therefore to work for better ecumenical relations between the Roman Catholic and Anglican traditions in order to reach a stage

---

1 The revocation of the Edict of Nantes in 1685 and the subsequent persecution of the French Protestants by the Roman Catholic government of Louis XIV is what is in the immediate background.

where Roman Catholics can be in communion with the Church of England and these problems no longer exist.

Objection 3

The third objection is that it is wrong for the monarch to appoint Church of England bishops.

This objection comes in two parts. The first part is an objection in principle to a bishop not being chosen by the Church itself. The second part is an objection to the fact that the Queen acts on the advice of the Prime Minister who may not be a member of the Church of England or even a Christian. As has been noted, the role of the Prime Minister in the appointment of bishops is currently under review, but at the moment he or she still has a necessary part to play in the appointment process.

In response to the first part of the objection the point that needs to be made is that in reality all bishops are chosen by the Church.

Two names are submitted to the Queen (who is in any case a lay member of the Church of England) by a diocesan bishop (in the case of suffragan bishops) or by the Crown Nominations Commission (in the case of diocesan bishops or archbishops).[1] On the advice of the Prime Minister, the Queen, exercising her responsibility for the well-being of the Church and the nation, either accepts one of the two names offered to her[2] or asks the Church to provide other names for consideration. In the case of archbishops and diocesan bishops the successful candidate is then formally elected, in accordance with ancient tradition, by the dean and chapter of the diocesan cathedral.[3]

Also in accordance with ancient tradition, election is then followed by confirmation of election. As the 2001 Church of England report *Working with the Spirit: Choosing Diocesan Bishops* explains:

---

1 There are two permanent officials, the Prime Minister's Appointments Secretary and the Archbishops' Secretary for Appointments who assist the bishops and Commission with the process of identifying suitable candidates.

2 The names are ranked in order of preference and the first name is almost always (or in the case of suffragan bishops, always) the one appointed.

3 For the history behind this see C. Podmore, 'The Choosing of Bishops in the Early Church and in the Church of England: An Historical Survey', in *Working with the Spirit: Choosing Diocesan Bishops*, London: Church House Publishing, 2001, pp. 113–38.

In the Church of England, the election of a diocesan bishop is confirmed by the archbishop of the province (or by his vicar-general acting on his behalf) and the election of an archbishop by a commission consisting of the senior bishops of the province and the archbishop of the other province. It is the confirmation of the election which actually makes the candidate bishop of the diocese and commits to him 'the care, government and administration of the Spirituals of the said Bishopric'.[1]

The purpose of the confirmation of election is to confirm that the wider Church is content that a fit and proper person has been elected as a bishop or archbishop, and what we see in the process as a whole is different branches of the Church of England each exercising their proper responsibility to ensure that a suitable person is appointed.

In response to the second part of the objection the point that needs to be made is that it is constitutionally necessary for the Prime Minister to be involved in the process because in this, as in other matters, the Queen has to act with the advice and consent of her ministers. If the Prime Minister had complete freedom of choice in the name to be recommended to the Queen then his or her own religious beliefs (or lack of them) might be an issue, but as the names recommended by the Prime Minister are those the Church itself has already judged to be fit to be bishops there can be no question of the Prime Minister imposing on the Church someone whom the Church considers to be unsuitable.

In addition, because a diocesan bishop is someone who is going to play an important role in the life of the nation and is potentially going to be a member of the House of Lords, the Prime Minister has a legitimate political interest in seeing that someone suitable is appointed just as he or she has a legitimate political interest in other senior public appointments.

To sum up, what takes place when a bishop is appointed is a process in which the Church, the Queen (herself a part of the Church) and the Prime Minister all have their own proper role to play in order to ensure that a suitable person is chosen to exercise episcopal ministry in the life of the Church and of the nation as a whole.

---

1 *Working with the Spirit*, p. 81.

What is true of the involvement of the Queen and the Prime Minister in the appointment of bishops is also true of their involvement in other Church of England appointments. In these cases as well, the Church, the monarch and the Prime Minister all have their proper role in seeing that a suitable person is chosen.

APPENDIX 1 – THE QUEEN'S CORONATION OATH OF 1953

The Queen having returned to her Chair (her Majesty having already on Tuesday, the fourth day of November, 1952, in the presence of the two Houses of Parliament, made and signed the Declaration prescribed by Act of Parliament), the Archbishop standing before her shall administer the Coronation Oath, first asking the Queen,
Madam, is your Majesty willing to take the Oath?

And the Queen answering,

I am willing,

The Archbishop shall minister these questions; and the Queen, having a book in her hands, shall answer each question severally as follows:

Archbishop: Will you solemnly promise and swear to govern the Peoples of the United Kingdom of Great Britain and Northern Ireland, Canada, Australia, New Zealand, the Union of South Africa, Pakistan and Ceylon, and of your Possessions and other Territories to any of them belonging or pertaining, according to their respective laws and customs?
Queen: I solemnly promise so to do.
Archbishop: Will you to the utmost of your power cause Law and Justice, in Mercy, to be executed in all your judgements?
Queen: I will.
Archbishop: Will you to the utmost of your power maintain the Laws of God and the true profession of the Gospel?
Will you to the utmost of your power maintain in the United Kingdom the Protestant Reformed Religion established by law?
Will you maintain and preserve inviolably the settlement of the Church of England, and the doctrine, worship, discipline, and government thereof, as by law established in England?
And will you preserve unto the Bishops and Clergy of England, and to the Churches there committed to their charge, all such

rights and privileges, as by law do or shall appertain to them or any of them?

Queen: All this I promise to do.

Then the Queen arising out of her Chair, supported as before, the Sword of State being carried before her, shall go to the Altar, and make her solemn Oath in the sight of all the people to observe the promises: laying her right hand upon the Holy Gospel in the great Bible (which was before carried in the procession and is now brought from the altar by the Archbishop, and tendered to her as she kneels upon the steps) [The Bible to be brought], and saying these words:

The things which I have here promised, I will perform, and keep. So help me God.

APPENDIX 2 – THE PROCESS FOR THE APPOINTMENT OF DIOCESAN BISHOPS FOLLOWING NOMINATION BY THE CROWN

After a bishop has been nominated by the Crown, the procedure is as follows:

(1) The Sovereign forwards to the dean and chapter of the diocese the *conge d'elire*, which is the licence giving them permission to elect. The licence is accompanied by a Letter Missive from the Sovereign, containing the name of the man chosen by the Crown and instructing the chapter to elect him. If it should refuse to elect, the Sovereign can proceed to appoint by Letters Patent. In fact the chapter invariably does elect the Royal nominee.

(2) The Crown instructs the archbishop of the province to confirm the election and, if the candidate is not already in episcopal orders, to consecrate. By convention, which seems to go back at least to the reign of Charles II, the Vicar General of the Province holds a court for the purpose of confirming the election, other than the election of an archbishop, which by statute is carried out by a Commission of bishops.

(3) The archbishop consecrates the new bishop, other bishops assisting, and it is then that he is admitted to the episcopate.

(4) Following the consecration, or the confirmation of election if

someone is already a bishop, the new bishop pays homage to the Queen and receives the temporalities of his office. The 'temporalities' are the property and revenues belonging to a bishop, which are administered by the Crown during an episcopal vacancy and are then restored to a new bishop. Traditionally these temporalities consisted in the episcopal residences and estates, but because these are now vested in the Church Commissioners as part of the historic assets of the Church, what they consist of today is the right to appoint incumbents to some of the benefices in the diocese.

(5) The newly appointed and consecrated bishop is enthroned in the cathedral church of his diocese. This ceremony possesses no legal significance, but it marks the ceremonial and public entry of the new bishop into his cathedral and diocese.

(based on Paul Welsby, *How the Church of England Works*, pp. 47–8)

FOR FURTHER READING

Avis, P., *Church, State and Establishment*, London: Church House Publishing, 2001.

Podmore, C., *Aspects of Anglican Identity*, London: Church House Publishing, 2005, Ch. 9.

Welsby, P., *How the Church of England Works*, London: Church Information Office, 1985, Ch. X.

Working with the Spirit: Choosing Diocesan Bishops, London: Church House Publishing, 2001.

6 The Church of England's Legal System

WHY A SYSTEM OF CHURCH LAW IS NEEDED

As Paul Welsby notes, the existence of a system of laws is a necessary part of the existence of the Christian Church:

> From the earliest times it has been conceded that a Church has the right to make its own laws for its members. Every society has its rules for the management of its own affairs, and the members of a particular society agree to abide by the rules of that society. In the case of the Church, however, there is a higher sanction for the formulation and enforcement of rules and regulations for its members. That sanction rests upon the commission given by Jesus Christ to his apostles: 'What things soever ye shall bind upon earth shall be bound in heaven; and what things soever ye shall loose on earth shall be loosed in heaven' (Matt. 18.18). The commission to 'bind' and to 'loose' means to 'declare forbidden' and to 'declare allowed'. The first apostles regarded rules and regulations as of considerable importance, and one only has to refer to St Paul's detailed rules for divine worship in the Church at Corinth (1 Corinthians) or to the regulations made at the first council of Jerusalem (Acts 15) concerning the admission of Gentiles into the Christian Church to see how necessary it was at a very early stage that corporate legislation needed to be promulgated. And so in every generation the Church, by virtue of Christ's commission, has made whatever rules have been necessary for the ordering of its corporate life. Now the Church is not a body of perfected saints but is made up of ordinary frail human beings. It follows, therefore, that unless chaos is to prevail the rules and regulations which it makes must be more than exhortations which anyone can set aside when he wishes. Instead, they must be laws that can be

enforced and to which are attached penalties for their non-observance.[1]

THE SOURCES OF CHURCH LAW

Because this is so, every particular church has developed its own system of laws and the Church of England is no exception. In the case of the Church of England this law is drawn from a number of different sources:

- First, there is statute law, that is to say Acts of Parliament or Measures of the Church Assembly or the General Synod, which have the same legal force as Acts of Parliament. This would now also include European legislation that forms part of English law.
- Secondly, there is subordinate legislation, such as Orders in Council or Statutory Rules and Orders that are made under the authority of an Act or Measure.
- Thirdly, there is common law, which is that part of the law relating to the Church that is based on custom and immemorial practice.
- Fourthly there are the current Canons of the Church of England.
- Fifthly, there is that part of the Church of England's Pre-Reformation Canon law that was allowed to remain in force when the law of the Church of England became subordinate to Royal authority by the Act of the Submission of the Clergy in 1533 and that has not subsequently fallen into disuse.

Different parts of the body of ecclesiastical law that is based on these sources apply to the clergy and the laity. To quote Welsby again:

(1) That part of ecclesiastical law which is embodied in Acts of Parliament and in Measures of the Church Assembly, and the General Synod, is binding upon both the clergy and the laity.

---

1 P. Welsby, *How the Church of England Works*, London: CIO Publishing, 1985, p. 68.

(2) Such pre-Reformation Canons and ancient usage which remain lawful are binding upon both the clergy and the laity.
(3) The Canons of 1969 are not legally binding upon the laity (other than certain lay officers), except in so far as they declare the ancient usage and law of the Church of England allowed in 1533.[1]

In the case of the Diocese in Europe the laws affecting the Church of England apply in so far as they are relevant to the specific settings in which the diocese operates. The diocese is also subject to the national laws of the countries in which it works although these rarely conflict with the laws governing the Church of England in general.

THE CHURCH'S SYSTEM OF COURTS AND TRIBUNALS

Diocesan courts and tribunals

Each bishop of the Church of England has a diocesan court for administering church law in his diocese. In every diocese except Canterbury this is called the Consistory Court and is presided over by a judge acting on behalf of the bishop who is known as the Chancellor. In the diocese of Canterbury the court is known as the Commissary Court and the judge is known as the Commissary General.

The principal role of these courts is the granting of faculties (official licences) for altering the fabric or furniture of churches in the diocese. When hearing these cases the Chancellor sits alone.

These courts also used to hear cases of misconduct against the clergy not involving matters of doctrine, ritual or ceremonial. Under the new Clergy Discipline Measure, when such cases involve deacons or priests they are now heard by a Bishop's Disciplinary Tribunal consisting of a legally qualified chairman sitting with two lay members and two members of the clergy appointed from a provincial panel. Cases involving bishops are heard at the provincial level.

---

1 Ibid., p. 71.

Provincial courts

The Provinces of Canterbury and York have their own provincial courts. In the case of Canterbury this is the Court of the Arches presided over by the Dean of the Arches and in the case of York this is the Chancery Court of York which is presided over by the Auditor. Under the Ecclesiastical Jurisdiction Measure of 1963 the Dean of the Arches and the Auditor must be the same person.

These provincial courts hear appeals from the consistory courts in the dioceses and from the disciplinary tribunals. When hearing appeals from the disciplinary tribunals the Dean of the Arches/ Auditor sits with four other judges, two of whom are clergy from the provincial panel and two of whom are lay people with judicial experience.

Complaints of misconduct against bishops are heard in the Court of the Vicar General for each province. This also has five judges, one of whom must be a bishop.

The Archbishop of Canterbury also has his own Court of Faculties that has certain specific functions, such as the granting of special marriage licences and the appointment of public notaries, which were transferred to the Archbishop from the Pope at the Reformation. The Dean of the Arches, acting as Master of the Faculties, presides over this court.

The Judicial Committee of the Privy Council hears appeals from the Court of the Arches and the Chancery Court. When cases have been referred from disciplinary tribunals there is no further right of appeal.

Cases involving doctrine, ritual and ceremonial

Cases involving matters to do with doctrine, ritual or ceremonial come under the Ecclesiastical Jurisdiction Measure.

When proceedings are brought against a member of the clergy in a case concerning such matters, his or her diocesan bishop may decide that no further action be taken or may decide to refer the case to a committee of enquiry consisting of one bishop, two clergy and two diocesan chancellors from the province concerned. If the committee recommends further action, the case goes to the Court of Ecclesiastical Causes Reserved.

This court consists of five judges appointed by the Crown. Two of the judges are communicant lay people of the Church of England who have held high judicial office and three of them are either serving or retired diocesan bishops. This court is also the court of appeal from the Consistory Courts in faculty cases that involve matters to do with doctrine, ritual or ceremonial.

Appeals from the Court of Ecclesiastical Causes Reserved are heard by a Commission of Review consisting of three Lords of Appeal (senior judges) who are communicant lay people of the Church of England and two diocesan bishops with seats in the House of Lords. Appeal is to the Commission of Review rather than to the Judicial Committee of the Privy Council on the grounds that it would be improper for spiritual or theological matters to be determined by a secular court.

The decisions of the courts and tribunals of the Church of England are legally binding in terms of English law, although sometimes it is necessary to seek orders from the secular courts in order to enforce them.

FOR FURTHER READING

Welsby, P., *How the Church of England Works*, London: Church Information Office, 1985, Ch. XIV (this does not cover the changes brought in under the Clergy Discipline Measure 2003).

7 The Doctrine of the Church of England

DOCTRINAL AUTHORITIES IN THE CHURCH OF ENGLAND

As we noted at the end of the first chapter, in the midst of all the changes that have taken place in the Church of England over the course of its history one of the things that has remained constant is its commitment to the faith 'uniquely revealed in the Holy Scriptures and set forth in the catholic creeds'. In this chapter we shall look at how the Church of England understands this faith.

The way that the Church of England understands this faith is set out in its most authoritative form in what are known as the 'historic formularies'. This term refers to three sixteenth- and seventeenth-century documents, The Thirty-Nine Articles, the Book of Common Prayer and the Ordering of Bishops, Priests and Deacons (commonly known as the Ordinal).

- The Thirty-Nine Articles is a set of thirty-nine doctrinal statements. In large part the work of Archbishop Cranmer, it dates in its final form from 1571. It was the English equivalent to the sixteenth-century Protestant statements of faith produced in continental Europe such as the Lutheran Augsburg Confession of 1530 or the Reformed Second Helvetic Confession of 1566.
- The Book of Common Prayer (BCP) is the Church of England's traditional service book. Once again it is largely the work of Cranmer, and it reached its current form in 1662.
- The Ordering of Bishops, Priests and Deacons consists of services for 'making, ordaining and consecrating' bishops, priests and deacons. Like the other two formularies it is for the most part the work of Cranmer and it too reached its current form in 1662.

The title page of an original 1662 edition of the Book of Common Prayer (Wing ESTZ R3118, B3622 (His Majesties Printers)) (courtesy of Lambeth Palace Library)

The role that these historic formularies have as doctrinal authorities for the Church of England is set out in A5 and A15 Canons, Canon A5 and Canon C15.

Canon A5 is entitled 'Of the Doctrine of the Church of England'. It states that:

> The doctrine of the Church of England is grounded in the Holy Scriptures, and in such teaching of the ancient Fathers and Councils of the Church as are agreeable to the said Scriptures.
>
> In particular such doctrine is to be found in the Thirty-nine Articles of Religion, the Book of Common Prayer and the Ordinal.

Canon C15 is entitled 'Of the Declaration of Assent'. It contains a declaration made by the clergy and some authorized lay ministers of the Church of England at the time when they begin their ministries or when taking up new ministerial appointments.

This Canon begins with a Preface that runs as follows:

> The Church of England is part of the One, Holy, Catholic and Apostolic Church worshipping the one true God, Father, Son and Holy Spirit. It professes the faith uniquely revealed in the Holy Scriptures and set forth in the catholic creeds, which faith the Church is called upon to proclaim afresh in each generation. Led by the Holy Spirit, it has borne witness to Christian truth in its historic formularies, the Thirty-nine Articles of Religion, the Book of Common Prayer and the Ordering of Bishops, Priests and Deacons. In this declaration you are about to make will you affirm your loyalty to this inheritance of faith as your inspiration and guidance under God in bringing the grace and truth of Christ to this generation and making Him known to those in your care?

In response to this Preface the person making the Declaration of Assent then replies:

> I, (Name), do so affirm, and accordingly declare my belief in the faith which is revealed in the Holy Scriptures and set forth in the catholic creeds and to which the historic formularies of the Church of England bear witness; and in public prayer and administration of the sacraments, I will use only the forms of service that are authorised or allowed by Canon.

If the two Canons are taken together we learn four things.

First, there is a threefold hierarchy of doctrinal authorities. The primary authority is the Holy Scriptures (also referred to as the 'Bible') in which the Christian faith is 'uniquely revealed'. The secondary authority is the teaching of the Fathers and Councils of the early church that is in agreement with the Scriptures, with the 'catholic creeds' being viewed as a summary of this teaching. The tertiary authority is the historic formularies.

Secondly, although the historic formularies are a tertiary authority they are nonetheless important. They are the means by which, under the guidance of the Holy Spirit, the Church of England has borne witness to the faith revealed in the Scriptures and reflected in the teaching of the early church as summarized in the creeds. As such they are said to be the place in which the doctrine of the Church of England is particularly (although not exclusively) to be found.

Thirdly, the historic formularies are not seen simply as historical statements of doctrine. Rather, they are viewed dynamically in the sense that they are seen as providing 'inspiration and guidance' in bringing the 'grace and truth of Christ' to today's world.

Fourthly, the Church is called to 'proclaim afresh' in each generation the faith revealed in the Scriptures and set forth in the creeds. What needs to be noted here is that the content of the proclamation remains the same in every generation; what changes is the way it is presented in each new generation. The old truth has to be proclaimed, but it has to be proclaimed in new ways in order to make fresh connections with each succeeding generation.

There is a range of other documents that contain material that can also claim to have some degree of doctrinal authority for the Church of England. Examples of such documents would include ecumenical agreements entered into by the Church of England and authorized liturgical material subsequent to the Book of Common Prayer.

It needs to be noted, however, that such documents, important though they are, do not have the same official status as the historic formularies. It is the historic formularies that are the Church of England's official doctrinal standards and subsequent material is authorized on the understanding that it is consonant with the doctrine that they contain. In this chapter we shall therefore focus on the teaching of the historic formularies as they provide us with the most authoritative statement of what the Church of England's doctrines are.

It is widely held, and often said, that the Church of England's theology is based on Scripture, tradition and reason. The account of the Church of England's doctrinal authorities just given refers to Scripture and tradition, but says nothing about reason. What then does the Church of England think about the place of reason in theology?

The answer is that the Church of England understands the importance of reason for theology in two ways. Firstly, reason is understood in terms of the human capacity for rational thought and in this sense it is fundamental to theology because without the capacity for rational thought no theology would be possible. As Richard Hooker put it:

Theology, what is it but the science of things divine? What science can be attained unto without the help of natural discourse and reason? 'Judge you of that which I speak,' saith the Apostle [1 Corinthians 10.15]. In vain were it to speak any thing of God, but that by reason men are able to judge of what they hear and by discourse to discern how consonant it is to truth.[1]

Richard Hooker by William Faithorne, line engraving, published 1662 or after (National Portrait Gallery, London)

1   R. Hooker, *The Laws of Ecclesiastical Polity*, III.VIII.11.

Secondly, reason has also come to be understood by some in terms of what a recent Anglican report has called the 'mind of a particular culture' with 'its characteristic way of seeing things, asking about them, and explaining them'.[1]

It is important to note that reason in both these senses is not an additional doctrinal authority on a par with Scripture and its interpretation in the tradition of the Church. Reason in the first sense is the instrument by which Scripture and tradition can be rightly understood. Reason in the second sense is the wider intellectual background against which theology operates and which it is called upon to address.

WHAT THE CHURCH OF ENGLAND BELIEVES

In this second section of the chapter we shall use the historic formularies as the basis for looking at what the Church of England believes about a number of key doctrinal topics.

... about the Bible

For the Church of England the Bible consists of 66 books that the Church as a whole has always accepted as canonical.

In the Old Testament these are: Genesis, Exodus, Leviticus, Numbers, Deuteronomy, Joshua, Judges, Ruth, 1 and 2 Samuel, 1 and 2 Kings, 1 and 2 Chronicles, Ezra, Nehemiah, Esther, Job, Psalms, Proverbs, Ecclesiastes, the Song of Solomon, Isaiah, Jeremiah, Lamentations, Ezekiel, Daniel, Hosea, Joel, Amos, Obadiah, Jonah, Micah, Nahum, Habakkuk, Zephaniah, Haggai, Zechariah and Malachi.

In the New Testament these are: Matthew, Mark, Luke, John, Acts, Romans, 1 and 2 Corinthians, Galatians, Ephesians, Philippians, Colossians, 1 and 2 Thessalonians, 1 and 2 Timothy, Titus, Philemon, Hebrews, James, 1 and 2 Peter, 1, 2 and 3 John, Jude and Revelation.

The Church of England holds that these books, although written by human authors, are given to us by God Himself in order

---

1 *The Virginia Report* of the Inter-Anglican Theological and Doctrinal Commission, in *The Official Report of the Lambeth Conference 1998*, Harrisburg, PA: Morehouse Publishing, 1999, p. 32.

that we might learn from them all that we need to know in order to be saved. Because this is the case, it follows that anything that is not in the Bible cannot be regarded as necessary for salvation: 'Holy Scripture containeth all things necessary to salvation: so that whatever is not read therein, nor may be proved thereby, is not to be required of any man, that it should be believed as an article of Faith, or be thought requisite or necessary to salvation.'[1]

As the Church of England sees it, in both the Old and New Testaments we have the one story of salvation that is offered to the human race through Jesus Christ. There is thus a unity rather than a contrast between them. The basic moral teaching of the Old Testament remains binding upon Christians even though with the coming of Christ they are not bound to observe the rites and ceremonies laid down in the Jewish law or those laws that relate directly to the social organization of Old Testament Israel.

In addition to the books listed above, the Church of England recognizes another collection of books known as the Apocrypha. The books that come in this category are 1 and 2 Esdras, Tobit, Judith, the Rest of Esther, the Wisdom of Solomon, Ecclesiasticus, Baruch, the Song of the Three Children, Susanna, Bel and the Dragon, the Prayer of Manasses, and 1 and 2 Maccabees. They are regarded as providing edifying instruction about how to live the Christian life, but not as having doctrinal authority.

The Church of England's belief about the Bible is set out explicitly in Articles VI and VII of the Thirty-Nine Articles. It is also reflected in the Book of Common Prayer and the Ordinal:

- in the Collect (special prayer) for the second Sunday in Advent;
- in the questions addressed to those who are ordained about their belief in the Bible;
- in the giving of the Bible to those who are ordained as a sign of their authority to preach the word, administer the sacraments and exercise pastoral care over the flock that has been committed to them;
- in the way in which provision is made for the Bible to be read in Church of England services and in which the words of the services are full of quotations from, or allusions to, the Bible; and

---

1   Article VI.

- in the way in which, in contrast to the practice of many Protestant churches, provision has always been made for the
reading in church services of portions of the Apocrypha.

. . . about the creeds

The Church of England's understanding of the authority of the
Bible is further reflected in its attitude to the creeds.

The Church of England makes use of three creeds that have
come down to us from the early church, the Apostles' Creed, the
Nicene Creed, and the Athanasian Creed. In the words of Article
VII, it holds that they '. . . ought thoroughly to be received and
believed: for they may be proved by most certain warrants of holy
Scripture'. What is important to note here is that the creeds are not
viewed as having an intrinsic authority of their own alongside
Scripture. Rather, they have a derived authority that consists in the
fact that they bear faithful witness to biblical teaching.

Because they are faithful witnesses to the teaching of the Bible,
provision is made for their regular recitation.

In the Book of Common Prayer the Apostles' Creed is recited at
Morning and Evening Prayer and also forms part of the Cate-
chism, the pattern of teaching to be learned by young people. The
Nicene Creed is recited at Holy Communion and the Athanasian
Creed is recited at Morning Prayer 14 times a year (including
Christmas Day, Easter Day and Trinity Sunday).[1]

. . . about God

In line with the teaching of the Bible and the creeds, the Church of
England believes that there is one eternal creator God who exists
eternally as Father, Son and Holy Spirit, each of whom possesses
the divine nature in all its fullness and therefore also possesses all
the characteristics or 'attributes' of that nature.

---

1 It should be noted that the Athanasian Creed is rarely used in the Church
of England today. This is both because it is felt to be too complex for
public recitation and because many people have doubts about the way in
which it seems to consign to eternal damnation those who cannot accept its
own precise formulation of the Christian faith. It should also be noted,
however, that the Church of England remains officially committed both to
its teaching and its use in church.

This belief is stated explicitly in Article I of the Thirty-Nine Articles:

> There is but one living and true God, everlasting, without body, parts or passions: of infinite power, wisdom, and goodness; the Maker and Preserver of all things both visible and invisible. And in unity of this Godhead there be three Persons, of one substance, power, and eternity; the Father, the Son and the Holy Ghost.[1]

It is also reflected in the Book of Common Prayer and the Ordinal:

- in the Collect for Trinity Sunday;
- in the use of the three creeds, which affirm a Trinitarian faith;
- in the Book of Common Prayer Catechism, which teaches a Trinitarian understanding of God;
- in the fact that baptism is 'in the name of the Father, Son and Holy Ghost';
- in the fact that glory is given to 'the Father, Son and Holy Ghost' at the end of Psalms and on other occasions;
- in the fact that the services of Morning and Evening Prayer close with the use of the Trinitarian grace from 2 Corinthians 13:14;
- in the fact that blessings are given in the name of the Father, Son and Holy Ghost;
- in the fact that in the litany (prayers of supplication) mercy for sinners is sought from the Holy Trinity.

. . . about Christ

The Church of England's beliefs about Jesus Christ also follow the teaching of the Bible and the creeds as well as the teaching contained in the Chalcedonian Definition, another statement of belief from the early church.

In line with these the Church of England believes that Jesus Christ is the eternal Son of God who took human nature upon Himself in the womb of the Virgin Mary. In consequence Christ is one person who has two natures, one divine and one human. In the words of Article II:

---

1 'Ghost' is simply an old English word for 'Spirit'.

The Son, which is the Word of the Father, begotten from everlasting of the Father, the very and eternal God, and of one substance with the Father, took man's nature in the womb of the blessed Virgin, of her substance: so that two whole and perfect natures, that is to say, the Godhead and manhood, were joined together in one person, never to be divided, whereof is one Christ, very God and very man . . .

It further believes that at the end of His earthly ministry Christ suffered and died for our salvation, descended to the place of the dead,[1] rose bodily from the grave and after forty days ascended into heaven. At the end of time He will return from heaven to judge the living and the dead. This further belief is set out in Articles II–IV of the Thirty-Nine Articles and is also reflected in the recitation of the creeds and in the Collects and readings for the major festivals of the Christian year in the Book of Common Prayer.

Although the beliefs of individual members of the Church of England may have been affected by some of the questions raised over the past two and a half centuries concerning the Christian Church's understanding of Christ and the historical truth of the accounts of His life contained in the New Testament, the Church of England as a whole has remained committed to the traditional view of the Christian Church on these matters.

. . . about the Holy Spirit

The belief of the Church of England concerning the Holy Spirit is declared in Article V ('Of the Holy Ghost'): 'The Holy Ghost, proceeding from the Father and the Son, is of one substance, majesty and glory, with the Father and the Son, very and eternal God.' This declaration is also reflected in what is said about the Holy Spirit when the Nicene and Athanasian creeds are recited in the services in the Book of Common Prayer. The two key points made in the Article and the creeds are (a) that the Holy Spirit is truly God just like the Father and the Son and (b) that He eternally proceeds from both the Father and the Son.

The latter point reflects the view of the Trinity accepted in the Western Church on the basis of Jn 14:26, 15:26 and 16:7 and the

---

1   This is what the Church of England understands by the use of the word 'hell' in the Apostles' Creed.

teaching of St Augustine of Hippo. The Church of England recognizes the difficulties that this view of the Trinity causes for the Orthodox churches, both because they believe it to be theologically mistaken and because it has led to what they see as a unilateral addition to the original text of the Nicene Creed. It has therefore authorized the omission of the words 'and the Son' on ecumenical occasions. However, it has not felt it right to modify its official theology or to abandon its own use of the Western version of the creed.

. . . about sin

The Church of England places a strong emphasis on the sinfulness of human beings. Thus the 'general confession' in the services of Morning and Evening Prayer in the Book of Common Prayer declares:

> Almighty and most merciful Father, We have erred and strayed from thy ways like lost sheep, We have followed too much the devices and desires of our own hearts, We have offended against thy holy laws, We have left undone those things which we ought to have done, And we have done those things which we ought not to have done. And there is no health in us . . .

Furthermore, the Church of England believes that it is not simply a case of individual human beings choosing to commit specific sins. It follows St Paul in passages such as Romans 5 and 7 and the subsequent teaching of St Augustine and holds that all human beings possess a fallen nature which means that they are internally divided in a way that means that they are incapable of living in complete obedience to God and deserve 'God's wrath and damnation'.[1] It also holds that this state of sinfulness persists even in those who are born again in Christ through faith and baptism.

This view of sin is set out in Articles IX and XV and, as already noted, it is reflected in the Book of Common Prayer in the general confession at Morning and Evening Prayer as well as in the general confession at the service of Holy Communion.

---

1 Article IX.

. . . about salvation

Because it takes this serious view of human sinfulness the Church of England also holds that human beings are incapable of achieving their own salvation. Drawing on the teaching of St Paul in Romans and Galatians and influenced by the theology of the Lutheran Reformers, it declares that, lost in sin, all human beings can do is have faith in the mercy of God offered to them in Christ, and when they do this God accepts them as righteous on account of the fact that Christ both paid the penalty for their sin on the cross and obeyed God's law on their behalf.

In the words of Article XI: 'We are accounted righteous before God, only for the merit of our Lord and Saviour Jesus Christ, by Faith, and not for our own works or deservings.' Or, as Archbishop Cranmer puts it in his homily *Of the Salvation of Mankind*:

> . . . all the good works that we can do be unperfect, and therefore not able to deserve our justification: but our justification doth come freely by the mere mercy of God, and of so great and free mercy, that, whereas all the world was not able of themselves to pay any part towards their ransom, it pleased our heavenly Father of his infinite mercy, without any our desert or deserving, to prepare for us the most precious jewels of Christ's body and blood, whereby our ransom might be fully paid, the law fulfilled, and his justice fully satisfied. So that Christ is now the righteousness of all them that truly believe in him. He for them paid their ransom by his death. He for them fulfilled the law in his life. So that now in him, and by him, every true Christian man may be called the fulfiller of the law; forasmuch as that which their infirmity lacked, Christ's justice hath supplied.[1]

The fact that the Church of England believes in justification by faith in the sense just described does not mean that it ignores the importance of good works. Rather, it stresses that they are what inevitably follow when a person has saving faith. Thus Article XII, 'Of Good Works', declares:

---

1 T. Cranmer, *A Sermon of the Salvation of Mankind*, text in J. H. Leith (ed.), *Creeds of the Churches*, rev. edn, Oxford: Blackwell, 1973, p. 242. This homily is specified by Article XI as explaining in greater detail the teaching contained in the article itself.

Albeit that Good Works, which are the fruits of Faith, and follow after Justification, cannot put away our sins, and endure the severity of God's Judgement; yet are they pleasing and acceptable to God in Christ, and do spring out necessarily of a true and lively faith; insomuch that by them a lively Faith may be as evidently known as a tree discerned by the fruit.

This teaching about salvation is found in the articles and homily already mentioned, and also in Articles XIII and XIV, which teach that works done by an individual before they have faith in Christ do not earn God's grace and that we cannot do any good works over and above God's commandments[1] that will earn us an additional reward from God.

It is taught implicitly in the Book of Common Prayer by the way in which the general confession at Morning and Evening Prayer is followed by the words of absolution in which the priest taking the service declares that 'God pardoneth and absolveth all them that truly repent and unfeignedly believe his holy Gospel.' It is also taught implicitly by the structure of the Book of Common Prayer communion service, which, as has been said, is a conscious attempt to give liturgical form to the doctrine of justification by faith.

In the words of Bishop Stephen Neill, in the communion service: 'We open soberly with the Words of the Law; we move forward through Gethsemane and Calvary, to the glory of the resurrection and the ascension.'[2] The believer participates in this journey through a liturgical sequence of repentance followed by the reception of God's gift of the broken body and shed blood of Christ through faith by the partaking of the bread and wine. This in turn leads the believer to respond to God by offering him or herself to God as a living sacrifice and asking for God's help to live a life of good works. What we have in this sequence are the key elements of justification, repentance, followed by acceptance in faith of God's gift of salvation and a response of self-dedication to God issuing in good works.

As is well known, at the Reformation the issue of justification was one of the key issues that divided those churches, including the Church of England, that embraced the Reformation from

---

1 Technically known as 'works of supererogation'.
2 S. C. Neill, *Anglicanism*, London: Mowbray, 1977, p. 76.

those that remained loyal to Rome. At the heart of this division was a perception by the Reformers that the late medieval teaching about justification confused justification with sanctification (the process by which we become holy people), and a perception by their opponents that the Reformers emphasized justification at the expense of sanctification.

One of the results of the ecumenical movement during the twentieth century has been a growth in agreement about justification which has led to a widespread acceptance that this should no longer be seen as a Church-dividing issue. An example of this growth in agreement is the joint Anglican–Roman Catholic statement *Salvation and the Church*, produced in 1986, which declares that justification and sanctification should be seen as distinct but necessarily linked together:

> Justification and sanctification are two aspects of the same divine act (1 Cor 6:11). This does not mean that justification is a reward for faith or works: rather, when God promises the removal of our condemnation and gives us a new standing before him, this justification is indissolubly linked with his sanctifying recreation of us in grace. This transformation is being worked out in the course of our pilgrimage, despite the imperfections and ambiguities of our lives. God's grace effects what he declares: his creative word imparts what it imputes. By pronouncing us righteous, God also makes us righteous. He imparts a righteousness which is his and becomes ours.[1]

. . . about predestination

The view of salvation just described has as its background a belief in predestination rooted in the teaching of St Paul in Ephesians 1:3–6, Romans 8:28–30 and 9:19–26 and the thought of St Augustine. This belief, which holds that our response of justifying faith to what Christ has done for us is the result of God's prior choice to save us, is set out in Article XVII, the first paragraph of which runs as follows:

---

1   ARCIC II, *Salvation and the Church*, 15.

Predestination to life is the everlasting purpose of God, whereby, before the foundations of the world were laid, He hath constantly decreed by His counsel secret to us, to deliver from curse and damnation those whom He hath chosen in Christ out of mankind, and to bring them by Christ to everlasting salvation as vessels made to honour. Wherefore they which be endued with so excellent a benefit of God be called according to God's purpose by His Spirit working in due season; they through grace obey the calling; they be justified freely; they be made sons of God by adoption; they be made like the image of His only-begotten Son Jesus Christ; they walk religiously in good works; and at length by God's mercy they attain to everlasting felicity.

The key point to note in this paragraph is its statement that we are chosen 'in Christ'. As Professor Oliver O'Donovan explains, this is:

. . . not to be understood as though we were chosen and he was merely the instrument by which our choosing was given effect. We are chosen in him, because he is the chosen one, the eternal object of the Father's good pleasure. Just as our predestination means our participation in his righteousness, so our pre-destination, our 'election', means our participation in his position as the object of the Father's favour from eternity.[1]

The claim is sometimes made that Article XVII (and hence the Church of England) is Calvinist in its theology. This claim is unsustainable because there are two key components of Calvinist theology that are missing from Article XVII and from the formularies as a whole.

The first component that is missing is a belief in *double* pre-destination. The article teaches single predestination, predestination to life, but it says nothing about predestination to damnation. In the words of O'Donovan 'the Article does not speak of the double decree. This silence is emphasized by its peculiar shape. "Predestination to life is the everlasting purpose of God", it

---

1 O. M. T. O'Donovan, *On The Thirty Nine Articles*, Exeter: Paternoster Press, 1984, p. 83.

begins; and we naturally await a balancing sentence, "Fore-ordination to death . . ." etc. But it never comes.'[1]

The second component that is missing is a belief in 'particular redemption', the belief that the saving action of God in Christ is for the benefit of a limited number of individuals rather than for humanity as a whole.

Such a belief is contrary to the teaching found elsewhere in the formularies. For example, the Catechism in the Book of Common Prayer teaches belief in: 'God the Son, who hath redeemed me, and all mankind' and the communion service declares that Christ's death was 'a full, perfect, and sufficient sacrifice, oblation and satisfaction, for the sins of the whole world'. It is also contrary to the final paragraph of Article XVII which teaches that '. . . we must receive God's promises in such wise as they be generally set forth to us in holy Scripture'. To quote O'Donovan again, what this means is that we are '. . . to understand the promises of God "generally", which is to say, generically, as addressed not to par-ticular individuals but to the class of human-beings who will hear and obey God's word. That individuals arbitrarily refuse to hear is not to be explained by reference to divine decrees.'[2]

. . . about the Church

Predestination is not simply a matter of elect individuals coming to salvation. It also means the coming into being of the Christian community, the Church. This link between predestination and the existence of the Church is made clear in the Collect for All Saints' Day in the Book of Common Prayer which begins with the words: 'O almighty God, who hast knit together thine elect in one com-munion and fellowship in the mystical body of thy Son Christ our Lord . . .'

This mystical body of Christ is not directly perceptible to human beings. This is both because it is a spiritual reality and because among its members are those who are dead and those whose membership of it is as yet known to God alone. However, it is manifested in this world in a human community that can be seen, the visible Church of God.

What the Church of England thinks this community looks like is

---

1 Ibid., p. 85.
2 Ibid., p. 86.

set out in Article XIX, 'Of the Church'. Drawing on earlier
Lutheran theology this declares that: 'The visible Church of Christ
is a congregation of faithful men, in the which the pure word of
God is preached and the sacraments be duly ministered according
to Christ's ordinance in all those things that of necessity are
requisite to the same.'

In order to understand Article XIX properly it needs to be
noted that in the sixteenth century the word congregation did not
have the same meaning as it has today.[1] Today we use it to
describe a group of people gathered together for worship. In the
sixteenth century it was simply used to describe any group of
people regardless of the size of the group and regardless of whether
or not they were gathered together in one place. What this means is
that Article XIX cannot be used to support the idea that the
Church of England holds to a congregational form of church
polity. To quote the Australian scholar Kevin Giles:

> To argue that article 19 defines the church as a local con-
> gregation and no more is a profound mistake. To do so is to
> read the word 'congregation' in this context anachronistically.
> Such an understanding of the church by any of the Reformers is
> untenable. The use of congregation to refer to the whole
> Christian community is common in this period. For example,
> Bishop Hooper writes, 'I believe and confess one catholic and
> universal church, which is an holy *congregation*, an assembly of
> all faithful believers.' While in the Belgic confession, the affir-
> mation is: 'we believe and confess one catholic or universal
> church, which is the holy *congregation* of true believers' (art. 27).
> This usage is also seen in the Authorized version of 1611, where
> 'congregation' is used to translate the Hebrew word *edah*,
> meaning all Israel, the covenant community.[2]

In Article XIX the word congregation is used in the same sense in
which it is used by Hooper and the Belgic Confession. It refers to

---

1   The same is, of course, true for the term 'men' which was used in the
sixteenth century as a generic term for both sexes.

2   K. Giles, *What on Earth is the Church?*, SPCK, 1995, p. 242.

the universal Church of which particular churches, such as the Church of England, are a local expression.[1]

Subsequent articles go on say more about the visible Church at both the universal and national levels. What they say can be summarized under two headings, positive and negative.

Positive

- The Church has the power to decide on matters of faith and order (Article XX).
- The traditions and ceremonies of the Church can vary over time 'according to the diversities of countries, times and men's manners' (Article XXXIV).
- The right to 'ordain, change and abolish' those rites and ceremonies of the Church: 'ordained only by men's authority' is something that belongs to the Church at the national level (Article XXXIV). It was in accordance with this principle that the Church of England introduced the new forms of service found in the Book of Common Prayer and the Ordinal.
- The Church has the right to exercise 'the power of the keys' (Mt. 16:19, 18:18, Jn 20:23) by excommunicating people for serious offences and those who are excommunicated ought to be regarded as outside the Christian community until they are restored to it by someone with the proper authority to do so (Mt. 18:15–20) (Article XXXIII).

Negative

- The Church does not have the right to command anything that is contrary to Scripture or to expound Scripture in such a way that one part becomes contrary to another (Article XX).

---

1 Article XIX could be seen as meaning that the Church of England believes that Christian bodies that do not have the sacraments, such as the Salvation Army or the Quakers, are not part of the Church. However, the Article does not need to be read this way. As O'Donovan notes, we can understand these marks:

> . . . not as *criteria* for any claim to be a church, but as *demands* that any church should seek to meet . . . Thus, with respect to the sacraments, for example, we can address the non-sacramental churches not with a curt definitional *fiat*, declaring that they are simply *not* churches, but with a challenge to them to join us in common obedience to the command of Christ. If they are to organise themselves as Christian believers, should they not do it in the way that Christ laid down? (Op. cit p. 96)

- The Church must not conduct worship in a language that people are unable to understand (Article XXIV). It is in accordance with this principle that the services in the Book of Common Prayer and the Ordinal are in English rather than in Latin as had been the case with the service books that were used prior to the Reformation.
- The Church is capable of error and has in fact erred. This is true both of particular churches and of General Councils held by the Church as a whole (Articles XIX and XXI).
- General Councils may only be held with the agreement of those with political authority (Article XXI). This is not just a pragmatic statement about the fact that in practice General Councils need political agreement in order to take place. It also reflects a belief that the well-being of the Church is something that is of vital importance to the whole of society and that therefore those with political power have a responsibility to see that General Councils are properly conducted.

What all this means is that the Church at both the universal and national levels possesses authority in matters to do with doctrine, ritual and discipline, but that this authority is limited by the teaching of Scripture, the need for worship to be in the vernacular so that people can understand it, the fact the Church may err and by a recognition of the responsibilities of those called to exercise political power.

. . . about the sacraments

The Church of England holds that there are two sacraments ordained by Christ. Thus the section on the sacraments in the Catechism in the Book of Common Prayer begins as follows:

Question. How many sacraments hath Christ ordained in his Church?

Answer. Two only, as generally necessary to salvation; that is to say, Baptism, and the Supper of the Lord.

Question. What meanest thou by this word *Sacrament*?

Answer. I mean an outward and visible sign of an inward and spiritual grace given unto us, ordained by Christ himself, as a means whereby we receive the same, and a pledge to assure us thereof.

The issue is sometimes raised about whether there are not also other actions (such as, for example, the laying on of hands at confirmation and ordination) that can be considered as 'sacramental' in the sense of being an outward and visible sign of an inward and spiritual grace. The Church of England's answer is that these are not sacraments in the strict sense because they are (a) not actions ordained by Christ Himself and (b) not 'generally necessary to salvation'.

The Catechism next goes on to explore in more detail how the Church of England understands the two sacraments.

Baptism

The section on baptism runs as follows:

> *Question.* What is the outward visible sign or form in Baptism?
>
> *Answer.* Water: wherein the person is baptized In the Name of the Father, and of the Son, and of the Holy Ghost.
>
> *Question.* What is the inward and spiritual grace?
>
> *Answer.* A death unto sin, and a new birth unto righteousness: for being by nature born in sin, and the children of wrath, we are hereby made the children of grace.
>
> *Question.* What is required of persons to be baptized?
>
> *Answer.* Repentance, whereby they forsake sin: and Faith, whereby they steadfastly believe the promises of God made to them in that Sacrament.
>
> *Question.* Why then are Infants baptized, when by reason of their tender age they cannot perform them?
>
> *Answer.* Because they promise them both by their Sureties: which promise, when they come to age, themselves are bound to perform.

There are three points that need to be noted here,

- In accordance with Mt. 28:19, the Church of England holds that baptism should be by water and in the name of the Holy

Trinity and, as has been noted previously, this is what we find in the baptism services in the Book of Common Prayer.

- Baptism is an effective means of grace, 'we are hereby made the children of grace'. However, as Article XXVII indicates, it is those who receive this gift of divine adoption 'rightly' who receive its benefits. What right reception means is specified by the Catechism in terms of repentance and faith.

- The Church of England believes that it is right to baptize infants, a belief that is stated explicitly in Article XXVII and is implied both in the Catechism and in the services for the baptism in the Book of Common Prayer. The baptism of infants might appear to be in tension with the need for a response of repentance and faith, but this response is made, firstly by the parents and godparents on the infant's behalf[1] and, secondly, by the infant him or herself when he or she is old enough to do so.

In the Church of England the formal liturgical occasion for making this adult response is confirmation. This is also the occasion at which those who are confirmed have hands laid on them by the confirming bishop with the prayer that they may receive the strength and the gifts of the Holy Spirit for a life of Christian discipleship.

The Eucharist

In the Catechism the second of the two dominical sacraments is described as the Lord's Supper (1 Cor. 11:20). Today, the primary term used for this sacrament in the Church of England is the Holy Communion, but it is also referred to as the Eucharist, the Lord's Supper or the Mass.

The account of this sacrament given in the Catechism is as follows:

Question. Why was the Sacrament of the Lord's Supper ordained?

Answer. For the continual remembrance of the sacrifice of the death of Christ and of the benefits which we receive thereby.

---

1   In the Baptism services in the Book of Common Prayer the promises are made only by the godparents, but today they are made by both parents and godparents.

Question. What is the outward part or sign of the Lord's Supper?

Answer. Bread and Wine, which the Lord hath commanded to be received.

Question. What is the inward part, or thing signified?

Answer. The Body and Blood of Christ, which are verily and indeed taken and received by the faithful in the Lord's Supper.

Question. What are the benefits whereof we are partakers thereby?

Answer. The strengthening and refreshing of our souls by the Body and Blood of Christ, as our bodies are by the Bread and Wine.

Question. What is required of them who come to the Lord's Supper?

Answer. To examine themselves, whether they repent them truly of their former sins, steadfastly purposing to lead a new life; have a lively faith in God's mercy through Christ, with a thankful remembrance of his death; and be in charity with all men.

There are four points to be noted here:

(1)   The description of the sacrament as a 'remembrance of the sacrifice of Christ' raises the issue of whether it is right to talk about the sacrament itself as being a sacrifice. Article XXXI specifically condemns the medieval practice of offering the 'sacrifices of Masses' because this practice was seen to involve the idea that the sacrifice of Christ was being re-peated each time the Mass was celebrated. However, the Anglican Reformers did not entirely rule out the use of sacrificial language in connection with the sacrament[1] and from the seventeenth century onwards many, although not all, Church of England theologians have felt it right to follow the lead of the early Fathers by using the language of Eucharistic sacrifice.

---

1   The language of sacrifice is used in relation to the sacrament, for example, by Nicholas Ridley, the reforming Bishop of London who was burned for his Protestant beliefs under Mary Tudor.

Thus the Archbishops of Canterbury and York write in a document of 1897 entitled *Saepius Officio*:

> . . . we truly teach the doctrine of Eucharistic sacrifice and do not believe it to be a 'nude commemoration of the Sacrifice of the Cross,' an opinion which seems to be attributed to us by the quotation made at that Council. But we think it sufficient in the Liturgy which we use in celebrating the holy Eucharist, – while lifting up our hearts to the Lord, and when now consecrating the gifts already offered that they may become to us the Body and Blood of our Lord Jesus Christ, – to signify the sacrifice which is offered at that point of the service in such terms as these. We continue a perpetual memory of the precious death of Christ, who is our Advocate with the Father, and the propitiation for our sins, according to His precept, until His coming again. For first we offer the sacrifice of praise and thanksgiving; then next we plead and represent before the Father the sacrifice of the cross, and by it we confidently entreat remission of sins and all other benefits of the Lord's Passion for all the whole Church; and lastly we offer the sacrifice of ourselves to the Creator of all things which we have already signified by the oblation of His creatures. This whole action, in which the people has necessarily to take its part with the Priest, we are accustomed to call the Eucharistic sacrifice.

(2) The Church of England holds that because the 'outward part or sign' of the sacrament is the two elements of bread and wine, the faithful are entitled to receive both the bread and the wine. As Article XXX puts it: 'The cup of the Lord is not to be denied to the Lay-people: for both the parts of the Lord's Sacrament, by Christ's ordinance and commandment, ought to be administered to all Christian men alike.'

(3) The Church of England further holds that at the Lord's Supper both the outward sign and the inward reality of the sacrament are received by the faithful. When the sacrament is rightly received what is received is both the bread and wine *and* the body and blood of Christ by which the souls of the faithful are strengthened and refreshed.

(4) The Church of England takes seriously the idea that the Lord's Supper has to be rightly received. Following the teaching of St Paul in 1 Corinthians 11:27–30 and also the teaching of St Augustine, it declares that if the sacrament is not rightly received then what is received is only the bread and wine and the person so receiving is in danger of condemnation from God. This point is made in both Article XXIX and in the words of exhortation spoken by the priest to the congregation in the Communion service in the Book of Common Prayer.

To avoid this danger what is required, as the Catechism says, is repentance, faith in the mercy of God based on a thankful remembrance of Christ's death for us and being in a state of love ('charity') with other people. In order that these requirements are met, the Book of Common Prayer prescribes a period of preparation for receiving the sacrament in which people are reconciled to God and to each other.

. . . about ministry

The basic principles of the Church of England regarding ministry as set out in the formularies are as follows:

- Only those who are properly authorized to do so may preach or minister the sacraments.
- Although it is important that discipline be exercised over those in ministry and that unsuitable ministers should be removed from office, nevertheless the personal unfitness of ministers does not render the preaching of the word or the celebration of the sacraments spiritually ineffective.
- The ministerial orders of bishop, priest and deacon can be traced back to the time of the Apostles, and the purpose of the Church of England's ordination rites is that these ancient orders should be: 'continued and reverently used and esteemed, in the Church of England'.
- Those who are ordained according to the rites of the Church of England are properly ordained.
- Those who are ordained as bishops, priests or deacons do not have to be celibate. Whether it is better to be married or single is a matter for the judgement of the individual minister concerned.

These principles are set out in Articles XXIII, XXVI, XXXVI and XXXII and in the Preface to the Ordinal.

Ministry in the Church of England today is looked at in more detail in the following chapter.

. . . about the state and Christian participation in civil society

The Church of England's theology of the relationship between Church and state has already been outlined in chapter five, but it is worth noting in this chapter that the formularies of the Church of England reveal three convictions about the Christian view of the state and Christian participation in civil society.

The first conviction, based on New Testament texts such as Rom. 13:1–7, 1 Tim. 2:1–4 and 1 Pet. 2:13–17, is that governmental authority (in the case of England the authority exercised by the British monarchy) is something that is given by God and that Christians should pray for those to whom it is given.

This conviction is reflected in Article XXXVII 'Of the Civil Magistrate' and in the many prayers for the Queen and other members of the royal family to be found in the Book of Common Prayer.

The second conviction, based on the example of the kings of Israel in the Old Testament and the Christian emperors in the later Roman Empire, is that the authority of those with governmental authority extends over the Church as well. This is what is meant when it is said that the Queen is the Supreme Governor of the Church of England.

This conviction is expressed in Article XXXVII which, as we noted in chapter five, declares that:

> Where we attribute to the Queen's Majesty the chief government, by which titles we understand the minds of some slanderous folks to be offended, we give not to our princes the ministering either of God's word or of sacraments, the which thing the Injunctions also lately set forth by Elizabeth our Queen doth most plainly testify: but that only prerogative which we see to have been given always to all godly princes in Holy Scriptures by God himself, that is, that they should rule all estates and degrees committed to their charge by God, whether they be ecclesiastical or temporal, and restrain with the civil sword the stubborn and evil-doers.

The third conviction is that neither the example of the early church as recorded in Acts 4:32–37 nor the teaching of Christ in Mt. 5:33–48 should be understood to mean that Christians should hold all their possessions in common, or should refuse to take oaths on all occasions, or should be pacifists. We can see this in Articles XXXVII–XXXIX.

The final two clauses of Article XXXVII declare that:

> The Laws of the Realm may punish Christian men with death for heinous and grievous offences.[1]

> It is lawful for Christian men at the commandment of the Magistrate to wear weapons and serve in the wars.

Article XXXVIII, 'Of Christian men's goods which are not common', states that:

> The riches and goods of Christians are not common, as touching the right, title, and possession of the same, as certain Anabaptists do falsely boast; notwithstanding every man ought of such things as he possesseth liberally to give alms to the poor, according to his ability.

Article XXXIX, 'Of a Christian man's Oath', teaches that:

> As we confess that vain and rash swearing is forbidden Christian men by our Lord Jesus Christ, so we judge that Christian religion doth not prohibit but that a man may swear when the magistrate requireth in a cause of faith and charity, so it be done according to the Prophet's teaching in justice, judgement, and truth.

. . . on life after death

In accordance with the teaching of the New Testament, the Church of England holds that God's saving work in the lives of the faithful will achieve its fulfilment at the end of time when God's

---

1 In Britain the death penalty has been abolished with the support of the Church of England. Nevertheless the Church of England accepts that those serving the Queen in the armed forces, the security services or the police may rightly be ordered to take life either in a war or in order to protect the lives of innocent people and so the principle of it being right for the state to take life in extreme circumstances still applies.

kingdom will be fully manifested and the faithful will enjoy life with God forever in both body and soul. This belief is given classic expression by the prayers at the end of the funeral service in the Book of Common Prayer which affirm a two stage view of life after death in which the souls of the faithful depart to be with God but still await the resurrection of the body at the last day.

In accordance with the Christian tradition as a whole, the Church of England has also traditionally taught that it is possible for human beings to reject God and so fail to attain eternal life. In the past two centuries many people have questioned this belief; however, in its 1995 report The Meaning of Salvation, the Church of England's Doctrine Commission re-affirmed the traditional position:

No one can be compulsorily installed in heaven, whose characteristic is the communion of love. God whose being is love preserves our human freedom, for freedom is the condition of love. Although God's love goes, and has gone to the uttermost, plumbing the depths of hell, the possibility remains for each human being of a final rejection of God, and so of eternal life.[1]

FOR FURTHER READING

Kaye, B., 'Anglican Belief', in I. Bunting, *Celebrating the Anglican Way*, London: Hodder & Stoughton, 1996.

O'Donovan, O. M. T., *On the Thirty Nine Articles*, Exeter: Paternoster Press, 1984.

Sykes, S. and J. Booty (eds), *The Study of Anglicanism*, London and Minneapolis: SPCK/Fortress Press, 1998, Part I.

---

1   *The Mystery of Salvation*, London: CHP, 1995, p. 198.

8 More than the Vicar – Ministry in the Church of England Today

NOT ALL MINISTERS ARE VICARS

In popular perception, ministry is understood almost exclusively in terms of ordained ministry. Ministry is what the 'vicar' does (vicar being used as a catch-all description of anyone entitled to wear a dog collar).

The problem with this popular view is that it does not do justice to the variety of forms of ministry that exist in the Church of England today. As we shall see in the course of this chapter, there are not only many different forms of ordained ministry but there are also many different forms of lay ministry and all of them are needed if the Church is to carry out its mission.

These different forms of ministry are not well understood (even within the Church) and so the purpose of this chapter is to explain what they are and how people are selected and trained to exercise them.

To start off with, however, we are going to look at what is meant by the term 'ministry'.

In response to what has been seen (rightly or wrongly) as the undue dominance of the Christian Church by the clergy with a corresponding devaluing of the role of the laity, it has been frequently argued over the course of the last century that 'ministry' is a term that should be used to describe the service that all Christians without exception are called to offer to God.

For example, the Swiss theologian Emil Brunner declares in his book *The Misunderstanding of the Church* that:

One thing is supremely important; that all minister, and that nowhere is to be perceived a separation or even merely a distinction between those who do and do not minister, between the active and the passive members of the body, between those who give and those who receive. There exists in the Ecclesia a universal duty and right of service, a universal readiness to serve, and at the same time the greatest possible differentiation of functions.[1]

The strength of Brunner's position is that it highlights the clear New Testament emphasis that all Christians without exception are called to serve God and one another in a whole variety of different ways. This emphasis is found, for instance, in passages such as Rom. 12:4–7, 1 Cor. 12:4–7, and 1 Pet. 4:10–11.[2]

However, this position also has three important weaknesses.

- The first weakness is the danger that if we equate 'ministry' with 'service' in an undifferentiated fashion we shall end up by making ministry such a comprehensive concept that it will be left without any specific content. If 'ministry' simply equals 'service' then it becomes a term that potentially describes the whole of the Christian life. This in turn means that there is nothing left that is not ministry and so the term then loses all meaning.
- The second weakness is that if the term ministry is used in this broad sense then we are left without any distinctive term to describe those liturgical, catechetical and pastoral activities which the term has traditionally been used to describe.
- The third weakness is that such an approach can encourage an individualism in which each individual insists on determining his or her own 'ministry' without reference to either the needs of the wider Christian community, or its discernment of how they may best use their gifts in God's service.

Because of these three weaknesses it is better to use a term such as 'discipleship' to describe that service of God that takes place in the whole of the life of a Christian, and to use the term 'ministry' in a more specific sense.

This chapter will follow the approach taken by the Church of

---

1 E. Brunner, *The Misunderstanding of the Church*, Lutterworth: Lutterworth Press, 1952, p. 50.
2 For an expansion of this point see G. Kuhrt, *An Introduction to Christian Ministry*, London: Church House Publishing, 2000, pp. 10–13.

England and the Methodist Church of Great Britain in their joint document *An Anglican–Methodist Covenant* and will use the term ministry to refer to: 'Work, undertaken in the service of the kingdom of God, that is actually acknowledged, either formally or informally by the Church.'[1]

This chapter will also distinguish between ordained and lay forms of ministry within the Church of England. In one sense all ministry is 'lay' ministry in the sense that it is carried out by those who are members of the *laos*, the people of God. However, a distinction has been made in the Church of England, as in most other churches, between ministry undertaken by those members of the *laos* who are ordained and ministry undertaken by those who are not, and this chapter will follow this traditional distinction.

ORDAINED MINISTRY IN THE CHURCH OF ENGLAND

(a) The three forms of ordained ministry

As was explained in the previous chapter, the Church of England has retained the three ministerial orders of bishop, priest and deacon that go back to the earliest days of the Church.

The clearest contemporary explanation of how it understands these three forms of ordained ministry is provided by the recently authorized *Common Worship Ordination Services*. As will be explained in the next chapter, *Common Worship* is the Church of England's authorized collection of contemporary liturgical material that exists alongside the Book of Common Prayer and as part of this the *Common Worship Ordination Services* is a collection of authorized ordination rites that exist alongside the traditional 1662 Ordinal.

Bishops

In the service for the ordination or, as it is generally known, the consecration of bishops, the role of a bishop (who must previously have been ordained as a priest) is explained as follows:

Bishops are called to serve and care for the flock of Christ.

---

1 An *Anglican–Methodist Covenant*, Peterborough and London: Methodist Publishing House/Church House Publishing, 2001, p. 44.

Mindful of the Good Shepherd, who laid down his life for his sheep, they are to love and pray for those committed to their charge, knowing their people and being known by them. As principal ministers of word and sacrament, stewards of the mysteries of God, they are to preside at the Lord's table and to lead the offering of prayer and praise. They are to feed God's pilgrim people, and so build up the Body of Christ.

They are to baptize and confirm, nurturing God's people in the life of the Spirit and leading them in the way of holiness. They are to discern and foster the gifts of the Spirit in all who follow Christ, commissioning them to minister in his name. They are to preside over the ordination of deacons and priests, and join together in the ordination of bishops.

As chief pastors, it is their duty to share with their fellow presbyters the oversight of the Church, speaking in the name of God and expounding the gospel of salvation. With the Shepherd's love, they are to be merciful, but with firmness; to minister discipline, but with compassion. They are to have a special care for the poor, the outcast and those who are in need. They are to seek out those who are lost and lead them home with rejoicing, declaring the absolution and forgiveness of sins to those who turn to Christ.

Following the example of the prophets and the teaching of the apostles, they are to proclaim the gospel boldly, confront injustice and work for righteousness and peace in all the world.

What this explanation tells us is that in the Church of England the bishops are the chief ministers of word, sacrament and pastoral care in the dioceses in which they minister. They share this ministry with the priests or presbyters (the two terms are used with the same meaning) and deacons of their dioceses, but they also have two key liturgical roles, one of which is confirmation and the other of which is the ordination of deacons, priests and their fellow bishops. In the Church of England only bishops may confirm and only bishops may ordain and they cannot transfer their authority in this regard to anyone who is not a bishop.

As was noted in Chapter 2 there are two types of bishops, diocesan bishops on the one hand and suffragan and assistant bishops on the other. They are both ordained to exactly the same type of ministry with the distinction between them being that diocesan bishops have overall responsibility for their dioceses and that suffragan or assistant bishops minister with the permission and under the authority of the diocesan.

A key role of the diocesan bishop that is not touched upon in the quotation given above, although it is reflected in other parts of the ordination service, is that of being the 'focus of unity'. This means a number of different things. First, it means that a diocesan bishop is called to foster the unity of his[1] diocese in the sense of fostering good Christian relationships between those who belong to it and seeking to ensure that they work together effectively in the service of God. Secondly, it means that the diocesan bishop is a sign and instrument of communion within his diocese because the other bishops, the other clergy and the laity of his diocese are in communion with him and through him with each other. Thirdly, it means that he is a sign and instrument of the unity of his diocese with the whole Church of Jesus Christ down the ages and across the world because he is part of a historic succession of bishops and is in communion with other bishops today.

As the 1990 Church of England report *Episcopal Ministry* puts it:

> In the local church the bishop focuses and nurtures the unity of his people; in his sharing in the collegiality of bishops the local church is bound together with other local churches; and, through the succession of bishops the local community is related to the Church through the ages. Thus the bishop in his own person in the diocese, and in his collegial relations in the wider church, and through his place in the succession of bishops in their communities in faithfulness to the Gospel, is a sign and focus of the unity of the Church.[2]

Priests

In the service for the ordination of priests or presbyters (who must first have been made deacons), the account given of their role is that:

---

1 The use of the male pronoun reflects the fact that all bishops in the Church of England are male. See 2(g) below.
2 *Episcopal Ministry*, London: Church House Publishing, 1990, p. 160.

Priests are called to be servants and shepherds among the people to whom they are sent. With their Bishop and fellow ministers, they are to proclaim the word of the Lord and to watch for the signs of God's new creation. They are to be messengers, watchmen and stewards of the Lord; they are to teach and to admonish, to feed and provide for his family, to search for his children in the wilderness of this world's temptations, and to guide them through its confusions, that they may be saved through Christ forever. Formed by the word, they are to call their hearers to repentance and to declare in Christ's name the absolution and forgiveness of their sins.

With all God's people, they are to tell the story of God's love. They are to baptize new disciples in the name of the Father, and of the Son, and of the Holy Spirit, and to walk with them in the way of Christ, nurturing them in the faith. They are to unfold the Scriptures, to preach the word in season and out of season, and to declare the mighty acts of God. They are to preside at the Lord's table and lead his people in worship, offering with them a spiritual sacrifice of praise and thanksgiving. They are to bless the people in God's name. They are to resist evil, support the weak, defend the poor, and intercede for all in need. They are to minister to the sick and prepare the dying for their death. Guided by the Spirit, they are to discern and foster the gifts of all God's people, that the whole Church may be built up in unity and faith.

What we learn from this is that, like bishops, priests are called to a ministry of word, sacrament and pastoral care. They lead worship, preach, preside at communion, baptize, absolve and bless the congregation in God's name and provide whatever pastoral care is required from them by the people for whom they are responsible. They are to resist evil and support the poor, the weak and the needy. Finally, under the guidance of the Spirit, they are called to identify and nurture the gifts of their people.

Deacons

The service for the ordination of deacons declares that:

Deacons are called to work with the Bishop and the priests with whom they serve as heralds of Christ's kingdom. They are to proclaim the gospel in word and deed, as agents of God's purposes of love. They are to serve the community in which they are set, bringing to the Church the needs and hopes of all the people. They are to work with their fellow members in searching out the poor and weak, the sick and lonely and those who are oppressed and powerless, reaching into the forgotten corners of the world, that the love of God may be made visible.

Deacons share in the pastoral ministry of the Church and in leading God's people in worship. They preach the word and bring the needs of the world before the Church in intercession. They accompany those searching for faith and bring them to baptism. They assist in administering the sacraments; they distribute communion and minister to the sick and housebound.

Deacons are to seek nourishment from the Scriptures; they are to study them with God's people, that the whole Church may be equipped to live out the gospel in the world. They are to be faithful in prayer, expectant and watchful for the signs of God's presence, as he reveals his kingdom among us.

What this declaration tells us is that deacons too are called to a ministry of word, sacrament and pastoral care. However there are two things that are distinctive about the ministry of deacons.

Firstly, diaconal ministry is an assistant ministry. Deacons work under the oversight not only of their bishops, but also of the priests with whom they minister. In the Church of England deacons lead non-Eucharistic worship, preach, lead prayers and assist with the distribution of the bread and wine at communion. However, they do not preside at communion nor give a blessing or absolution, and they are not the normal ministers of baptism (although they may baptize when they are authorized to do so).

Secondly, diaconal ministry is a bridge-building ministry. As the description of the deacon's role quoted above notes, deacons have a special responsibility for reaching out to the '. . . poor and weak, the sick and lonely and those who are oppressed and powerless' and also for '. . . bringing to the Church the needs and hopes of all the people'. They thus act as a bridge between the Church and the needs and concerns of the world.

In the Church of England there are two sorts of deacons. The majority of deacons are what are known as 'transitional' deacons.

Because the Church of England practises a pattern of sequential ordination in which bishops first have to be priests and priests first have to be deacons, most deacons are undertaking a year of diaconal ministry before going on to be ordained as priests.

However, there are also those who are distinctive deacons. These are people who minister as deacons but do not intend to go on to be ordained as priests. There are two reasons why people choose to be distinctive deacons. Some are people who simply feel that the distinctive diaconal ministry of assistance and bridge-building is the particular form of ordained ministry to which God has called them. Others are women who believe that God has called them to ordination as deacons, but hold that is not right for women to be ordained as priests.

(b) Stipendiary and non-stipendiary ministry

As well as the basic traditional distinction between bishops, priests and deacons there is a further distinction between ordained ministers, which is that some are stipendiary ministers while others are non-stipendiary (or 'self-supporting' ministers).

The majority of ordained ministers are stipendiary ministers. What this means is that they receive a payment or 'stipend' that enables them to live and to provide for their families while engaging in full-time ministry. It is important to note that a stipend is not a salary. Ordained ministers in the Church of England are not employees, either of the Church or of the state. They are technically speaking 'office holders' who receive money so that they can carry out the duties of their office. It is also important to note that in the Church of England stipendiary ministers are expected to live in the parish or diocese in which they hold office and that, to ensure that this is possible, they receive appropriate rent-free accommodation in addition to their stipend.

A minority, although a growing minority, of clergy are non-stipendiary ministers. These ministers, for whom the abbreviation NSM is often used, do not receive a stipend although they do receive expenses. A term which is increasingly used to describe these ministers today is 'self-supporting ministers'. This term is used to make the point that these ministers should be defined, not by the negative fact that they do not receive a stipend, but by the positive fact that they support themselves.

According to the 1994 Regulations for Non-Stipendiary Ministers there are two main categories of NSMs:

(1)   Those in secular employment whose chief area of ministry is the context of their employment, commonly called ministers in secular employment . . .

(2)   Those in secular employment, and those retired from or not engaged in secular employment, whose chief area of ministry is in the context of a parish or chaplaincy.[1]

NSM priests and deacons are ordained into exactly the same ministry as their stipendiary colleagues and it is possible for people to move between stipendiary and NSM forms of ministry during the course of their ministerial career.

(c) Ordained Local Ministry

Ordained Local Ministry (or OLM) is a particular form of NSM ministry that has developed in some dioceses in the Church of England over the past two decades. As Ferial Etherington explains, the term 'refers to those local ministers who are priests or deacons called by, and from within, their local community, who hold the bishop's licence to serve specifically within and for that local community in the context of a local ministry team'.[2] This definition highlights the two distinctive features of OLMs.

First, their call to the ordained ministry takes place within the context of the formation of a local ministry team. The idea is that a parish, or group of parishes, with the support of their diocese, forms a ministry team drawn from lay members of the congregation. Once this team is in existence a process of discernment then takes place in which it is decided which member(s) of the team have the potential to serve within the team as ordained ministers and which should serve as lay ministers. OLMs are then selected from those people who it is believed have the potential to serve as ordained ministers.

---

1   Advisory Board of Ministry, Regulations for Non-Stipendiary Ministers (1994), quoted in G. Kuhrt (ed), *Ministry Issues for the Church of England*, London: Church House Publishing, 2001, p. 219.

2   F. Etherington, ' Local Ministry and Ordained Local Ministry', in ibid., p. 224.

Secondly, OLMs are selected and ordained on the understanding that they will serve in their home parish or group of parishes within the ministry team out of which they have come, rather than going to serve in another parish and being nationally deployable as is the normal practice with stipendiary and NSM clergy.[1]

(d) The selection and training of ordained ministers

Selection

In order to be considered for selection, candidates for ordination have to have the support of their own parish or parishes and to be sponsored by their diocesan or area bishop. Bishops are helped in deciding whom to sponsor by their diocesan directors of ordinands who, as their name suggests, have responsibility within dioceses for those who are seeking ordination.

Once their bishop has agreed to sponsor them, candidates for ordination attend a two-and-a-half-day residential Bishops' Selection Conference. Over fifty of these conferences are organized each year on behalf of the bishops by the Church of England's Ministry Division.

At these conferences, those seeking ordination go through a series of interviews and other individual and group tests and exercises that are designed to allow a team of selectors to test whether a candidate is a suitable person to be ordained. As a result of these interviews and exercises, the selectors assess each candidate against a set of eight criteria which cover a candidate's knowledge and experience of the Church of England and his or her spiritual, intellectual and psychological fitness for the demands of ordained ministry.[2] Once the selectors have decided whether or not to recommend a candidate,[3] this decision is then reported to the candidate's sponsoring bishop. If the selectors decide not to

1 The two key documents that explain OLM ministry are *Local NSM* (London: Church House Publishing, 1991) and *Stranger in the Wings* (London: Church House Publishing, 1998).

2 A summary of the criteria can be found in Kuhrt, op. cit., pp. 112–13.

3 There are three possible outcomes – recommended, conditionally recommended (which means that the candidate has to fulfil certain specified conditions before starting their training) and not recommended (which means that the selectors do not consider someone to have a vocation to the ordained ministry).

recommend a candidate the bishop has the right to overrule their decision.

In the case of candidates for OLM ministry, selection may take place by the method described above, in which case the candidate will attend a national selection conference at which special provision has been made for OLM candidates. Alternatively, candidates may be assessed at a local bishops' selection conference held within their diocese.

The key difference between this selection process and secular forms of selection is that all stages of the process are set in the context of seeking God's will through prayer and the exercise of Christian discernment.

Training

Those recommended by selection conferences are recommended for training. This is not simply a matter of giving candidates for ministry academic knowledge of theology or specific skills in liturgy or pastoral care, but is concerned with what is known as 'formation': the overall growth of the candidates towards the ministry in the Church and the wider world to which God has called them.

There are four forms of training available.

Training at a residential theological college

Most candidates who are recommended for training for stipendiary ministry attend one of the 12 residential theological colleges. These colleges are independent institutions that are recognized by the bishops as providing suitable training for ordained ministry. With two exceptions these colleges represent the different traditions in the Church of England outlined in chapter one of this book and they aim to provide a training which reflects that tradition. For example, St John's College, Nottingham is a college in the Evangelical tradition while St Stephen's House, Oxford is a college in the Anglo-Catholic tradition. The two exceptions are the Queen's Foundation, Birmingham, which provides a specifically ecumenical form of training jointly offered by the Methodist and United Reformed churches alongside the Church of England, and St Michael's College, Llandaff in Wales, which would not describe itself as being affiliated to any one tradition.

Depending on their age, their previous studies and their academic potential, candidates will spend either two or three years at

*St John's College, Nottingham. Photograph reproduced with permission of
St John's College, Nottingham*

theological college. For most students, training at theological
college takes place on a full-time basis. Participation in the life of
the college community is regarded as a key component of the
training that is offered.

Training on a regional training course

Most candidates who are recommended for training for non-
stipendiary ministry, and a minority of students training for
stipendiary ministry, train part time on one of the 12 regional
training courses. Regional courses are owned and managed by the
dioceses in the regions that they cover. Whereas candidates are free
to go to any one of the theological colleges with the agreement of
their bishop, students are normally expected to attend the regional
training course that is in their own area.

Training on a regional course normally lasts three years and is
usually based on a combination of evening classes combined with
residential weeks and weekends.

Training on a diocesan training course
Most candidates for OLM ministry train for three years on part-time courses that are organized within their dioceses and that often also provide training for various forms of lay ministry.

Mixed mode training
Two schemes for what is known as 'mixed mode' training are offered by St John's College, Nottingham (one of the residential colleges) and by the East Anglian Ministerial Training Course. These courses are known as 'mixed mode' because they offer a form of training that mixes placement in a parish with more formal theological training.

The Theological Institute of the Scottish Episcopal Church in Edinburgh is an accredited institution which is recognized as offering appropriate training for ministry although it does not come within the framework for training described above.

Whichever route is taken, training will involve a combination of academic theological study (incorporating subjects such as biblical studies, doctrine, church history and spirituality), vocational training (including subjects such as liturgy, preaching, evangelism and pastoral psychology), and placements in parishes and in other contexts such as hospitals, prisons or local community projects.

In the case of all the colleges and regional courses and an increasing number of the diocesan courses, the training will be validated by a university as well as by the Church. Many of the students at the colleges take university degrees as part of their training and attend university lectures and classes. Conversely, many of the lecturers at the colleges are also university lecturers whose lectures and classes are attended by university students who are not training for ministry. Suitably qualified candidates may take research degrees up to doctoral level as part of their training.

Currently, forms of training are becoming increasingly fluid, with relevant qualifications or experience possessed by candidates being taken into account in the construction of their training programmes, and with different types of training increasingly being combined in order to produce specific forms of training suitable for particular candidates.

Mention has already been made of the ecumenical nature of the training offered at the Queen's Foundation, but this is only one aspect of the increasingly ecumenical nature of ordination training.

As David Way explains, the ecumenical nature of training takes a number of different forms:

> Colleges may be working closely with institutions sponsored by other Churches or may choose to appoint staff from different Churches. Courses are often ecumenical in terms of students or even in terms of their constitution. The Ministry Division's educational validation service now works regularly with the Methodist Church and the United Reformed Church where we share educational programmes, and there have been some moves to work together in a more structured way in the financial area. At a denominational level, the Ecumenical Strategy Group for Ministerial Training, a group which usually meets at staff level, has been a useful forum for liaison and for promoting ecumenical partnerships nationally and regionally.[1]

A recent development that will affect the way in which ordination training in the Church of England is delivered is the emergence of the concept of Regional Training Partnerships (RTPs). This concept was first proposed in a 2003 report entitled *Formation for Ministry Within a Learning Church*.[2] As part of a wider set of proposals for the development of patterns of lifelong learning for the clergy and for wider access to theological education for both clergy and laity alike, the report proposed the 'creation of new institutional arrangements for training through structured and effective partnerships, drawing on diocesan training establishments (including OLM schemes), theological colleges and courses, in collaboration both with other churches and with UK higher education'.[3]

The report also suggested that these partnerships should be organized on a regional basis and coined the term Regional Training Partnerships to describe them. At the moment concrete proposals for the establishment of RTPs are being discussed in the regions concerned. It is not yet clear precisely how they will work in practice.

---

1   D. Way, 'Initial Ministerial Education', in Kuhrt, *Ministry Issues*, p. 141.
2   This is often referred to as the 'Hind report' because the Bishop of Chichester, John Hind, chaired the working party that produced it.
3   *Formation for Ministry Within a Learning Church*, summary of the report, p. 12.

(e) Ordination and beyond

At the completion of training a recommendation is made by the college or course to the sponsoring bishop as to whether or not a candidate should be ordained. As with the recommendation of a selection conference, the bishop has the right to overrule a recommendation. In the final instance, it is the bishop who determines who shall be ordained.

Candidates who are accepted for ordination are ordained as deacons, normally by the diocesan bishop or by a suffragan or assistant bishop. The ordinations of deacons take place in cathedrals, but the ordinations of priests take place either in cathedrals or in parish churches. Ordinations are traditionally held at Petertide (i.e., in the octave of St Peter's Day on 29 June) or at Michaelmas (in the octave of St Michael's Day on 29 September) or, less frequently, at Advent. In order to be ordained a candidate has to have a specific ministry to go to. This ministry is known as a 'title post' and normally involves ministry in a parish. If a candidate does not have a title post to go to, s/he cannot be ordained.

After a year as a deacon, those who are not remaining as distinctive deacons and who have shown themselves to be suitable are ordained as priests. The arrangements for priestly ordinations follow the same pattern as those for the ordination of deacons.

According to the Canon C3 of the Canons of the Church of England, deacons normally have to be at least 23 years old before they can be ordained and priests normally have to be at least 24.

Those who are ordained as priests generally serve another two or three years in the same post into which they were ordained as a deacon. The period of time that they serve in their first parish is colloquially known as a curacy[1] and during this period their training as ministers continues in two ways. First, the incumbent or priest in charge of the parish (known as the training incumbent) acts as a mentor, offering them advice, support and, where necessary, constructive criticism. Secondly, they take part in a programme of Continuing Ministerial Education (CME) organized by their diocese. This will have three aims: to provide support for the newly ordained, to help them to address practical

---

1 Technically speaking, it is an *assistant* curacy since all priests are curates in that they have a 'cure', that is to say, a pastoral responsibility, together with their bishop, for the pastoral care of a parish or congregation.

issues relating to ministry, and to encourage their continuing theological development.

Although there is a particular focus on the continuing ministerial education of those in their first years of ministry, this is something that is also regarded as important for all ordained ministers throughout their ministries, and opportunities of various kinds, including study days and the provision of study leave, are made available to facilitate it. Ordained ministers are also helped in the development of their ministries by a regular process of ministerial review in which they discuss with a bishop or other senior priest from their diocese how their ministry is developing.

Most clergy are engaged in parochial ministry and this is the focus of their ministerial training. However, there are opportunities for some priests to take on senior diocesan posts such as archdeacons or deans. In addition, priests and deacons may be called to other forms of non-parochial ministry such as theological education, the administration of the Church at the diocesan or national level, or work with children and young people; or into chaplaincy work in, for example, the health service, the prison service or the armed forces.

In addition, as has already been noted, there are NSMs for whom their workplace is their primary field of ministry.

A new category of ordained ministry that has emerged recently is the category of 'ordained pioneer minister'. These will be priests or deacons whose primary ministerial focus will be to pioneer what are known as 'fresh expressions of Church', this is to say, new ways of being the Church which respond creatively to the challenges of mission in twenty-first-century England. Discussions are currently under way about how these new types of ordained ministers may best be selected, trained and deployed.[1]

(f) Bishops

The ways in which bishops are chosen and the role of the Crown in the process were explained in chapter five. However, there are a number of points to be noted in this chapter.

---

1 For more details on the proposals for this type of ministry see the paper *Guidelines for the Identification, Training and Deployment of Ordained Pioneer Ministers*, at www.freshexpressions.org.uk.

- First, according to Canon C2 bishops have to be at least 30 years old.
- Secondly, just as deacons and priests are ordained to a particular post, so are bishops. This means that no one is selected simply to be a bishop. They are always selected to be the bishop of somewhere because it is felt that they will meet the needs of that particular post. (A bishop who subsequently moves to another post is described as having been 'translated'.)
- Thirdly, bishops are ordained by at least three bishops, one of whom is the archbishop of the province in which the bishop is to serve or a bishop representing him. Episcopal ordinations generally take place in a cathedral in the province concerned.
- Fourthly, there is no separate training for bishops any more than there is for priests. However, once they have been appointed, bishops receive help in coming to terms with what their new role involves and there is a CME programme for bishops that is designed with their specific needs in mind.

(g) The ordination of women

From 1861 women in the Church of England were permitted to be deaconesses on the grounds that deaconesses had existed in the early church. Women were not permitted, however, to be deacons, priests or bishops.

After a long campaign by supporters of women's ordination, women in the Church of England were first ordained as deacons in 1987 and priests in 1994. Since then, women's ordained ministry has become widely accepted and in 2006 more women were ordained than men, with 244 women being ordained compared to 234 men[1]. There are now women deans and women archdeacons.

However, when the ordination of women as priests was finally agreed in 1993, it was also agreed that this was in the context of an 'open period of reception' in which the Church of England submitted its decision to the eventual judgement of the universal Church. It was also agreed that those opposed to the ordination of

---

1 It should be noted that the fact that a greater number of women than men were ordained in 2006 reflects the greater number of women than men being ordained to non-stipendiary and OLM ministry. It remains the case that significantly more men than women are being ordained for stipendiary ministry.

women would continue to have an equal place in the Church of England alongside those who support it, and today some 15–20 per cent remain opposed.[1]

What this means in practice is that no one is barred from ordination or from serving as a bishop, priest or deacon in the Church of England because he or she cannot accept the ordination of women. It also means that provision is made for those parishes which are opposed. This provision takes three forms. They can pass resolution A stating that they do not want a woman priest to preside at Holy Communion or pronounce absolution. They can pass resolution B saying that they do not want a woman as their incumbent. Finally, they can ask their diocesan bishop for extended episcopal care from a bishop who is also opposed to women's ordination.

This extended episcopal care is provided in three ways: through arrangements made within dioceses; through regional arrangements covering more than one diocese; and through the ministry of the Provincial Episcopal Visitors (PEVs). The three PEVs (commonly known as 'flying bishops') are the Bishops of Ebbsfleet, Richborough and Beverley. They are suffragan bishops of the Archbishops of Canterbury and York who are charged with providing episcopal ministry to parishes that are opposed to the ordination of women. The Bishops of Ebbsfleet and Richborough serve parishes in the Province of Canterbury and the Bishop of Beverley serves parishes in the Province of York.

Women are not permitted to be ordained as bishops in the Church of England. Since February 2005 an official debate has begun within the Church of England about whether, and, if so, how, women bishops should be introduced. At the moment it is not possible to predict what the eventual outcome of this debate will be.[2]

---

1 For this percentage see I. Jones, *Women and Priesthood in the Church of England Ten Years On*, London: Church House Publishing, 2004.

2 For details of the issues involved in this debate see *Women Bishops in the Church of England?*, London: Church House Publishing, 1994.

LAY MINISTRY IN THE CHURCH OF ENGLAND

(a) The different forms of lay ministry in the Church of England

There are a large number of different forms of lay ministry in the Church of England and a helpful way of beginning to get to grips with the differences between them is to distinguish between those forms of ministry that have national authorization, those that have diocesan authorization, and those that are authorized at the parochial level.

Lay ministries authorized by the Church of England as a whole

There are three forms of lay ministry that come into this category.

- The first of these is the ministry of readers, which is authorized under Canons E4–6.[1]
- The second is the ministry of accredited lay workers, who are authorized to serve as lay workers under Canons E7 and E8.[2]
- The third is the ministry of Church Army officers, who are admitted to the office of evangelist in the Church of England under Canon E7 (2).[3]

Because the ministry of readers, accredited lay workers, and Church Army officers is recognized by the Church of England as a whole, it is transferable across the dioceses and candidates for these ministries are selected and trained according to nationally agreed criteria.

Ministries with diocesan authorization

There are four types of ministry with diocesan authorization.

---

1 For details of reader ministry see G. W. Kuhrt and P. Nappin (eds), *Bridging the Gap: Reader Ministry Today*, London: Church House Publishing, 2002.
2 See H. Unwin, 'Accredited Lay Workers', in G. Kuhrt (ed.), *Ministry Issues for the Church of England*, London: Church House Publishing, 2001, pp. 216–18. The numbers of ALMs are tiny, with one being authorized every now and then.
3 See P. Johanson, 'The Church Army', in ibid., pp. 258–61.

- The first of these is the ministry of churchwardens who, under the terms of Canon E1, are officers of the diocesan bishop.
- The second is the ministry of those who under the terms of Canon B12(3) are authorized by the bishop to 'distribute the holy sacrament of the Lord's Supper'.
- The third is the ministry of those who can be generically referred to as 'pastoral assistants' – also known as 'pastoral auxiliaries', 'lay pastors', 'parish assistants', 'licensed local ministers' and 'diocesan evangelists' – whose ministry has some form of formal diocesan authorization.[1]
- The fourth is those who are part of local ministry teams, but who are not Ordained Local Ministers (OLMs) or readers.[2]

These ministries do not involve any form of nationally agreed selection or training, except for the fact that under the Church-wardens (Appointment and Resignation) Measure 1964, church-wardens have to be chosen by the joint consent of the minister of the parish and a meeting of the parishioners.

For the other ministries involved, the criteria for selection and training are instead set by the diocese involved. The scope of ministry anticipated, and the extent of training, vary enormously from diocese to diocese.[3] Such ministries are not transferable between dioceses.

Another form of ministry that could be said to come under this category would be that of lay mission partners from mission agencies such as CMS and Crosslinks working with different communities in this country. They would be appointed following agreement between the diocese and parish(es) involved and the mission agency concerned and there might well be some form of diocesan authorization.

Ministries with parochial authorization
There are a number of different types of ministry which have a

---

1 For details of these forms of ministry see *Formal Lay Ministry* (London: Church of England Board of Education, 1999) and J. Cox, *Authorised Lay Pastoral Ministry* (London: Church of England Board of Education, 2002).
2 For details of what is meant by local ministry teams and OLMs see Advisory Board of Ministry, *Stranger in the Wings*, London: Church House Publishing, 1998.
3 Further details are available in a discussion paper by J. Cox, *Authorized Lay Pastoral Ministry* (September 2002).

purely parochial authorization in the sense that the people involved are authorized to act by a local parish or group of parishes, rather than by the diocese or by the Church of England nationally.

Such ministries include:

- Youth and children's workers
- Evangelists
- Community workers and community development workers
- Parish administrators
- Choirmasters or worship leaders
- Young people working with schemes such as Time for God or Oasis House Group, Cell Group or Alpha Group leaders

Those involved in such ministries might receive some form of episcopal commissioning, but they would not be formally authorized at a diocesan level, and their recognition would not be transferable outside the parish or parishes involved.

The fact that the term 'evangelist' has been used with reference to national, diocesan, and parochial forms of lay ministry means that the use of the term in the Church of England requires a brief explanation at this point.

In the Church of England, as we have said, Church Army officers are admitted to the nationally recognized office of evangelist. In the Diocese of Rochester, for example, there is also a Diocesan Fellowship of Evangelists, whose members receive training and authorization at diocesan level.[1] In a number of parishes there are people who are authorized to undertake evangelistic activity in their local area. Finally, there are those who engage in a ministry of evangelism and in that sense can be called evangelists even if they are not formally authorized to act as such, or are officially authorized to perform some other form of ministry such as, for example, being a priest.

The College of Evangelists is different again. In the words of the *Church of England Year Book*:

The national College of Evangelists was founded in 1999 to support and give the accreditation of the Archbishops of Canterbury and York to evangelists in the Church of England. To

---

1 For details see www.evangelists.diocese-rochester.org.

qualify, evangelists will be involved in evangelistic missions (not just training or teaching about evangelism) and will be operating nationally or regionally.[1]

(b) What activities do these ministries involve?

It is impossible to give a precise description of what activities are involved because these will vary according to the type of lay ministry concerned and the particular circumstances in which a particular form of ministry is exercised.

However, it is possible to give a general list of the kind of activities in which lay ministers are involved and this list includes both liturgical and non-liturgical activities:

Liturgical activities
- Conducting Morning and Evening Prayer and other non-sacramental services
- Preaching
- Reading the Epistle and sometimes the Gospel
- Leading the people in prayer
- Administering the elements at the Holy Communion
- Leading a service of Holy Communion by extension
- Leading the music for services and training singers and musicians
- Reading the banns of marriage in certain circumstances
- Taking funerals.

Non-liturgical activities
- Evangelism
- Leading home groups
- Church administration
- Pastoral visiting
- Pastoral counselling
- Marriage and baptism preparation
- Visiting the bereaved
- Children and young people's work
- Hospital and prison chaplaincy
- Working with the elderly

---

1 *The Church of England Year Book 2003*, London: Church House Publishing, 2003, p. 279.

- Working with the unemployed, the homeless and refugees, and other groups such as those suffering from alcohol and drug addiction.

Churchwardens and sidesmen have particular responsibilities set out in Canons E1 and E2 which involve representing the laity, working with the incumbent to promote 'true religion' in the parish, taking care of the property of the Church and maintaining 'order and decency' in the church and churchyard 'especially during the time of divine service'.

During vacancies, churchwardens are responsible (together with the rural dean) for ensuring that services continue to take place in the parish.

(c) Training for lay ministry

As has already been indicated, those lay ministers whose ministry has national authorization will be trained according to nationally agreed criteria, and the training they receive will be monitored by the Ministry Division.

This training will involve an extensive grounding in theology and pastoral studies and, in the case of Church Army officers, evangelism as well.

Church Army officers are trained at the Wilson Carlile College of Evangelism in Sheffield. Accredited Lay Ministers are selected and trained alongside candidates for ordained ministry. Readers are trained on diocesan training schemes which are nationally moderated. These may involve them training alongside both candidates for Ordained Local Ministry and those training for other ministries with diocesan recognition, such as pastoral assistants.

Pastoral assistants whose ministry has diocesan authorization will be trained according to diocesan criteria and these vary greatly from diocese to diocese. There is no national standard for this training, though training for lay ministries not recognized by canon law comes within the remit of the Education Division, and much current national work relates to discussion among dioceses of appropriate structures and the sharing of good practice.

Three examples will serve to illustrate this varied diocesan practice.

- In the diocese of Carlisle, 'commissioned ministers' are trained by means of an 'apprenticeship model' in which those in training engage in a 'vocational journey', acquiring their skills and their theological knowledge as they begin to engage in ministry under the supervision of those who are already experienced ministers.
- In the diocese of Southwell, 'recognised lay ministers' study for a bishop's certificate in lay ministry alongside those training to be readers and then do a final year of specialist training in one of the following areas: children's work, youth work, pastoral care, workplace ministry, community ministry, helping adults learn, witness and evangelism, leading music and worship.
- In the diocese of Truro, 'local worship leaders' undertake a 'core training' module which gives a basic understanding of the theology of worship, of communication and the theory and practice of leading services. They are then encouraged to take a second, optional module which focuses on assisting at the Eucharist and on services for special occasions and, after they are commissioned as part of a parish team, continuing training is provided by means of occasional sessions on topics such as leading all-age worship, the use of liturgical space and the use of desktop publishing to produce orders of service.

Churchwardens do not normally receive any kind of formal training, though many dioceses offer some short induction or training sessions. The same is generally true of those authorized to distribute the elements at Holy Communion although in the Diocese of Chichester those authorized to undertake this ministry have to have undergone a training course provided by the diocese.

The pattern of training for those undertaking ministries with parochial authorization is even more varied than the training for ministries with diocesan authorization. Training for parochially authorized ministries may be arranged 'in house' by the parish or parishes concerned; or those involved may participate in various diocesan training schemes alongside those training for other forms of ministry; or they may participate in training courses on specific topics offered by organizations such as Alpha, Scripture Union, Crusade for World Revival, or the Royal School of Church Music.

In addition to undertaking training for specific ministries, many people engaged in lay ministry in the Church of England undertake study in areas such as theology, pastoral counselling or youth work by taking courses at universities, theological colleges and Bible colleges or by making use of the various distance-learning courses that are now provided by bodies such as the Open Theological College and St John's College, Nottingham. This kind of study will generally be of good academic standing and may lead to a nationally recognized qualification such as a degree, diploma or certificate in the area of study concerned. The recommendations of the Hind Report will extend the availability of such study, especially with the proposals for 'Education for Discipleship'.

(d) Patterns of authorization for lay ministry

As Joanna Cox notes in a paper on the recognition and authorization of lay ministries,[1] the authorization of ministries is important for a number of reasons. It gives those involved formal permission to act, and it gives affirmation to them and to the particular form of ministry involved. It can help to clarify the nature and purpose of a particular form of ministry, and what is expected of those involved in it, and it makes it clear that what is being undertaken is being undertaken on behalf of the Church.[2]

Patterns of authorization vary between the various types of ministry involved.

In the case of readers, Church Army officers and accredited lay workers, authorization takes the form laid down in Canons E6 and E8 of admission by the diocesan bishop to the office of reader or lay worker in the Church of England, and licensing by the bishop to a particular post.

In the case of other lay ministers, the appointment may be by the bishop, the archdeacon, or the parish minister or, in the case of churchwardens and sidesmen, as a result of an election; and, as Joanna Cox further notes, it may take a number of different forms:

- It may be authorization for a particular task (such as churchwarden) or a more general role (such as pastoral assistant), and there may or may not be a specific job description or parish agreement involved.

---

1 J. Cox, 'Local Recognition and Authorisation of Lay Ministries Not Recognised by Canon', unpublished paper.
2 Ibid., pp. 2–4.

- It may involve authorization for a fixed period of time or for an indefinite period.
- It may involve authorization for a pattern of ministry which exists across a diocese, or for a form of ministry that is specific to a particular parish or group of parishes.[1]

WHAT ARE THE DIFFERENCES BETWEEN THESE VARIOUS FORMS OF LAY MINISTRY AND ORDAINED MINISTRY?

The differences between them are not in terms of full or part time, paid or unpaid, or qualified or less qualified.

Just as there are part-time and non-stipendiary ordained ministers, so there are full-time and paid lay ministers; and many lay ministers may be at least as well qualified for what they do as their ordained counterparts.

The differences are not concerned with issues of value or status. There is fundamentally only one ministry, which is the ministry of Christ in His Church and, as 1 Cor. 12:4–26 indicates, every manifestation of this ministry has its own distinctive part to play in the well-being of the Church and the performance of its mission.

It is clear that the Church of England would simply not be able to carry out its God-given mission effectively without the work undertaken by its thousands of lay ministers. The ordained clergy simply could not do the task on their own.

The differences are not a matter of national as against local recognition. Readers and Church Army officers have national recognition, just as much as bishops, priests and deacons.

Neither are the differences between them a matter of sacramental as against non-sacramental ministry. It is true that lay ministers are not authorized to baptize or to preside at the Eucharist. However, lay ministers are frequently involved in Eucharistic ministry in the sense that they are authorized to 'distribute the holy sacrament of the Lord's Supper to the people'[2] and to take services of Holy Communion by extension.

Finally, the differences between lay and ordained ministers cannot be related without careful qualification to the four creedal

1 Ibid., pp. 4–6 .
2 Canons B12 (3), E4 2 (c) and E 7 4(b).

marks of the Church, that is, to the fact that the Church is one, holy, catholic and apostolic.

The 1997 House of Bishops report *Eucharistic Presidency* shows that the role of the ordained ministry can be related to these four marks. For example, on the unity of the Church it states that:

> The Church is one in that it has been given to share in, and is called to grow deeper into the unity of the triune God . . . The ordained minister as leader carries a specific responsibility to foster the unity-and-diversity which we believe God seeks to bring about in his Church for the sake of the world. In addition, the ordained leader is to be a focus of unity for the particular congregation(s) for which he or she is responsible. The leader not only speaks and acts in the name of Christ, but also for the community in its plurality, as 'one on behalf of the many'. The Church is represented in that person as he or she carries the concerns of the flock. The ordained person can be both a means of renewing unity and a sign of it.[1]

It then goes on to show in a similar fashion how the other three marks also relate to the ordained ministry.[2]

The question therefore is whether this *only* applies to ordained ministers, and this is more difficult to maintain.

Thus it can be argued that lay ministers too are responsible for fostering the unity of the Christian community in which they serve; that they serve its apostolicity and catholicity by teaching the apostolic and catholic faith and by their involvement in, and promotion of, the Church's apostolic vocation to bear witness to Christ; and that they are responsible for promoting the holiness of the Church through their teaching and personal example.

It is, however, true that the existence of the threefold ministry of bishop, priest and deacon witnesses to the Church of England's commitment to being part of the one, holy, catholic and apostolic Church in two ways that the existence of its lay ministries does not.

First, the retention by the Church of England of the threefold pattern of ministry that has been a central feature of the life of by far the greater part of the Church from apostolic times onwards

---

1 *Eucharistic Presidency*, London: Church House Publishing, 1997, p. 32.
2 Ibid., pp. 32–3.

witnesses to the Church of England's commitment to being in unity with the whole Church of God across time and space.

Secondly, the way in which ministers are ordained into this threefold pattern of ministry bears further witness to the Church of England's commitment to the principles of catholicity and apostolicity.

We can see this latter point if we look at what the 1994 House of Bishops occasional paper *Apostolicity and Succession* tells us about the significance for the Church of England of the way its bishops are ordained:

> To ordain by prayer and the laying on of hands expresses the Church's trust in its Lord's promise to empower disciples and it expresses the Church's intention in response to be faithful in carrying out the apostolic ministry and mission. The participation of three bishops in the laying on of hands witnesses to the catholicity of the churches. The laying on of hands by bishops who have had hands lain on them in succession signifies continuity back to the Apostles. Both the act of consecration and the continuity of ministerial succession witness to the Church's fidelity to the teaching and mission of the Apostles. This continuity is integral to the continuity of the Church's life as a whole.[1]

What is said in this quotation about the significance of the way bishops are ordained also applies to the way priests and deacons are ordained. In their case the laying on of hands by a bishop who has himself been ordained in the way described above bears witness to the catholicity of the Church, in that the bishop acts on behalf of the Church Catholic, ordaining ministers not just for the Church of England but for the Church of God, and to its apostolicity in that the bishop also represents the apostolic continuity of the Church of England as part of the universal Church.

In the light of the above, what can we therefore say are the differences between the lay and ordained ministries of the Church of England? As lay ministries have come to assume ever greater importance in the life of the Church of England, and as lay people have been permitted to exercise more and more ministerial roles

---

1 *Apostolicity and Succession*, London: Church House Publishing, 1998, p. 22.

that were once restricted to those who were ordained, this question is being asked more and more.[1]

The Anglican Roman Catholic International Commission report 'Ministry and Ordination' declares that ordained ministers share through baptism in the common priesthood of the whole people of God, but it also argues that:

> . . . their priesthood is not an extension of the common Christian priesthood but belongs to another realm of the gifts of the Spirit. It exists to help the Church to be 'a royal priesthood, a holy nation, God's own people, to declare the wonderful deeds of him who called [them] out of darkness into his marvellous light'. (1 Pet. 2:9)[2]

This argument makes sense if it is seen in terms of the teaching of St Paul that, although all ministry is an embodiment of the one ministry of Christ, God does not call people to exercise this ministry in a single undifferentiated fashion, but instead gives various different forms of ministry to the Church through the Spirit in order that, through their exercise, the Church as a whole may be built up (see 1 Corinthians 12:27–3, Ephesians 4:9–13). However, recognizing that this is the case still leaves unanswered the question of what is distinctive about the particular ministry that is exercised by those who are ordained.

A helpful way to approach this question may be to start with the recognition that there are large areas of ministry where there is no difference between the ministry exercised by those who are lay and those who are ordained. This is true, for example, of the areas of preaching, evangelism, catechesis and the provision of various kinds of pastoral care.

There are also areas in which there is both an overlap and a distinction between the ministries exercised by lay people and by those who have been ordained. For example, lay people can lead services but only those who have been ordained as priests can pronounce absolution or give a blessing; lay people can help

---

1 See, for example, the discussion of the relationship between readers and Ordained Local Ministers (OLMs) in *The Reader*, Spring 2005, Vol. 102, No. 2, pp. 27–8.
2 Anglican Roman Catholic International Commission, *The Final Report*, London: CTS/SPCK, 1982, p. 36.

prepare people for marriage but only those who have been ordained as deacons or priests can officiate at weddings; and lay people can assist in the administration of Holy Communion but only those who have been ordained as priests can preside.

However, there are four ways in which the ministry of those who are ordained remains distinctive.

First, the ministry exercised by those who are ordained is more comprehensive in scope than that exercised by lay ministers. If we look at what the Church of England requires of its ordained ministers as set out in its Ordinals and in its selection criteria for those offering for ordained ministry, we find that they are called to manifest a Christian character by living distinctively holy lives, to exercise sensitive pastoral care, to teach the Christian faith in an effective manner and to give leadership in mission. Each of these requirements can obviously also be found in lay people, but what is distinctive about the ordained is that they are required to exhibit all four as well as fostering their development in others.

Secondly, bishops, priests and deacons are authorized to perform a wider range of ministerial functions than lay ministers. Thus:

- Deacons can take weddings and can baptize while lay ministers cannot take weddings and can only baptize in an emergency.
- Priests can preside at the Eucharist, pronounce absolution and give a blessing and have pastoral oversight of parishes while lay ministers cannot.
- Bishops can ordain, confirm and have pastoral oversight of dioceses while lay ministers cannot.

Thirdly, bishops, priests and deacons have a ministry that is bestowed for life. The theological reason for this lies in the fact that those who are ordained are called to point in a distinctive fashion, both to the relationship of Christ to His people and the response that they are called to make to Him. In this context, the lifelong vocation of those who are ordained embodies both the total commitment of Christ to His Church and the total and lifelong commitment to Him that He asks for from His people. It is true that others in the Church, such as members of religious orders, also have a lifelong vocation, but this does not negate the significance of this vocation in the case of the ordained.

Fourthly, bishops, priests and deacons are part of the historic threefold order of ministry and have some degree of ecumenical recognition within the universal Church. This bears witness, in the two ways described above, to the commitment of the Church of England to being part of the one, holy, catholic and apostolic Church.[1]

In his book *After our Likeness: The Church as the Image of the Trinity*, the American theologian Miroslav Volf writes:

> Every Catholic church is charged with maintaining and deepening its ties to other churches past and present. The church that refuses to do thus would not be a church at all. Openness to other churches should lead to a free networking with those churches, and as the image of the net also suggests, these mutual relations should be expressed in corresponding ecclesial institutions.[2]

In the Church of England the three ordained ministries of bishop, priest and deacon are among the key ecclesial institutions through which these mutual relations are symbolized and maintained.

RELIGIOUS COMMUNITIES IN THE CHURCH OF ENGLAND

Another form of ministry that exists in the Church of England, but that is often overlooked, is the ministry undertaken by members of the Church of England's religious communities, who live out their Christian faith in the context provided by obedience to a monastic rule.

The medieval monastic communities that existed prior to the Reformation were closed down by Henry VIII, the last to close being Waltham Abbey in Essex in 1539. There was a very small and very brief monastic revival during the reign of Mary Tudor but, this apart, religious communities ceased to exist in the Church of England until the nineteenth century when they were

---

1 It needs to be noted, however, that the Church of England has historically recognized Christian bodies lacking the traditional threefold ministry as nevertheless being part of the one Church of Jesus Christ and that, as its ecumenical agreements make clear, it continues to do so today.

2 M. Volf, *After our Likeness: The Church as the Image of the Trinity*, Grand Rapids: Eerdmans, 1998, p. 275.

reintroduced as part of the Catholic revival in the Church of England that resulted from the Oxford Movement.

In 1841 two women took vows and in 1863 an Anglican Benedictine monastery for men was opened. From these small beginnings the number of religious communities grew throughout the rest of the century. In the Church of England today there are some 1,200 men and women living in over 40 religious communities, some of which are for men, some of which are for women and some of which are mixed communities.

As the *Church of England Year Book* explains:

Each Community has its own history and character; some follow one of the traditional Rules, and others those written by more recent founders, but all have one thing in common: their daily life based on the work of prayer and living together centred in their Daily Office and the Eucharist. The work grows from the prayer, depending on the particular Community.

Some Communities are 'enclosed'. The members do not normally go out, but remain within the convent or monastery and its grounds, seeking and serving God through silence and prayer, study and work. Other Communities share the basic life of prayer and fellowship and may also be involved in work outside the Community.[1]

As it also notes:

Most Community Houses offer a place where people can go for a time of Retreat, either alone or with a group, for a day, several days, or occasionally for longer periods of time. They offer a place of quiet to seek God, grow in prayer and find spiritual guidance.[2]

The religious communities of the Church of England relate to the structures of the Church of England in a number of ways.

First, each community comes under the oversight of the diocesan bishop of the diocese in which it is situated.

---

1   *The Church of England Year Book*, 2006, London: Church House Publishing, 2005, p. 249.
2   Ibid., p. 249.

Secondly, each of the communities has a bishop (who may or may not be the diocesan bishop) as its Visitor. These episcopal Visitors 'are the guardians of the Constitutions of the community and guarantors to the Church at large of the community's sound administration, stability and right to confidence'.[1]

Thirdly, there is also an Advisory Council on the Relations of Bishops and Religious Communities. This serves the Church of England as a whole and its functions are:

(1) to advise bishops on (a) questions arising about the charters, constitutions and rules of existing Communities, (b) the establishment of new communities, (c) matters referred to it by a diocesan bishop; (2) to advise existing Communities or their Visitors in any matters they may wish to refer to it; (3) to give guidance to those who wish to form communities.[2]

Fourthly, as we noted in chapter three, the religious communities have four places assigned to them in the Church of England's General Synod.

In common with religious communities across the Western Church, the religious communities in the Church of England, such as the Community of the Resurrection, the Society of St Francis, the Order of the Holy Paraclete and the Community of St Mary the Virgin, currently have problems in recruiting new members, but they remain a valued and distinctive part of its life.

FOR FURTHER READING

Avis, P., *A Ministry Shaped by Mission*, London: T&T Clark, 2005.
Kuhrt, G., *Ministry Issues for the Church of England*, London: Church House Publishing, 2000.
Ministry in the Church of England, www.cofe.org/lifeevents/ministry/ministryinthecofe.
Sceats, D., 'Orders and Offices in the Church', in I. Bunting (ed.), *Celebrating the Anglican Way*, London: Hodder & Stoughton, 1996.

---

1 Advisory Council on the Relations of Bishops and Religious Communities, *A Handbook of the Religious Life*, Norwich: Canterbury Press, 2004, p. 50.
2 *Church of England Year Book*, 2006, p. 249.

APPENDIX 1 – RECOGNIZED INSTITUTIONS FOR ORDINATION TRAINING IN THE CHURCH OF ENGLAND

(a) Theological colleges

- College of the Resurrection, Mirfield
- Cranmer Hall, Durham
- Oak Hill Theological College, London
- Queen's Foundation for Ecumenical Theological Education, Birmingham (including the West Midlands Ministerial Training Course)
- Ridley Hall, Cambridge
- Ripon College, Cuddesdon, Oxford (incorporating the Oxford Ministry Course)
- St John's College, Nottingham
- St Michael's College, Llandaff, Cardiff
- St Stephen's House, Oxford
- Trinity College, Bristol
- Westcott House, Cambridge
- Wycliffe Hall, Oxford

The Theological Institute of the Scottish Episcopal Church, Edinburgh is described as an 'accredited institution'.

(b) Regional courses

- Carlisle and Blackburn Diocesan Training Institute
- Eastern Region Ministry Course
- East Midlands Ministerial Training Course
- North East Oecumenical Course
- Northern Ordination Course
- North Thames Ministerial Training Course
- South East Institute for Theological Education
- Southern Theological Education and Training Scheme
- South West Ministry Training Course
- Queen's Foundation for Ecumenical Theological Education including the West Midlands Ministerial Training Course
- West of England Ministerial Training Course

(c) Ordained Local Ministry Schemes

- Blackburn OLM Scheme
- Canterbury OLM Scheme
- Coventry OLM Scheme
- Gloucester OLM
- Guildford Diocesan Ministry Course
- Hereford Local Ministry Scheme
- Lichfield OLM Scheme
- Lincoln OLM Scheme
- Liverpool OLM Scheme
- Manchester OLM Scheme
- Newcastle OLM Scheme
- Norwich OLM Scheme
- Oxford OLM Scheme
- St Edmundsbury and Ipswich Diocesan Ministry Course
- Salisbury OLM Scheme
- Southwark OLM Scheme
- Wakefield Ministry Scheme

APPENDIX 2 – STATISTICS FOR MINISTRY AND ORDINATION IN THE CHURCH OF ENGLAND

These statistics, which are the latest available, are taken from the *Church of England Year Book 2008*. They clearly indicate the importance of licensed lay ministry (especially reader ministry) in the Church of England and the growth in the numbers of female, NSM and OLM ordinands.

Church of England Licensed Ministries 2006

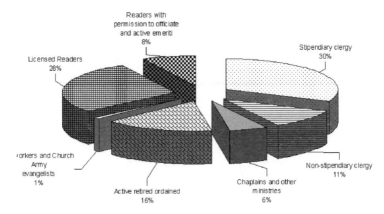

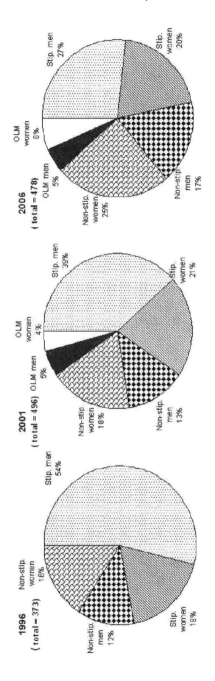

1996 (total = 373)
Stip. men 54%
Stip. women 18%
Non-stip. men 12%
Non-stip. women 16%

2001 (total = 496)
Stip. men 39%
Stip. women 21%
Non-stip. men 13%
Non-stip. women 18%
OLM men 5%
OLM women 4%

2006 (total = 478)
Stip. men 27%
Stip. women 20%
Non-stip. men 17%
Non-stip. women 25%
OLM men 5%
OLM women 6%

Ordinations 2004–2006

	1994	1995	1996	1997	1998	1999	2000	2001	2002	2003	2004	2005	2006
Stipendiary men	244	245	201	186	174	199	223	190	199	181	143	155	128
Stipendiary women	72	65	67	57	67	78	90	105	112	120	92	99	95
Non-stipendiary men	55	30	46	69	73	61	81	65	67	55	63	81	82
Non-stipendiary women	34	42	59	67	87	76	107	89	104	77	93	108	118
OLM men					27	40	25	27	34	24	31	31	24
OLM women					40	27	43	20	24	36	47	31	31
Totals	405	382	373	379	468	481	569	496	540	493	469	505	478

9 Worship in the Church of England

THE RULES GOVERNING WHICH SERVICES MAY BE USED

Canons B1–5a set out the rules governing which forms of service are authorized for use in the Church of England. What these canons tell us is that there are a number of different forms of service that may be used.

- First there are the services contained in the Book of Common Prayer, either in their full form or in the form of the shorter versions of Morning and Evening Prayer authorized in 1872 (Canon B1).
- Secondly, there are special services authorized by Royal Warrant for use on the anniversary of the accession of the Monarch (Canon B1).
- Thirdly, there are forms of service approved for use by the General Synod (Canon B2). Services that are being prepared for use in this way may be authorized for experimental use by the Archbishops of Canterbury and York after consultation with the House of Bishops and General Synod (Canon B5a).
- Fourthly, there are forms of service approved by the Convocations of Canterbury and York, by the Archbishops of Canterbury and York or by diocesan bishops for use on occasions for which there are no services provided either in the Book of Common Prayer or in the services authorized by the General Synod (Canon B4).
- Fifthly, on occasions where there are no services provided by the sources already noted, a Church of England minister may use other forms of service that he or she considers suitable and may permit another minister to use them as well (Canon B5).

Services other than those contained in the Book of Common Prayer are used on the basis that they are 'neither contrary to, nor indicative of, any departure from, the doctrine of the Church of England on any essential matter'[1] and in the case of services authorized under Canon B5, on the additional basis that they are 'reverent and seemly'.[2]

In parish churches, the decision about the forms of service to use for the normal pattern of church services is taken jointly by the minister and the parochial church council.

The decision about which forms of service to use for the Occasional Offices, that is to say, weddings, funerals and baptisms, is normally made by the minister who is conducting the service in conjunction with the parties involved.

The decision about the form of service to use for confirmation and ordination is made by the bishop or archbishop concerned.

THE BOOK OF COMMON PRAYER

The 1549 Prayer Book

As the Roman Catholic Church historian Eamon Duffy explains in his book *The Stripping of the Altars*,[3] by the time of the Reformation centuries of development had produced a rich and vibrant pattern of worship in the English church. As he also explains, however, at the Reformation, this pattern was almost entirely dismantled and reconstructed.

The reasons for this process of dismantling and reconstruction are set out in the section entitled 'Concerning the Service of the Church' in the preface to the Book of Common Prayer.

This section first of all explains what the English Reformers saw as wrong with the late medieval patterns of worship that the Book of Common Prayer replaced. It argues that a 'godly and decent' order of worship had been developed by the early Fathers, but that subsequently:

. . . this godly and decent order of the ancient Fathers hath been so altered, broken, and neglected, by planting in uncertain Stories, and Legends, with multitude of Responds, Verses, vain

---

1 Canons B2:1, B4:2, B5:3.
2 Canon B5:3.
3 E. Duffy, *The Stripping of the Altars*, New Haven and London: Yale University Press, 1992.

Repetitions, Commemorations, and Synodals; that commonly when any Book of the Bible was begun, after three of four Chapters were read out, all the rest were unread. And in this sort the Book of *Isaiah* was begun in *Advent*, and the Book of *Genesis* in *Septuagesima*; but they were only begun, and never read through: after like sort were other Books of holy Scripture used. And moreover, whereas St *Paul* would have such language spoken to the people in the Church, as they might understand, and have profit by hearing the same; the service in this Church of *England* these many years hath been read in Latin to the people, which they understand not; so that they have heard with their ears only, and their heart, spirit and mind, have not been edified thereby. And furthermore, notwithstanding that the ancient Fathers have divided the *Psalms* into seven portions, whereof every one was called a *Nocturn*: now of late time a few of them have been daily said, and the rest utterly omitted. Moreover, the number and hardness of the Rules called the *Pie*, and the manifold changings of the service, was the cause, that to turn the book only was so hard and intricate a matter, that many times there was more business to find out what should be read, than to read it when it was found out.

If we look carefully at this statement we find four criticisms of medieval practice:

- The biblical books were not read through in their entirety.
- Most of the Psalms were not read.
- The services were read in Latin rather than in the vernacular.
- The rules governing which parts of the service to use were very difficult to follow.

Having made these criticisms the section goes on to explain how the new service book responds to them:

These inconveniences therefore considered, here is set forth such an order, whereby the same shall be redressed. And for a readiness in this matter, here is drawn out a Calendar for that purpose, which is plain and easy to be understood; wherein (so much as may be) the reading of holy Scripture is so set forth, that all things shall be done in order, without breaking one piece from another. For this cause be cut off Anthems, Responds,

Invitatories, and such like things as did break the continual course of the reading of the Scripture.

Yet, because there is no remedy, but that of necessity there must be some Rules; therefore certain Rules are here set forth; which, as they are few in number, so they are plain and easy to be understood. So that here you have an Order for Prayer, and for the reading of the holy Scripture, much agreeable to the mind and purpose of the old Fathers, and a great deal more profitable and commodious, than that which of late was used. It is more profitable, because here are left out many things, whereof some are untrue, some uncertain, some vain and superstitious; and nothing is ordained to be read, but the very pure Word of God, the holy Scriptures, or that which is agreeable to the same; and that in such a language and order as is most easy and plain for the understanding both of the readers and hearers. It is also more commodious, both for the shortness thereof, and for the plainness of the order, and for that the rules be few and easy.

And whereas heretofore there hath been great diversity in saying and singing in Churches within this Realm; some following *Salisbury* Use, some *Hereford* Use, and some the Use of *Bangor*, some of *York*, some of *Lincoln*; now from henceforth all the whole Realm shall have but one Use.

Looking carefully at this statement what we find is that the new book embodies four principles:

- It is biblically based and those things that are untrue, uncertain, vain or superstitious have been left out.
- The biblical books are to be read through continuously rather than being broken up into disconnected pieces.
- It is in a language that can be understood, i.e., in English rather than Latin (although the use of Latin was still allowed in contexts where it would be understood, such as the universities).
- The rules that govern the service are few and simple.

There is also to be one uniform liturgy for the whole country rather than a diversity of local rites. This was what was meant by the term 'common prayer'.

The first large-scale attempt to embody these principles was the 1549 Prayer Book. Archbishop Cranmer had produced a litany (a sequence of prayers asking for God's help) in English in 1544 and in 1548 he also produced an English Order for Communion which was inserted into the Latin Mass. What was different about the 1549 book was that it did not simply contain supplementary material, but replaced the existing Latin orders of service in their entirety.

The key features of the book were that:

- It contained a new lectionary from which non-Scriptural readings were eliminated and in which the Psalms were read through once a month, the Old Testament was 'read through every year once, except certain books and chapters, which be least edifying, and might best be spared' and the New Testament was 'read over orderly every year thrice . . . except the Apocalypse (Revelation), out of which there be only certain lessons appointed upon diverse proper feasts'.
- It compressed the seven traditional monastic daily services into the two daily services of Morning and Evening Prayer.
- It replaced the Mass with a new service of Holy Communion.
- It provided new forms of the services for baptism, confirmation, marriage and funerals.

Scholars continue to debate how much of this book was written by Cranmer himself, and how much was contributed by others, but as Professor Diarmaid MacCulloch writes: 'Whatever help of this sort Cranmer received, he should take credit for the overall job of editorship and the overarching structure of the book.'[1] The sources underlying the book also continue to be debated, but it is generally accepted that a variety of different sources were used. Marion Hatchett declares, for example, that:

> The sources cover a broad spectrum, the early Church Fathers, Eastern liturgies that had recently come into print in Latin, various uses of the medieval Roman rite, the Reformed Breviary of the Roman Catholic Cardinal Francisco Quiniones, various German Church Orders, especially the *Consultation*, various

---

1 D. MacCulloch, *Thomas Cranmer*, New Haven and London: Yale University Press, 1996, p. 417.

English Reformation formularies, and Cranmer's two earlier drafts for Daily Offices.[1]

However, as she also notes: 'Very few texts were retained from earlier sources without editing or without revision in the process of translation.'[2]

The revision of 1552

The 1549 Prayer Book has become the basis of the prayer books of a number of Anglican churches such as the Scottish Episcopal Church and the Episcopal Church in the United States of America. In England itself, however, it was the revised 1552 edition of the Book of Common Prayer that became the basis for the worship of the Church of England.

This revised edition is often characterized as a distinctively Protestant revision influenced by the continental Protestant scholars Martin Bucer and Peter Martyr, who were the Regius Professors of Divinity at Cambridge and Oxford respectively. The truth, however, is more complicated. On the one hand there are elements in the 1552 revision that do mark a move in a Protestant direction. For example, all prayers for the dead are removed from the funeral rite and in the service of Holy Communion the emphasis in the rite shifts from the idea of sacrifice and real presence to that of commemoration and communion. On the other hand, as Hatchett points out,[3] there are also elements in the revision that are conservative. For example, the medieval customs of the Epistle being read by the priest rather than the parish clerk and the people receiving communion kneeling were reintroduced.

It seems that either Cranmer was seeking to make alterations that would please both Protestants and conservatives in different ways or, perhaps more likely, that he was simply following through his own liturgical vision and this was one that included both Protestant and traditional elements within it.

---

1   M. Hatchett, 'Prayer Books', in S. Sykes and J. Booty (eds), *The Study of Anglicanism*, London and Minneappolis: SPCK/Fortress Press, 1988, p. 122.
2   Ibid., p. 122.
3   Ibid., p. 127.

The Ordinal

The 1549 Prayer Book did not have an ordinal. A separate ordinal was subsequently produced in 1550 and this too was revised in 1552. As with the services in the main Book of Common Prayer the ordination services contain both traditional and Protestant elements. Thus on the one hand the rites are specifically aimed at perpetuating the traditional Catholic threefold order of bishops, priests and deacons, while on the other hand the medieval minor orders vanish from view and, in the 1552 revision, the practice of giving priests a cup and bread and bishops a pastoral staff as symbols of their new ministry was abolished in favour of giving them only the Bible.

From 1559 to 1662

The reign of Mary Tudor saw a return to the medieval Sarum Rite – the Latin rite that was most commonly used in England prior to the Reformation and was the authorized rite for the Church of England from the breach with Rome until the introduction of the 1549 Prayer Book[1] – but after the accession of Queen Elizabeth I, the 1552 Book of Common Prayer was reintroduced in 1559 with four changes, which seem to have been designed to conciliate those with conservative leanings.

- The prayer in the Litany asking deliverance from the Bishop of Rome and all his enormities was dropped.
- An 'Ornaments Rubric'[2] restored the liturgical vestments, the distinctive dress worn by the clergy when performing the services of the Church, that had been used in: 'the Second year of the Reign of King Edward the Sixth'.
- The words at the reception of the bread and wine at communion in the 1552 book, 'Take and eat this in remembrance that Christ died for thee, and feed on him in thy heart with thanksgiving' and 'Drink this in remembrance that Christ's blood was shed for thee and be thankful', were combined with

---

1 It was called the Sarum rite because it was the rite used at the cathedral in Salisbury ('Sarum' in Latin).
2 A rubric is an instruction in a service book. It is called a rubric because such instructions were often written in red (Latin *ruber*) to distinguish them from the main text.

the words from the 1549 book 'The Body of our Lord Jesus Christ which was given for thee, preserve thy body and soul unto everlasting life' and 'The Blood of our Lord Jesus Christ, which was shed for thee, preserve thy body and soul unto everlasting life.'

- A declaration attached to the 1552 revision (the so called 'Black Rubric') indicating that kneeling at Communion did not indicate a belief in the real presence of Christ in the Eucharistic elements was omitted.

In addition, a new liturgical calendar was introduced in 1561, which contained more than sixty 'Black Letter Days' (lesser, mainly non-Scriptural, Saints Days), and in 1562 a metrical version of the Psalter, which also contained a few hymns and metrical settings of certain Prayer Book texts, was authorized for use before and after services and sermons in an attempt to please those who were enthusiastic about the metrical psalmody of the continental Reformed churches.

During the remainder of Elizabeth's reign the Puritan element in the Church of England argued for further revision of the Church of England's worship in a Protestant direction. As John Moorman notes, to them:

The Prayer Book of 1559 smelt of popery. It was 'an imperfect book, culled and pricked out of the popish dunghill.' It allowed such improper ceremonies as the use of the sign of the cross in Baptism, the imposition of hands in Confirmation and the ring in Marriage. It preserved the veneration of the saints through its Calendar and tolerated such customs as bowing at the Name of Jesus and kneeling at the Communion. Moreover, with the Prayer Book went certain discreditable adjuncts of worship especially the use of organs and other musical instruments and antiphonal singing – 'the singing, ringing and trowling of psalms from one side of the choir to the other.' But the greatest dislike of all was of the vestments in which the priest clothed himself. The Ornaments Rubric in the Prayer Book of 1559 had allowed for the wearing of alb and chasuble or cope at the Eucharist and the surplice for the choir offices.[1] The Puritans greatly

---

1 That is, Morning and Evening Prayer.

disapproved of this and many of the clergy whose sympathies lay with this party found themselves prevented by their consciences from appearing in church in even so innocent a garment as a surplice, while [Archbishop] Edmund Grindal was doubtful whether he could accept a bishopric because it would necessitate the wearing of robes.[1]

However, during the reigns of Elizabeth and her successor James I no concessions were made to these objections. When James' son Charles I came to the throne in 1625 matters grew worse from a Puritan point of view with Charles and his Archbishop of Canterbury, William Laud, insisting that Puritan clergy observe the Church of England's rules and with Laud insisting that the Communion table be placed against the east end of the church where the altar had stood in pre-Reformation times and be fenced in with altar rails rather than being placed lengthways in the chancel as had become the accepted practice since the reign of Elizabeth I.

Between 1645 and 1662 the Book of Common Prayer was officially abolished by Parliament. It was replaced by the *Directory for the Public Worship of God* which, unlike the Book of Common Prayer, did not contain detailed liturgy, but was instead an outline of the necessary elements for each of the services that was to be developed by each minister as they felt appropriate.

During the Civil War and the Commonwealth period loyalty to the Book of Common Prayer came to be identified with loyalty to the Royalist cause. Consequently, when the monarchy was restored in 1660 there was strong pressure from the triumphant royalists for the restoration of the Prayer Book as well. After the failure of the Savoy Conference of 1661 to reach agreement about a way forward for the Church of England's worship, the Book of Common Prayer in a modified form was reintroduced by Act of Parliament in 1662. There were about 600 alterations to the 1559 version in all, but these were mostly matters of detail. The key changes were:

- A number of additional prayers including new collects (prayers that sum up the particular theme of the service) and prayers of thanksgiving.

---

1 J. R. H. Moorman, *A History of the Church of England*, Harrisburg, PA: Morehouse Publishing, 1980, pp. 208–9.

- The introduction of a service of adult baptism to respond to the needs of native converts in the new English plantations overseas and those who had not been baptized during the Commonwealth period.
- The restoration of the 'Black Rubric' of 1552 but in an altered form which ruled out not the 'real and essential' but the 'corporal' (i.e. 'material') presence of Christ in the bread and wine at Communion.
- Changes in the rubrics for the Communion service, many of which were taken from the Scottish Prayer Book of 1637 and which represent a move towards a more traditional 'catholic' view of the sacrament. For example, the Eucharistic prayer is called the 'prayer of consecration' and any consecrated bread and wine that is left over is to be 'reverently' consumed by the priest and other communicants in church rather than being taken home by the priest for his own use.[1]

The 1550 Ordinal was also reintroduced in a modified form, the key changes here being:

- A change to the Preface to the Ordinal making it clear that no one should be accepted as a bishop, priest or deacon in the Church of England unless they had been ordained according to the form contained in the Ordinal itself or 'hath had formerly Episcopal Consecration or Ordination'. The words just quoted were new and were intended to rule out ministers who had not been ordained by a bishop from serving in the Church of England without re-ordination as had very occasionally happened in the sixteenth and seventeenth centuries.
  The main point of this change was to prevent those ordained during the Commonwealth period from serving as clergy in the Church of England without receiving episcopal ordination.
- Changes to the order for the 'ordaining or consecrating of an Archbishop or Bishop' intended to make it clear that the episcopate was a distinct order of ministry from the priesthood. For example, the word 'ordaining' in the title of the rite was introduced in 1662 and was intended to make it clear that a bishop was being ordained into a new order of ministry and not

---

1 For full details of the changes to the rubrics see Hatchett, in Sykes and Booty, op. cit, p. 130.

simply consecrated to exercise his existing priestly ministry in a new way.[1]

THE 1928 PRAYER BOOK AND THE *ALTERNATIVE SERVICE BOOK*

The Book of Common Prayer as modified in 1662 is the one that is still used in the Church of England and remains its fundamental liturgical standard, although today it is only used at a minority of services. For over three hundred years after 1662 the Book of Common Prayer also contained the Church of England's only legally authorized liturgical material. However, this does not mean that nothing changed in the worshipping life of the Church of England during that time.

First, the Evangelical revival in the eighteenth century meant that congregational hymn singing became a key part of the services in many Church of England services, something that was not envisaged in the Book of Common Prayer.

Secondly, in 1859 certain state services, such as the service of thanksgiving for the deliverance from the Gunpowder Plot of 1605, were abolished.

Thirdly, in 1871 the lectionary in the Book of Common Prayer was replaced with a revised lectionary.

Fourthly, in 1872, in response to concerns about how the Church of England could more effectively reach out to the millions of people who did not come to church, an Act of Parliament was passed that allowed for a shortened form of the services of Morning and Evening Prayer. This Act also allowed for an additional more informal 'third service' on special occasions, provided it used only the words from the Bible and the Prayer Book plus hymns. In 1892 the Convocations went further and permitted the use of other materials that were 'substantially in agreement with Scripture and the Prayer Book'.

Fifthly, and perhaps most importantly, by the end of the nineteenth century many of those influenced by the development of Anglo-Catholicism in the Church of England were deliberately going beyond or departing from what was laid down in the Book of

---

1   For full details of the changes to the rite for ordaining bishops and their significance see P. Bradshaw, 'Ordinals', in ibid., pp. 147–50.

Common Prayer. From their perspective the nature of the Church of England was determined by its continuity with the Church of the patristic and medieval periods rather than by what took place at the Reformation. Consequently, they felt it was legitimate to introduce or reintroduce elements into Church of England services that expressed this Catholic continuity. For example, they introduced the use of incense and candles, of wafers instead of ordinary bread, the stations of the Cross, the invocation of the saints, prayers for the dead, the reservation of the consecrated elements from communion and the offering of devotion before these. Some went even further and used the Latin Mass for the celebration of Communion.

These examples and many others went way beyond the most elastic interpretation of what was permitted in the Prayer Book and the question that this raised was what should be done about it. Prosecutions of wayward clergy under the Public Worship Regulation Act of 1874 failed to solve the problem. In the words of Moorman: 'Undeterred by episcopal denunciations and legal threats, clergy went on their own individualistic ways, determined to do what they themselves thought best despite the demands of law and obedience.'[1]

From 1904–06 the Royal Commission on Ecclesiastical Discipline considered the matter. It concluded that the root of the problem was that: 'the law of public worship in the Church of England is too narrow for the religious life of the present generation'. In response to this conclusion an entirely new Prayer Book intended to replace the Book of Common Prayer was agreed by the Church Assembly of the Church of England in 1927.

This had a number of features that were intended to meet the concerns of the Anglo-Catholics:

- Limited provision was made for the reservation of the consecrated elements from Communion. This was ostensibly in order to provide communion for the sick and housebound.
- There was an alternative order for Holy Communion in which the Prayer of Consecration at Holy Communion was similar to the more 'Catholic' 1549 service rather than following the more 'Protestant' 1552 rite.

---

1 Moorman, op. cit, pp. 426–7.

- Prayers for the dead were included in the intercessions at Holy Communion as well as in the funeral service.

In spite of the fact that the National Assembly had voted in favour of the new book by a majority of 517 to 133 there was a vigorous campaign both inside and outside the Church of England to get Parliament to reject it. This campaign was spearheaded by Evangelicals who felt that the Catholicizing tendencies of the new book represented a betrayal of the English Reformation, but it also received support from Anglo-Catholics who felt that the book was not Catholic enough and was likely to be more rigorously enforced than the old Prayer Book had been. In the end, although the House of Lords passed the Prayer Book Measure authorizing the book, the House of Commons rejected it in 1927 and, in a slightly amended form, in 1928.

In response to this rejection the Church of England's bishops agreed to publish the book anyway as an unauthorized text and issued a statement saying that its use in the present 'emergency' would be regarded as being in accordance with the mind of the Church. On this basis, parts of the book, especially the occasional offices, came to be widely used. However, the use of an unauthorized alternative to the Book of Common Prayer was clearly an unsatisfactory long-term solution and so the bishops also sought to avoid a repeat of 1928 by finding ways of authorizing new forms of worship without having to get them through Parliament.

The Prayer Book (Alternative and Other Services) Measure of 1965 and the Church of England (Worship and Doctrine) Measure of 1974 eventually provided a solution to the problem. These Measures meant that power to authorize its own liturgical material was delegated by Parliament to the Church of England and introduced the current situation referred to at the beginning of the chapter, in which the Book of Common Prayer remains normative, but in which services that are alternative to the ones it contains and other additional services can also be legally authorized for use in the Church of England providing that their contents are judged to be in line with the doctrine of the Church of England as expressed in the Prayer Book and the other historic formularies.

This new situation led first of all to a series of alternative and additional services that were produced between 1965 and 1972. These were known as Series 1, 2 and 3 and were published in leaflet form and with a limited life span. Following the passing of the 1974 Measure it became possible to produce something on a more permanent basis and on this basis the *Alternative Service Book* (the *ASB*) was introduced with a ten-year authorization in 1980.[1] As its name suggests, it provided a series of services that were alternative to those contained in the Book of Common Prayer and the 1662 Ordinal. It also provided an alternative lectionary. It was in modern English (for example, it addressed God as 'you' rather than 'thou'), and it reflected the current state of liturgical scholarship both in the Church of England and ecumenically.

Unlike most of the services in the Book of Common Prayer[2] it also contained a number of different forms of the services and options within them so that they could be varied according to circumstances or liturgical preference.

For example, there were three rites for Holy Communion. There was Rite A, which followed the pattern of the traditional Western Eucharistic rite from which the Book of Common Prayer had departed at the Reformation, used modern language and offered a choice of four possible Eucharistic Prayers. There was Rite B, which also followed the pattern of the traditional Western rite, but used traditional language (addressing God as 'thou' rather than 'you'). Finally, there was the 'Order following the pattern of the Book of Common Prayer', which, as its name suggests, followed the order of the Prayer Book rite, but used modern language.

Publication of the *Alternative Service Book* was followed by the publication of additional material. *Ministry to the Sick* was published in 1983, books of services for Lent and Easter and the winter seasons, *Lent, Holy Week and Easter* and *The Promise of His Glory*, were published in 1986 and 1991 respectively, and *Patterns for Worship*, a book of services intended to be more accessible to less literate worshippers and to those in Urban Priority Areas, was published in 1995. Because the seasonal services and *Patterns for Worship* were not alternatives to material in the Book of Common Prayer they were not authorized by the General Synod, but

---

1 Its authorization was renewed for another ten years in 1990.
2 The exception in the Book of Common Prayer would be the baptism service where there are various forms of the service depending on whether the service is private or public and whether a child or an adult is being baptized.

'commended' for use by the House of Bishops following Synod debates.

COMMON WORSHIP

The Church of England could have extended the authorization of the *Alternative Service Book* after 2000 or produced a new volume to replace it. It the event it rejected both alternatives. It felt that not all the material in the *ASB* had proved successful and that therefore it was not sufficient simply to extend its authorization. It also accepted the advice of the Liturgical Commission that it would be a mistake to follow the pattern of the *ASB* by trying to include all the Church's modern liturgical materials in a single big volume.

What it decided to do instead was to produce *Common Worship*, a library of liturgical materials that have been made available 'in printed volumes, in separate booklets, of varying sizes, on congregational card, as computer discs (both as text-only discs and as the Church's *Visual Liturgy* service composing programme) and on the Internet'.[1] The material that has been produced is as follows:[2]

(1) ***Common Worship: Services and Prayers for the Church of England***
This is the main volume. It contains services and resources for use on Sundays, Principal Feasts and Holy Days, and Festivals, in both contemporary and traditional language, together with the *Common Worship* Psalter.

The Psalter is a new version of the Psalms that draws on the insights of modern Old Testament scholarship and yet also consciously builds on a tradition of translating the Psalms for use in worship that goes back to the Psalter of Bishop Miles Coverdale that is found in the Book of Common Prayer.

This volume also contains a lectionary that offers three sets

---

1   M. Earey and G. Myers (ed.), *Common Worship Today*, London: Harper-Collins, 2001, p. 114.
2   The description of the various volumes of *Common Worship* that follows is based on the description of them given on the *Common Worship* section of the Church of England website.

of readings for use at the Principal, Second and Third services on each Sunday, principal feast, holy day and festival.

A *Common Worship* weekday lectionary has also been authorized. The booklets published annually that contain both the *Common Worship* and Book of Common Prayer lectionary readings are based on this weekday lectionary.

(2) *Common Worship: The President's Edition*
This volume contains the Holy Communion and Baptism services, the Collects and Post Communions[1] that appear in the main volume, and:
- Collects and Post Communions for Lesser Festivals and Special Occasions;
- additional Proper Prefaces and Blessings;
- music for the Eucharistic Prayers.

(3) *Common Worship: Pastoral Services*
The services and resources for Wholeness and Healing, Marriage, and Funerals are contained in this volume.

(4) *Common Worship: Initiation Services*
This volume contains the Baptism and Confirmation services together with related material.

(5) *Common Worship: Daily Prayer*
This volume contains orders of service for morning, evening and night prayer for each day of the week and each season of the Church's year. There is also a wealth of seasonal variants, Collects, psalms and other devotional materials.

(6) *Common Worship: Times and Seasons*
This is a collection of seasonal services and resources.

(7) *Common Worship: Festivals*
This is a collection of services and resources for the festivals of the Christian year.

(8) *Common Worship: Collects and Post Communions*
This volume contains all of the *Common Worship* Collects and Post Communions, including the Additional Collects authorized in 2004.

(9) *Common Worship: Ordination Services*
This is published in a study edition that contains the *Common Worship* ordination rites, the 1662 Ordinal, a history of

---

1 The Collects and Post Communions are the set prayers which are said before the readings from the Bible and after the people have received communion.

ordination rites, a commentary by the Liturgical Commission and a practical guide to organizing ordination services.

(10) *New Patterns for Worship*

This volume contains guidance on planning worship, resources for use on a variety of occasions and sample services.

(11) *Public Worship with Communion by Extension*

This material, commended by the House of Bishops, is designed to provide a form of service for occasions when a group of worshippers need to receive the sacrament using bread and wine that has already been consecrated in a previous service of Holy Communion.

The distinctive features of the material contained in *Common Worship* are as follows:

- It is a mixture of alternative material that has been authorized by General Synod and additional material that has been commended for use by the House of Bishops.
- It contains material from the Book of Common Prayer plus contemporary language material.
- Like the *Alternative Service Book*, it contains various different forms of the services and various options within them. For example, there are two orders for Holy Communion. There is Order One that follows the order of the Western rite and offers a choice of eight Eucharistic Prayers, and there is Order Two that follows the order of the Book of Common Prayer as normally used and has both traditional and modern language versions.
- It expands the range of Eucharistic and seasonal material.
- In the 'Service of the Word' in the main volume it provides a very flexible pattern for worship that is to some extent reminiscent of the outlines contained in the *Directory of Public Worship*.
- The material is authorized or commended for an indefinite period of time.

THE REQUIREMENTS FOR THE HOLDING OF WORSHIP IN THE CHURCH OF ENGLAND

Canons B10–14a lay down the requirements for the holding of services in the cathedrals and parish churches of the Church of England.

In cathedrals Morning and Evening prayer has to be said or sung every morning and evening with the Litany being recited on appointed days and the Holy Communion being celebrated as a minimum every Sunday and on all other Feast Days and on Ash Wednesday. It is also to be celebrated '. . . on other days as often as may be convenient, according to the statutes and customs of each church' (Canon B13).

In parish churches Morning and Evening Prayer is to be said or sung in church at least every Sunday and on other principal Feast Days, Ash Wednesday and Good Friday. On every other day, Morning and Evening Prayer is to be said or sung either in church or in some other place agreed after consultation between the parish minister and the parochial church council. Holy Communion is to be celebrated in every church as a minimum every Sunday and on all principal Feast Days, Ash Wednesday and Maundy Thursday.

Canon B14a allows dispensations from the requirements for parish churches on either an occasional or regular basis. This is to allow for circumstances such as rural benefices with multiple churches where it would be impractical to hold a service in every church either every day or every week. The giving of such dispensations depends on the availability of services in other places in the benefice and is also on the basis that no church shall cease to be used for public worship altogether unless and until it is formally declared redundant.

The requirement in the canons for the regular celebration of Holy Communion is a relatively new development in the life of the Church of England. In the post-Reformation Church of England, Morning and Evening Prayer were the normal Sunday services and Holy Communion was celebrated infrequently. The current canonical requirements represent a conscious return to the ancient idea that Holy Communion is the central and distinctive service in the Christian Church and should therefore be celebrated every Sunday.

MUSIC IN THE CHURCH OF ENGLAND

Canon B20:3 states that:

> It is the duty of the minister to ensure that only such chants, hymns, anthems, and other settings are chosen as are appropriate, both the words and music, to the solemn act of worship and prayer in the House of God as well as to the congregation assembled for that purpose: and to banish all irreverence in the practice and in the performance of the same.

The wording of this quotation highlights three things about the use of music in the worship of the Church of England.

First, the Church of England emphasizes the importance of using appropriate music and performing it in a reverent fashion. Music is an integral part of the worship offered to God and as such is to be taken with due seriousness.

Secondly, the wide range of musical terms used emphasizes the fact that there are a wide variety of musical styles employed in worship in the Church of England. These styles range from the choral setting of the words of the Book of Common Prayer to be found in cathedrals and other institutions with a strong choral tradition such as Oxford and Cambridge colleges, through traditional congregational hymn singing with organ accompaniment, to music in a modern musical idiom shaped by influences such as the music of Taizé or the music produced by the charismatic movement.

Thirdly, the lack of precise instruction about the music or words to be used indicates that there is not and never has been official authorization of musical material within the Church of England. The liturgy may be authorized but the music is not. There is no equivalent in the Church of England to the official hymn books produced in other churches. The music that is used is determined at a parochial or cathedral level as a result of agreement between the minister with overall responsibility for a service and the person such as the choir master or director of music directly responsible for the musical element.

The hymn books used in the Church of England range from specifically Church of England works such as *Hymns Ancient and Modern*, *The English Hymnal* or *One Church, One Faith, One Lord*, to books such as *Mission Praise*, *Songs and Hymns of Fellowship* or

The Bridge that are designed for use by churches from a variety of traditions. Many churches, particularly in the Evangelical tradition, are also moving away from the use of hymn books altogether and are choosing to use an eclectic range of sources with the words put up on a screen using overhead or digital projection.

The Royal School of Music, which was founded in 1927, exists to support music in the Church of England and around the world through the provision of 'education, training, publications, advice and encouragement'. It supports more than 9,000 churches, schools and individuals in this country and elsewhere. The work undertaken by the School covers both traditional and modern forms of music.

PREACHING

Canon B18 states:

(1) In every parish church a sermon shall be preached at least once every Sunday, except for some reasonable cause approved by the bishop of the diocese.
(2) The sermon shall be preached by a minister, deaconess, reader or lay worker duly authorized in accordance with Canon Law. At the invitation of the minister having the cure of souls another person may preach with the permission of the bishop of the diocese given either in relation to the particular occasion or in accordance with diocesan directions.
(3) The preacher shall endeavour with care and sincerity to minister the word of truth to the glory of God and to the edification of the people.

These words reflect three things about preaching in the Church of England.

First, the Church of England regards preaching as a very important part of its worship. That is why a sermon is normally required in every parish church at least once every Sunday and why the third section of the Canon stresses that the preacher must endeavour to 'minister the word of truth' with 'care and sincerity'.

Secondly, however, the Church of England does not hold that a sermon is a necessary part of every act of worship. That is why it is not stated that a sermon must be preached at every service. It is frequently the case, for example, that there are no sermons at the formal choral services mentioned in section 6 above. In these services the word of God is proclaimed through the liturgy, the prayers and the music, without the need for a sermon.

Thirdly, in the Church of England it is not only ordained people who are allowed to preach. As section 2 of the Canon indicates, authorized lay people are allowed to preach as well. It is important to note, however, that there does have to be authorization. Because the Church of England takes the importance of preaching seriously it does not permit anyone who feels like it to preach at its services. Authorization is a means of seeking to ensure that only people carrying the authority of the wider Church may preach in Church of England pulpits.

It also needs to be noted that although traditional forms of preaching are still highly valued in the Church of England, nevertheless alternative forms of communication have also increasingly been used in recent years. Thus use is made of drama and audiovisual presentations either to replace or to complement the sermon, and sermons themselves have become more inter-active with the inclusion of dialogue, group discussion and per-sonal testimonies. The use of these alternative forms of communication reflects the fact that the tradition of listening to extended public speeches is something that is now culturally alien to most people in Britain today

VESTMENTS

As has already been noted, vestments are the distinctive dress worn when performing the services of the Church. The main vestments that are worn in the Church of England today by members of the clergy, readers and members of choirs are as follows:

- The alb: an ankle-length garment in white linen fastened round the middle with a girdle or 'cincture'. This is worn by some priests or bishops when presiding at Holy Communion.
- The cassock: an ankle-length coat which is normally black for readers, priests and deacons, purple for bishops and scarlet for chaplains to the Queen.
- The cassock alb: a combination of the cassock and the alb that has come to be used by some members of the clergy since the 1970s, particularly when presiding at Holy Communion.

- The chasuble: a large garment shaped like a poncho that is worn over an alb by some priests and bishops when presiding at Holy Communion. The colour of the chasuble will vary according to the season of the Church's year.
- The cope: a ceremonial cloak, often ornately embroidered, that is worn over a cassock and surplice.
- The mitre: a liturgical headdress worn by bishops with heraldic panels in the shape of inverted shields at the front and back and two fringed flaps or 'lappets' hanging down at the back.
- The scarf: a ceremonial scarf worn with the ends hanging down in front. Scarves worn by the clergy are black while those worn by readers are blue. Clergy and readers who have degrees sometimes wear their degree hood under their scarf.
- The stole: a ceremonial scarf worn as a sash by deacons and with the ends hanging down in front by priests. The colour of the stole will vary according to the service being taken and the season of the Church's year.
- The surplice: a white linen garment with wide sleeves that is worn over a cassock. The surplice is worn by clergy and readers when taking Morning and Evening Prayer and some priests and bishops wear it when presiding at Holy Communion.
- Members of robed choirs will wear cassocks in a variety of colours and surplices. (Scarlet is restricted to the Chapels Royal and Royal Peculiars.)

The alb, chasuble and stole, together with the cope and mitre, have their origins in the priestly and episcopal robes of the medieval Western Church, which were in turn adapted from the ceremonial dress of the later Roman Empire. The cassock, surplice, scarf and hood have their origins in traditional academic dress.[1]

In the history of the Church of England since the Reformation the use of vestments has been a matter of dispute between different groups within the Church. As was noted earlier in this chapter, one of the reasons that the Puritans objected to the Prayer Book in the

---

1 Two further garments worn as ceremonial dress by bishops as part of their formal insignia are the rochet, which is a white garment like a surplice but with gathered sleeves, and a chimere: a long sleeveless gown of black or scarlet wool, silk or satin, open down the front, gathered in at the back between the shoulders, and with slits for the arms. The chimere is worn over the rochet with a black scarf and possibly an academic hood.

sixteenth century was because of the requirement to wear vestments, and in the nineteenth and twentieth centuries the issue was a battleground between Anglo-Catholics and Evangelicals, with the dispute between them focusing on the question of what vestments were permitted under the Ornaments Rubric of the 1559 Prayer Book.

Underlying this dispute about the interpretation of the rubric was a deeper theological dispute, with Anglo-Catholics seeing the traditional vestments as a sign of the continuity between the ministry of the Church of England and the ministry of the Church in the early and medieval periods and Evangelicals seeing them as unbiblical and as representing a false sacerdotal view of the ministry centred on the offering of the sacrifice of the Mass.

The present position of the Church of England on the matter of vestments is set out in Canon B8. This runs as follows:

(1) The Church of England does not attach any particular doctrinal significance to the diversities of vesture permitted by this Canon, and the vesture worn by the minister in accordance with the provision of this Canon is not to be understood as implying any doctrines other than those now contained in the formularies of the Church of England.

(2) Notwithstanding the provisions of this Canon no minister shall change the form of vesture in use in the church or chapel in which he officiates unless he has ascertained by consultation with the parochial church council that such changes will be acceptable. Provided always that in the case of disagreement the minister shall refer the matter to the bishop of the diocese, whose direction shall be obeyed.

(3) At the Holy Communion the presiding minister shall wear either a surplice or alb with scarf or stole. When a stole is worn other customary vestments may be worn. The epistoler and gospeller (if any) may wear surplice or alb to which other customary vestments may be added.

(4) At Morning and Evening Prayer on Sundays the minister shall normally wear a surplice or alb with scarf or stole.

(5) At the occasional Offices the minister shall wear a surplice or alb with scarf or stole.

The significance of this Canon is fourfold.

First, it attempts to defuse the traditional disputes about vestments by insisting that vestments do not carry any particular doctrinal significance and that wearing them does not imply any doctrinal position other than that held by the Church of England as a whole.

Secondly, it allows Evangelicals to wear their preferred vestments of surplice and scarf while also permitting Anglo-Catholics to wear albs, stoles and other 'customary vestments' such as chasubles.

Thirdly, it protects the customary practice of particular churches with regard to vestments, insisting that ministers can only change this if consultation reveals that there is agreement to do so. This section of the Canon is designed to prevent a new minister simply riding roughshod over local practice as happened in some places in the past.

Fourthly, while it lays down that vestments should be worn on specific occasions, the use of the word 'normally' in section 4 and the fact that only specific services are listed gives room for ministers to dispense with vestments on an occasional basis on Sundays and not to wear them at all for services other than Holy Communion and Occasional Offices during the week, if the local situation makes this appropriate. Thus it would be legal under the Canon for a minister not to wear vestments for an informal family service on Sundays or during the week.

FOR FURTHER READING

Bradshaw, P. (ed.), *Companion to Common Worship*, Vol. 1, London: SPCK, 2001.

Earey, M. and G. Myers (eds), *Common Worship Today*, London: Hodder & Stoughton, 2001.

Hatchett, M., 'Prayer Books', in S. Sykes and J. Booty (eds), *The Study of Anglicanism*, London and Minneapolis: SPCK/Fortress Press, 1998.

In Tune With Heaven, The Report of the Archbishops' Commission on Church Music, 1992.

10 Paths to Unity – The Church of England and the other Christian Churches

This chapter will look at the network of relationships that the Church of England has with other churches in this country and around the globe. These 'ecumenical' relationships form part of a quest for the visible unity of the Christian Church as a whole, and we shall begin by looking at the history behind their development.

THE HISTORY OF THE SEARCH FOR UNITY WITH OTHER CHURCHES

It is sometimes suggested that the search for unity is a recent development, with Christians huddling together for sustenance and protection in an increasingly hostile world. This suggestion is misleading. Throughout its history the Church of England has understood itself as belonging to the One, Holy, Catholic and Apostolic Church. It has therefore seen itself as under an obligation to maintain as close a relationship as possible with the other churches that also form part of the universal Church.

The story of how it has sought to respond to this obligation can be divided in two parts: relations with churches outside England and relations with other churches in England.

Relations with churches outside England

In the pre-Reformation period, the Church of England played its full part in the life of the Western Church and in the twelfth century there was an English Pope, Hadrian IV (c. 1100–59).

After the break with Rome the Church of England sought to develop relations with the Continental Protestant churches. During the reign of Henry VIII in the sixteenth century, for example, there were unsuccessful negotiations between the Church of England and the German Lutheran churches of the Schmalkaldic League, and during the reign of Edward VI Archbishop Cranmer corresponded with the Protestant Reformers Heinrich Bullinger, Philip Melancthon and John Calvin in order to try convene a conference that would produce an agreed pan-Protestant confession of faith.

After the death of Edward VI and the accession of the Roman Catholic Mary I, Cranmer's project had to be abandoned and it was never subsequently revived. However, the Church of England continued to try to maintain relationships with the Continental Protestant churches, and members of the Church of England also tried to develop relationships with the Orthodox churches and with Roman Catholics.

Thus, at the beginning of the seventeenth century, delegates from the Church of England took part in the Synod of Dort convened by the Dutch Reformed Church, while towards the end of the century the Church of England chaplain at Smyrna, Isaac Basire, sought to foster relations between the Church of England and the Orthodox churches in Greece and the Middle East.

In the early eighteenth century the Archbishop of Canterbury, William Wake, sought to promote unity with the Swiss Reformed churches and the churches of the Unitas Fratrem (the Bohemian Brethren), and also proposed a scheme for unity between the Church of England and the Roman Catholic Church in France. The nineteenth century saw the coming into being of the Anglican Communion and the establishment of a short-lived joint bishopric in Jerusalem by the Church of England and the United Protestant Church of Prussia. It also saw the increasing development of contacts between members of the Church of England and the churches of the Orthodox tradition. At the end of the century, conversations took place between the English High Churchman Lord Halifax and the French priest Abbe Portal in an attempt to heal the breach between the Church of England and the Roman Catholic Church. (These are known as the Malines Conversations, after the place in Belgium where they were held.)

The twentieth century has been dubbed 'the ecumenical century', during which the Church of England was fully involved in the development of the worldwide ecumenical movement. It was a founder member of both the World Council of Churches and the Conference of European Churches, and it also took part in a number of bilateral and multilateral conversations with other churches. These conversations resulted in a series of ecumenical agreements that are detailed later on in this chapter.

The twenty-first century has seen the continuation of twentieth-century developments, but it has also seen the emergence of new challenges as new divisions have opened up within and between churches on issues such as the ordination of women and homosexuality.

Relations with other churches in England

The division of the English church at the Reformation was not intentional. At the Reformation the idea was that the reformed Church of England would be the church of all the people of England, but this idea never became reality because the Reformation settlement was rejected both by those who remained loyal to Rome and later also by Protestants of various kinds who felt that the English Reformation had not been radical or thorough enough.

Consequently a situation developed in which a number of other churches existed in England alongside the Church of England. The initial reaction of the Anglican state was persecution. Those who would not conform to the Church of England were punished with fines, imprisonment or even death. In the case of most Protestant dissenters this period of persecution ended with the Toleration Act of 1689, and in the case of Roman Catholics it gradually came to an end during the eighteenth century.

However, even after this change in the legal position, the attitude of the Church of England towards other churches in England remained ambivalent. On the one hand, there is evidence of good relations and cooperation in mission and Christian service between Christians of the Church of England and Christians of other churches and there is also evidence of some degree of informal recognition of other churches and their sacraments and ministries.[1]

---

1 As an example, see the accounts of good historical relations between Anglicans and Baptists in Ch. 2 of *Pushing at the Boundaries of Unity: Anglicans and Baptists in Conversation*, London: Church House Publishing, 2005.

On the other hand, there is also evidence of members of the Church of England continuing to ignore the existence of other English churches or being positively hostile towards them.

After 1920, however, there was a permanent change for the better in the relations between the Church of England and the other churches in England. This followed the 'Appeal to all Christian People' issued that year by the bishops of the Anglican Communion, including those of the Church of England. In this appeal the bishops declared: 'We acknowledge all those who believe in our Lord Jesus Christ, and have been baptized into the name of the Holy Trinity, as sharing with us membership in the Universal Church of Christ which is his Body.'[1] They also declared:

> The time has come, we believe, for all the separated groups of Christians to agree in forgetting the things which are behind and reaching out towards the goal of a reunited Catholic Church. The removal of the barriers which have arisen between them will only be brought about by a new comradeship of those whose faces are definitely set this way.[2]

In the changed atmosphere following the issuing of this appeal the Church of England formally agreed that on special occasions members of other churches should be invited to preach and pray in Church of England churches. This small beginning then led in time to the Church of England making formal canonical provision in Canons B43 and 44 for a considerable degree of shared life and ministry between the Church of England and other churches in England, and to the Church of England allowing baptized members of other churches to receive Communion in Church of England churches.

The changed atmosphere also led to the Church of England playing a leading role in the British Council of Churches and in its successor bodies, Churches Together in Britain and Ireland, and Churches Together in England.

The Church of England has continued to believe, however, that ultimately there should be only one church in England, which

---

1 R. Coleman (ed.), *Resolutions of the Lambeth Conferences 1867–1988*, Toronto: Anglican Book Centre, 1992, pp. 45–6.
2 Ibid., p. 46.

would be a part of that 'reunited Catholic Church' called for in the 1920 appeal. In pursuit of this goal it has taken part in a series of multilateral and bilateral conversations with other churches. These have not always been successful, but in recent years they have resulted in ecumenical agreements with the Moravian and Methodist churches and a proposal for the development of a closer relationship with the churches of the Baptist Union of Great Britain. These recent developments are described in more detail later on in this chapter.

THE CHURCH OF ENGLAND'S ECUMENICAL PRINCIPLES

The basic principles underlying the Church of England's ecumenical relationships are set out in Canon A8:

> Forasmuch as the Church of Christ has for a long time past been distressed by separations and schisms among Christian men, so that the unity for which our Lord prayed is impaired and the witness to his gospel is grievously hindered, it is the duty of clergy and people to do their utmost not only to avoid occasions of strife but also to seek in penitence and brotherly charity to heal such divisions.

These principles are expressed in more detail in The Reuilly Common Statement, agreed in 1999 by the British and Irish Anglican Churches and the French Lutheran and Reformed Churches. This declares that:

> In order to be truly itself and to fulfil its mission the Church must be seen to be one. The missionary imperative entails the overcoming of the divisions which have kept our churches apart. As our churches grow in faith into the fullness of Christ, so they will grow together in unity (Ephesians 1). This unity will reflect the different gifts God has given to his Church in many nations, languages, cultures and traditions.
>
> Perfect unity must await the full realization of God's kingdom, in which all will be completely obedient to God and therefore totally reconciled to one another in God. But in a fallen world we are committed to strive for the 'full visible unity' of the body of Christ on earth. We are to work for the manifestation of unity at every level, a unity which is grounded in the

life of the Holy Trinity and is God's purpose for the whole of creation.[1]

The Church of England's commitment to the 'full visible unity of the body of Christ on earth' raises the obvious issue of what this unity should look like. This is something about which members of the Church of England have had differing views.[2] However, the vision of unity that has determined the Church of England's official ecumenical activity has remained that set out in the 'Appeal to all Christian People' referred to above.

Drawing on an earlier statement concerning the basis for the reunion of the churches, the Appeal states:

> We believe that the visible unity of the Church will be found to involve the wholehearted acceptance of:
>
>> The Holy Scriptures, as the record of God's revelation of himself to man, and as being the rule and ultimate standard of faith; and the Creed commonly called Nicene, as the sufficient statement of the Christian faith, and either it, or the Apostles' Creed as the baptismal confession of belief;
>>
>> the divinely instituted sacraments of Baptism and the Holy Communion, as expressing for all the corporate life of the whole fellowship in and with Christ;
>>
>> a ministry acknowledged by every part of the Church as possessing not only the inward call of the Spirit, but also the commission of Christ and the authority of the whole body.[3]

Referring to the last of these points, the Appeal then goes on to ask:

> May we not reasonably claim that the episcopate is the one means of providing such a ministry? It is not that we call in

---

1 *Called to Witness and Service*, London: Church House Publishing, 1999, p. 21.
2 See M. Davie, 'Anglican Ecumenism: The Liberal Catholic Consensus and the Conservative Evangelical Challenge', in P. Avis (ed.), *Paths to Unity – Explorations in Ecumenical Method*, London: Church House Publishing, 2004, pp. 29–51.
3 Coleman (ed.), op. cit, p. 47.

question for a moment the spiritual reality of the ministries of those Communions that do not possess the episcopate. On the contrary we thankfully acknowledge that these ministries have been manifestly blessed and owned by the Holy Spirit as effective means of grace. But we submit that considerations alike of history and of current experience justify the claim which we make on behalf of the episcopate. Moreover, we would urge that it is now and will prove to be in the future the best instrument for maintaining the unity and continuity of the Church.[1]

To this day the Church of England has continued to see these four elements (often referred to as the 'Lambeth quadrilateral'), as constituting the necessary basis for a reunited Church.

It is important to note that the emphasis on the importance of the episcopate in this approach to the reunion of the churches is not based on a belief that a body of Christians lacking bishops is not a church and lacks a spiritually fruitful ministry. The 1920 appeal sees the importance of bishops rather in terms of their role in maintaining the unity and continuity of the Church. That is to say, because a pattern of ministry including bishops is the one that is the most ancient and widespread, Anglicans believe that it is the one that provides the most effective sign of the unity of the Church as a whole across time and space.

It is also important to note that the Church of England has not taken an 'all or nothing' approach towards unity. It has not insisted that all four of the elements listed above have to be in place in another church before the Church of England can start to move towards unity with it. It has instead taken a gradualist approach in which it has recognized non-episcopal churches as churches and developed increasingly close relations with them, while still holding that full unity will only be possible when both churches have a mutually accepted and interchangeable pattern of ministry involving bishops in historic succession.

---

1   Ibid., p. 47.

THE CHURCH OF ENGLAND'S CURRENT ECUMENICAL RELATIONSHIPS

(a) Churches with which the Church of England is in communion

The Anglican Communion

The largest body of churches with which the Church of England is in communion are the churches of the Anglican Communion. This is a group of 38 self-governing churches made up of about 500 dioceses, 30,000 parishes and 64,000 individual congregations in 164 countries. The other member churches of the Anglican Communion are:

- The Anglican Church in Aotearoa, New Zealand and Polynesia
- The Anglican Church of Australia
- The Church of Bangladesh
- The Episcopal Anglican Church of Brazil
- The Church of the Province of Burundi
- The Anglican Church of Canada
- The Church of the Province of Central Africa
- The Anglican Church of the Central American Region
- The Church of the Province of Congo
- The Holy Catholic Church in Hong Kong
- The Church of the Province of the Indian Ocean
- The Church of Ireland
- The Anglican Communion in Japan
- The Episcopal Church in Jerusalem and the Middle East
- The Anglican Church of Kenya
- The Anglican Church in Korea
- The Church of the Province of Melanesia
- The Anglican Church of Mexico
- The Church of the Province of Myanmar (Burma)
- The Church of Nigeria (Anglican Communion)
- The Church of North India
- The Church of Pakistan
- The Anglican Church of Papua New Guinea
- The Episcopal Church in the Philippines
- The Church of the Province of Rwanda
- The Scottish Episcopal Church
- The Province of the Anglican Church of South East Asia

- The Church of the Province of Southern Africa
- The Anglican Church of the Southern Cone of America
- The Church of South India
- The Church of the Province of the Sudan
- The Anglican Church of Tanzania
- The Church of the Province of Uganda
- The Episcopal Church of the United States of America
- The Church in Wales
- The Church of the Province of West Africa
- The Church in the Province of the West Indies.

In addition there are a number of extra-provincial dioceses and other churches that are part of the Anglican Communion. These are:

- The Anglican Church of Bermuda
- The Church of Ceylon (Sri Lanka)
- The Episcopal Church of Cuba
- The Ethiopian Episcopal Church
- The Lusitanian Church (The Portuguese Episcopal Church)
- The Spanish Episcopal Reformed Church
- The Anglican Church in Venezuela
- The Episcopal Church of Puerto Rico
- The Falkland Islands.

All the churches listed possess the four elements of the Lambeth quadrilateral and are linked, via a complex history of colonization and missionary activity, to the three churches in the British Isles, the Church of England (then covering both England and Wales), the Church of Ireland and the Scottish Episcopal Church, that in the sixteenth and seventeenth centuries accepted the Reformation but also retained episcopacy. The Churches of North and South India and Pakistan are united churches into which Anglican churches have been incorporated.

The churches of the Anglican Communion are also linked by what are known as the four 'instruments of unity'. These are:

- The ministry of the Archbishop of Canterbury. He is acknowledged as the senior Anglican bishop. All the churches of the Anglican Communion are in communion with him and he has rights of jurisdiction in some of them.

- The Lambeth Conference. This is the meeting of the bishops of the Anglican Communion that was first held in 1867 and is now held every ten years. The decisions ('resolutions') of the Lambeth Conferences are not legally binding but are accepted as having moral authority.
- The Anglican Consultative Council. This is a meeting of bishops, clergy and laity from all the provinces of the Communion that meets every two or three years: 'It fills a liaison role, consulting and recommending and at times representing the Communion.'[1]
- The Primates Meeting. This is the regular consultative meeting of the Primates (the presiding bishops) of the churches of the Communion, set up at the request of the Lambeth Conference of 1978.

The work of the instruments of unity is supported by the Anglican Communion Office which is based in London.

The procession in Canterbury Cathedral for the Opening Service of the 1998 Lambeth Conference (courtesy ACNS)

---

1 *The Church of England Yearbook 2006*, London: Church House Publishing, 2006, p. 342.

As well as these historical and institutional links there is also a multitude of other personal and organizational links across the Communion. For example, the Anglican Mission Agencies such as the United Society for the Propagation of the Gospel (USPG) and the Church Mission Society (CMS) work in churches across the Communion and many dioceses in the Church of England are linked to dioceses in other Anglican churches. More details about the Mission Agencies and diocesan links can be found in chapter twelve.

In spite of these links the unity of the Anglican Communion has come under great strain in recent years because of divisions over the issue of homosexuality. In response to this, the Lambeth Commission on Communion set up by the Primates produced the *Windsor Report* in 2004. As well as producing recommendations to deal with the immediate causes of division, this report also recommended the strengthening of the instruments of unity and the introduction of an Anglican Covenant which would cover 'the acknowledgement of common identity; the relationships of communion; the commitments of communion; the exercise of autonomy in communion; and the management of communion affairs (including disputes)'.[1] The recommendations contained in the report are currently under discussion by the churches of the Communion.

The Old Catholic Churches

Under the Bonn Agreement of 1931 the Church of England is in communion with the Old Catholic Churches of the Union of Utrecht. This is a union of independent episcopal churches which, for a variety of reasons, separated from the Roman Catholic Church during the eighteenth and nineteenth centuries.

The churches involved are the Old Catholic Churches in Austria, Croatia, the Czech Republic, France, Germany, Italy, the Netherlands, Poland and Switzerland.

The Bonn Agreement was based on three statements:

(1) Each Communion recognises the catholicity and independence of the other and maintains its own.
(2) Each Communion agrees to admit members of the other Communion to participate in the sacraments.

---

1 *The Windsor Report*, London: Anglican Communion Office, 2004, p. 62.

(3)   Intercommunion does not require from either Communion
the acceptance of all doctrinal opinion, sacramental devotion, or liturgical practice characteristic of the other, but
implies that each believes the other to hold all the essentials
of the Christian faith.[1]

An Anglican/Old Catholic International Coordinating Committee was established in 1998, and good relations between the
churches involved are also fostered by the Society of St Willibrord.

There is full Eucharistic communion and interchangeability of
ministries with the churches of the Bonn Agreement.

The Porvoo Churches

Under the Porvoo Agreement of 1992 the Church of England,
along with the Church in Wales, the Church of Ireland and the
Scottish Episcopal Church, is in communion with a number of
episcopally led Nordic and Baltic Lutheran churches. These
churches are:

- The Church of Norway
- The Church of Sweden
- The Estonian Evangelical-Lutheran Church
- The Evangelical-Lutheran Church of Finland
- The Evangelical-Lutheran Church of Iceland
- The Evangelical-Lutheran Church of Lithuania

The Porvoo Agreement built on previous ecumenical agreements going back to the 1920s. The communion which it established involves 'common membership, a single interchangeable
ministry and structures to enable the Churches to consult each
other on significant matters of faith and order, life and work'.[2]

The implementation of the Porvoo Agreement is coordinated by
the Porvoo Contact Group and the Porvoo Panel oversees its
implementation within the life of the Church of England. In

---

1   G. K. A. Bell, *Documents on Christian Unity*, 3rd series, Oxford: Oxford
University Press, 1948, p. 60.
2   *The Church of England Year Book 2006*, London: Church House Publishing, 2006, p. 426. For the text of the Porvoo Agreement see *The Porvoo
Common Statement*, London: Council for Christian Unity, 1993.

addition, the Primates of the Porvoo churches meet regularly to consult on matters of common concern.

The Philippine Independent Church and the Mar Thoma Syrian Church of Malabar

The Church of England is also in communion with the Philippine Independent Church and the Mar Thoma Syrian Church of Malabar.

The former is a church of some seven million people that was established in 1902 as a church that was independent from the Roman Catholic Church but which retained catholic faith and order. Full communion on the basis of the Bonn Agreement was established between it and the Church of England in 1963.

The latter is that part of the ancient church of South India that underwent reformation during the nineteenth century under the influence of missionaries of the CMS. As a result of this reformation it retained a generally Eastern form of liturgy but removed certain elements such as the invocation of the saints and prayers for the dead that were considered unbiblical. It has been in communion with the Church of England since 1974.

(b) Other ecumenical relationships

In addition to being in communion with the churches listed above, the Church of England also has developing ecumenical relationships with a number of other churches.

Under the terms of the Meissen Agreement of 1988 and the Reuilly Agreement of 1999, the Church of England has entered into relationships of mutual recognition with the member churches of the Evangelical Church in Germany and with the Lutheran and Reformed Churches in France.[1] These agreements commit the churches involved 'to share a common life and mission. We will take steps to closer fellowship in as many areas as possible, so that all our members together may advance on the way to full visible

---

1   The Reuilly Agreement also involved the Church of Ireland, the Church in Wales and the Episcopal Church of Scotland.

unity.'[1] The development of these relationships is overseen by the Meissen Commission and the Reuilly Contact Group.

Both the Meissen relationship, and the Porvoo relationship mentioned earlier, involve Church of England people in many different spheres of activity. Their most important expression is in the many parish, diocesan and individual links that these agreements encourage, and the opportunity to engage with issues of life and faith, European and global, with Christians from other countries. An enthusiastic network of diocesan European Officers sustains this work. At the national level, the agreements bring together church leaders, ordained and lay, in bishops' meetings, delegation visits, specialist consultations and theological conferences. Details of these activities are available via the Council for Christian Unity website[2] and the monthly European bulletin issued by the Council.

The Church of England has also entered into similar relationships of mutual recognition with two British churches, the Moravian Church in Great Britain and Ireland and the Methodist Church of Great Britain.

The Fetter Lane Agreement of 1995 between the Church of England and the Moravian Church follows the wording of the Meissen Agreement and declares: 'We commit ourselves to share a common life and mission. We will take all possible steps to unity in as many areas of life and witness as possible.'[3]

The agreement between the Church of England and the Methodist Church in 2002 took the form of a covenant between the two churches in which they committed themselves 'to overcome the remaining obstacles to the organic unity of our two churches, on the way to the full visible unity of Christ's Church'.[4]

The implementation of the Fetter Lane Agreement is overseen by the Church of England–Moravian Contact Group, and the

1   The Meissen Agreement, 17:B, in *The Meissen Agreement – Texts*, London: Council for Christian Unity, 1992, p. 20, and The Reuilly Declaration B, in *Called to Witness and Service*, London: Church House Publishing, 1999, p. 37.

2   www.cofe.anglican.org/info/ccu/index.html.

3   The Fetter Lane Declaration b, in *Anglican–Moravian Conversations*, London: Council for Christian Unity, 1996, p. 31.

4   Commitments 1, in *Anglican–Methodist Covenant*, Peterborough and London: Methodist Publishing House/Church House Publishing, 2001, p. 61.

implementation of the Anglican–Methodist Covenant is being taken forward by a Joint Implementation Commission.

The reason that the Church of England does not describe these relationships in terms of its being 'in communion' with the other churches involved is because there is not yet interchangeability of ministry and membership between these churches and the Church of England.

The Church of England's Council for Christian Unity has also been in conversations with representatives from the Baptist Union of Great Britain. These conversations have not produced an ecumenical agreement along the lines of the Fetter Lane Agreement or the Anglican–Methodist Covenant. What they have produced instead is a report entitled *Pushing at the Boundaries of Unity*[1] that points towards closer practical collaboration in mission between Anglicans and Baptists and puts a series of far-reaching challenges to both communions, especially with regard to their respective baptismal practices. It is hoped that this report will encourage discussion and response within and between the Church of England and the Baptist Union as part of a developing relationship between them.

The Council for Christian Unity is also involved in informal conversations with the Lutheran Council of Great Britain, the body that represents and co-ordinates the common work of 10 different Lutheran churches that have congregations or chaplaincies in Britain, and with the Church of Scotland. It is involved in regular discussions on issues of faith in order with the community of Protestant churches in Europe and also participates in a joint study group with the United Reform Church looking at the 1984 Anglican Reformed report 'God's Reign and Our Unity'.

Representatives of the Church of England also meet regularly with representatives of the Roman Catholic Church in England and Wales under the auspices of the English Anglican–Roman Catholic Committee (English ARC). This exists for: 'The positive fostering of Roman Catholic and Anglican relations in England, and the coordination of future work undertaken for this purpose by our two churches.' Issues that the English ARC has addressed have included joint schools, mixed marriages and the discipline

---

1 *Pushing at the Boundaries of Unity*, London: Church House Publishing, 2005.

of the Roman Catholic Church concerning Eucharistic inter-communion between Roman Catholics and those of other Christian traditions.

A good example of the work that has been produced by English ARC is the 1990 document *Twinnings and Exchanges* that was published jointly by English ARC and its counterpart in France. This document provides agreed guidelines for Anglicans and Roman Catholics taking part in both civil and religious twinnings and exchanges, and is intended to help groups of Anglicans and Roman Catholics visiting France or England to 'use all available opportunities to worship together while respecting those whose discipline may differ from their own'.[1]

(c) Multilateral dialogues

Representatives of the Church of England have been and are involved in a series of multilateral dialogues between the Anglican Communion and the following:

- The Roman Catholic Church: The Anglican–Roman Catholic International Commission (ARCIC) and now also the International Anglican–Roman Catholic Commission on Unity and Mission (IARCCUM)
- The Orthodox Churches: The International Commission of the Anglican–Orthodox Theological Dialogue (ICAOTD)
- The Oriental Orthodox Churches: The Anglican–Oriental Orthodox International Commission
- The Old Catholic Churches: The Anglican–Old Catholic International Coordinating Council (AOCICC)
- The Lutheran World Federation: The Anglican–Lutheran International Commission (ALIC)
- The World Alliance of Reformed Churches: The Anglican–Reformed International Commission
- The Baptist World Alliance: The International Conversations between the Anglican Communion and the Baptist World Alliance.

---

1 *Twinnings and Exchanges*, London: The Anglican–Roman Catholic Committees of France and England, 1990, p. 6.

A number of important statements of ecumenical theology have been produced by these multilateral dialogues[1] and the ARCIC reports on 'Eucharistic Doctrine' and 'Ministry and Ordination' (together with the subsequent 'Elucidations' which were produced to clarify aspects of these reports) were declared to be 'consonant in substance' with the faith of the Church of England by General Synod in 1986 and need to be taken into account when the Church's teaching about these issues is considered.[2]

(d) The ecumenical Canons

A number of aspects of joint ecumenical activity between the Church of England and other churches at the local level are governed by the two 'ecumenical Canons', Canons B43 and B44.

- Canon B43, 'Of relations with other Churches', permits and regulates clergy and lay ministers of other churches taking part in Church of England services and clergy and lay ministers of the Church of England taking part in the services of other churches. It also permits and regulates the use of Church of England parish churches and cathedrals by other churches for services of joint worship or for their own services.
- Canon B44, 'Of Local Ecumenical Projects', permits and regulates Church of England participation in what are now known as Local Ecumenical Partnerships, that is to say, the sharing of life, ministry and worship on a long-term basis by Christians belonging to two or more churches.

There is a specified list of churches to which the provisions of Canons B43 and 44 apply. The list is as follows:

- The Archdiocese of Thyateira and Great Britain (Greek Orthodox)

---

1 See, for example, from the Anglican–Orthodox dialogue *The Moscow Agreed Statement* (London: SPCK, 1977), from the Anglican–Reformed dialogue, *God's Reign and Our Unity* (London: SPCK, 1984), and from the Anglican–Baptist dialogue, *Conversations Around the World 2000–2005* (London: Anglican Communion Office, 2005).

2 For the texts of these reports and their elucidations see *ARCIC: The Final Report*, London: CTS/SPCK, 1982.

- The Assemblies of God in Great Britain and Ireland
- The Baptist Union
- The Church of the Augsburg Confession of Alsace and Lorraine
- The Congregational Federation
- The Council of African and Afro-Caribbean Churches
- The Evangelical-Lutheran Church of France
- The Free Church of England
- The Independent Methodist Churches
- The International Ministerial Council of Great Britain
- The Lutheran Council of Great Britain
- The member churches of the Evangelical Church in Germany (EKD)
- The Methodist Church
- The Moravian Church
- The New Testament Church of God
- The Reformed Church of Alsace and Lorraine
- The Reformed Church of France
- The Roman Catholic Church in England and Wales
- The Russian Orthodox Church (Diocese of Sourozh)
- The Southam Road Evangelical Church, Banbury
- The United Reformed Church.

The Council for Christian Unity has produced brief guides to Canons B43 and 44 and these are included as an Appendix below.

APPENDIX – BRIEF GUIDES TO CANONS B43 AND B44

B43 – Yes, you may!

How any Church of England parish can share worship with Christians of other traditions.

A Mini-guide to Canon B43: Of Relations with other Churches

Canon B43 was passed in 1989 so that Church of England churches can lawfully share in worship with churches of other traditions.

Canon B43 applies to all Church of England congregations and places of worship.

Canon B43 provides the ground rules for when Church of England churches share in worship in the context of local 'Churches Together', or when they have signed a Declaration of Ecumenical Welcome and Commitment, or at any other time.

Canon B43 provides a foundation in worship to enable Church of England congregations to begin to work more closely with other Christians in mission and service.

A: Invitations to other Christians

Church of England incumbents, with the approval of their PCC, may invite ministers and lay people of other churches on an occasional basis to take part in the worship of the Church of England in a number of ways.

Those who are invited must be baptized and in good standing with their own churches. They must also be authorized to undertake similar duties in their own church.

They may be invited to:

- Say or sing Morning or Evening Prayer or the Litany
- Read Holy Scripture at any service
- Preach at any service
- Lead intercessions at Holy Communion
- Lead prayers at any other service
- Assist at Baptisms and Weddings
- Conduct a Funeral Service
- Assist in distributing the sacrament (bread or wine) at Holy Communion

Where the person invited is not baptized (e.g. a member of the Salvation Army or a Quaker), the bishop must give permission.

The bishop must also give permission for regular invitations, and when someone is invited to preside at Holy Communion or take part in an Ordination. Baptisms, weddings and funerals obviously also require the consent of the families concerned.

B: Invitations from other churches
Church of England clergy, lay workers and Readers may accept invitations from other churches to share in their worship, provided that it only involves the kind of duties they perform in a Church of England church.

Before accepting any invitation they will need the approval of the incumbent of the parish where the service is to take place, together with the approval of both the bishop and the PCC in that parish if the invitation is to take part in leading worship on a regular basis.

The bishop will need to be sure there are special circumstances before allowing a priest to accept an invitation to preside at Holy Communion in another church. Most bishops will now regard the Anglican–Methodist Covenant as a 'special circumstance' when the invitation comes from a Methodist church.

C: Hospitality for other Christians
Incumbents may invite other churches to use Church of England churches for services in their own tradition, either on special occasions or more regularly.

The invitation needs the approval of the PCC and the bishop – and the bishop will indicate any special conditions for the arrangement.

If a regular arrangement seems likely to become permanent, an agreement under the Sharing of Church Buildings Act may be appropriate.

D: First steps on a journey
As local churches of different traditions grow together, developing a common life and witness, it may be appropriate to work towards establishing a Local Ecumenical Partnership. The provisions of Canon B44 will then apply.

B44 – Yes, you may!

How the Church of England shares in Local Ecumenical Partnership with other churches.

A Mini-guide to Canon B44: Of Local Ecumenical Projects

Six categories of LEP
Since 1994 Churches Together in England has identified six categories of Local Ecumenical Partnership:

1. Single congregation partnerships between more than one denomination.
2. Local covenant partnerships where several congregations covenant to work together.
3. Shared Building agreements
4. Partnerships for chaplaincy work in institutions
5. Partnerships for missionary engagement (e.g. Industrial Mission)
6. Partnerships in educational work.

Any individual partnership may appear in more than one of these categories, e.g. many single congregation partnerships will operate in the context of a Shared Building agreement.

The bishop must agree
Canon B44 authorizes the bishop of a diocese to make an agreement with other churches designated under the Church of England (Ecumenical Relations Measure) 1989 so that the Church of England may be a partner in a Local Ecumenical Partnership. Partnerships can operate in a variety of contexts.

a) Parishes (or parts of parishes)
Canon B44 (1) sets out how this is possible in relation to a parish or part of a parish (and indicates how it can be extended to more than one parish).

In practice, detailed proposals are likely to be worked out between the parish or local congregation and representatives of its prospective partner churches, in the form of a Declaration of Intent or a Covenant, together with a Constitution for the new Partnership. This is what will be brought to denominational bodies for approval. In the Church of England, therefore, for a parish, or part of a parish, to become involved in a Local Ecumenical Partnership – whether single congregation (Category 1) or a multi-congregational Covenant (Category 2):

(i)   The incumbent must agree
(ii)   The PCC must agree by at least a 75 per cent majority
(iii)   The parish's annual meeting (or a special meeting) must agree
(iv)   The Deanery Synod and Standing Committee must agree
(v)   The Diocesan Pastoral Committee must agree.

To enable Church of England participation, the Constitution will need to include clauses reflecting the provisions of Canon B44 (2) namely:

(i)   The Partnership shall be subject to review and renewal after not more than seven years.
(ii)   Any extension or amendment to the Partnership (e.g. by including additional parishes) must also have the consent of
   • the incumbents concerned
   • the PCCs concerned
   • the Diocesan Pastoral Committee
For a proposed single-congregation Partnership, many other practical matters will have to be resolved including:
   • possible pastoral reorganization;
   • possible Shared Building Agreement;
   • financial considerations;
   • possible ministry by a minister from another church;
   • provision of housing for such a minister.

Special guidance leaflets are available by email from the Council for Christian Unity ccu@c-of-e.org.uk:

C-1 Authorisation of ministers from another church,
C-2 Housing of ministers,
C-3 Finance and LEPs

See also below on the provisions of Canon B44 (4) and (5) in relation to worship and ministry in a single-congregation LEP.

b) Cathedrals

Canon B44 (6) sets out how all this is varied if a cathedral is involved.

c) Non-parochial LEPs

Canon B44 (7) sets out how all this is possible extra-parochially. This is normally taken to cover Church of England participation in Local Ecumenical Partnerships in Categories 4, 5 and 6.

The clause in the Canon, however, specifically refers to 'institutions' (without defining the word) where 'a clerk in Holy Orders is licensed under section 2 of the Extra-Parochial Ministry Measure 1967 in respect of that institution'. The arrangements for any partnership in these circumstances simply need the approval of the Diocesan Pastoral Committee.

Shared buildings

A Shared Building Agreement allows two or more congregations to 'time-share'. Where there is no separate written agreement in line with Canon B44 (1) & (2) there is, strictly speaking (as the Church of England uses the expression), no Local Ecumenical Partnership. Shared buildings are, however, listed as Category 3 LEPs by Churches Together in England.

Shared Building Agreements can be made under the Sharing of Church Buildings Act 1969 with any of the Churches designated under the Act.

Churches not designated under the Ecumenical Relations Measure 1989 may hold their own services on the basis of the Sharing Agreement (which relates solely to the building). Shared worship, however, will be regulated by Canon B43 and is thus limited to those churches designated under the 1989 measure.

Worship and ministry in a single-congregation LEP

Clause 4 & 5 of Canon B44 normally only come significantly into play in the case of single-congregation LEPs (Category 1).

They may also sometimes be thought relevant in the case of Category 4 chaplaincies where there is regular provision of public worship. They can also sometimes be usefully applied in the context of Category 2 covenant partnerships. The latter part of Clause 5, however, refers only to parishes.

A bishop may in these circumstances, by making an instrument in writing, make special provision as to worship and ministry in the partnership. This will, among other things, make it possible for a minister of another church to lead worship on a regular basis and be engaged in the cure of souls.

Copies of a Draft Instrument reflecting the provisions of Canon B44 (4) and (5) are available from the Council for Christian Unity.

The Instrument will be the means by which, in relation to a Church of England place of worship, the bishop:

- exercises his powers of discretion in relation to various canonical obligations to do with the conduct of Church of England services – 4 (1) (b);
- authorizes ministers of other participating churches to baptize – 4 (1) (c);
- authorizes a Church of England priest to use rites of Holy Communion authorized by a partner church – 4 (1) (d);
- permits joint services with other participating churches, e.g. baptism and confirmation – 4 (1) (e);
- authorizes ministers of other participating churches to preside at services of Holy Communion – 4 (1) (f);

For these last three the bishop must be satisfied that the rite used is essentially in line with Church of England doctrine – 4 (2).

The Instrument will also draw attention to clause 4 (3) as follows:

- Details shall be published in advance, 'so far as practicable', when a minister of another church is to preside at Holy Communion;
- It must be understood that, even if that minister uses a Church of England rite (as authorized under Canon B1), it is not a service 'according to the use of the Church of England';
- Bread and wine consecrated at these services may not be reserved, and may only be used for sick communion if the communicant expressly wishes it.

A guidance leaflet is available in relation to diocesan authorization of ministers of other churches (leaflet C-1) – including ways of meeting the requirements of Canon B44 (5).

For all other categories of LEP, a bishop's Instrument will not normally be necessary. The provision of non-Anglican worship by non-Anglican ministers (and the participation in non-Anglican worship by Anglican ministers) will be covered by Canon B43.

The Bishop's signature on the LEP agreement under these circumstances may be regarded as giving permission for whatever is allowable under Canon B43 'on a regular basis' in relation to the partner churches in the LEP.

FOR FURTHER READING

Avis, P. (ed.), *Paths to Unity: Explorations in Ecumenical Method*, London: Church House Publishing, 2004.

Bell, G. K. A., *Documents on Christian Unity*, Series I–III, Oxford: Oxford University Press, 1931–48.

'Council for Christian Unity', www.cofe.anglican.org/info/ccu.

Podmore, C. (ed.), *Community – Unity – Communion: Essays in Honour of Mary Tanner*, London: Church House Publishing, 1998.

11 Interfaith Relationships[1]

THE CHURCH OF ENGLAND'S INVOLVEMENT IN INTERFAITH RELATIONS

The Church of England, in partnership with other Christian churches, seeks to build up good relations with people of other faiths, and to cooperate with them where possible in service to society, recognizing that good relations between members of different faiths are of key importance to peace and social harmony. In recent years, the increasing numbers of immigrants from other faiths has meant that the issue of interfaith relations has become correspondingly important. As long ago as 1981, the General Synod endorsed the Four Principles of Inter Faith Dialogue agreed ecumenically by the British Council of Churches:

- Dialogue begins when people meet each other.
- Dialogue depends upon mutual understanding and mutual trust.
- Dialogue makes it possible to share in service to the community.
- Dialogue becomes the medium of authentic witness.

The Anglican commitment to working ecumenically in interfaith relations remains strong, and the Church of England is a member of the Churches' Commission for Inter Faith Relations, one of the commissions of Churches Together in Britain and Ireland. Through CCIFR, the Church of England is also in membership of the Inter Faith Network for the UK, which works to build good relations between the communities of all the major faiths in Britain: Baha'i, Buddhist, Christian, Hindu, Jain, Jewish,

---

1 This chapter draws on the material on interfaith relations on the Church of England website.

Muslim, Sikh and Zoroastrian.[1] The Bishop of Southwark is currently one of the two Co-Chairs of the Network.

Until recently the Church of England was represented on the Inner Cities Religious Council (ICRC), a body in the Department for Environment, Transport and the Regions bringing together representatives of faith communities with a substantial presence in England's inner cities to work together with the government in tackling the problems facing deprived urban areas. The ICRC has now been ended and has been merged into a new body: The Faiths Consultative Council. This was originally located within the Home Office, but is now managed by the Cohesion and Faith Communities Unit in the new Department for Communities and Local Government.

The Archbishop of Canterbury is Chair of the Presidents of the Council of Christians and Jews, and Church of England bishops, clergy and lay people are involved in several other national

Interfaith leaders at Lambeth Palace, 2005 (courtesy Rosenthal photos)

---

1 It is worth noting that the convention that the Church of England follows is to use the term 'other faiths' to refer to the religious traditions on the Inter Faith Network list. Thus Bahai, Buddhism, Hinduism, Jainism, Judaism, Islam, Sikhism and Zoroastrianism are 'other faiths'. Everything else, Scientology for example, comes into the category of 'New Religious Movements'.

interfaith initiatives, including the newly launched Christian–Muslim forum of which the Bishop of Bolton is one of the two Chairs.

The Church of England is also in touch with interfaith issues internationally through being a member church of the worldwide Anglican Communion, which includes churches in very diverse situations of religious plurality. The Network for Inter Faith Concerns of the Anglican Communion (NIFCON) which is part of the Anglican Communion Office, draws together the wide range of interfaith issues facing Anglicans across the Communion.

Both the current Archbishop of Canterbury and his immediate predecessor have shown that the holder of that office can play an important role in inter-religious dialogue, internationally and domestically. For example, Archbishop George Carey negotiated the Alexandria Declaration of 2002 in which Christian, Muslim and Jewish leaders pledged to work together for peace in the Holy Land,[1] and Archbishop Rowan Williams has delivered significant addresses on interfaith issues in Pakistan, at the Al Azhar University in Cairo and the General Assembly of the World Council of Churches at Porto Allegre. At home, the Archbishop of Canterbury uses his position as the senior religious figure in England to convene gatherings of other religious leaders on significant national occasions.

Across the country, a network of Inter Faith Advisers and contacts in each diocese provide specialist advice and encouragement for church leaders and members seeking to develop good relations with members of different faiths. Bishops often have a particularly important role to play alongside other religious leaders and ecumenical colleagues in speaking for the faith communities. Some of the ways in which local churches are involved in interfaith work include:

- practical partnerships, e.g. caring for homeless people or asylum seekers; urban regeneration schemes; young people's projects; groups to fight racism;
- building up links with mosques, synagogues, temples, or gurdwaras nearby – arranging visits, exchanging seasonal greetings, and so on;

---

1 The text of the declaration can be found at www.anglicannifcon.org/Alexand-Declaration.htm.

- combating misinformation, prejudice and bigotry about other faiths;
- responding constructively to requests to use church halls and other premises;
- studying interfaith issues and reflecting theologically on them;
- forming small groups where people of different faiths can meet to share experiences in trust, friendship and prayer.

The Church of England also has a major involvement in such areas as education, healthcare, the prison service, and civic life; in all of these dimensions of communal life the presence of significant numbers of people from other faiths is leading to new patterns of pastoral ministry and spiritual care. As was noted in chapter two, Church of England schools are open to members of all faiths and they seek to respect the beliefs and practices of those of other faiths while at the same time seeking to maintain their own distinctive Christian ethos. The same is also true of the Church's colleges and universities.

THEOLOGICAL REFLECTION ON THE SIGNIFICANCE OF OTHER FAITHS

Increased contact with those of other faiths has raised ever more insistently the question of the place of these faiths in the purposes of God. While there have been, and still are, a range of different views on this issue, the Church of England as a whole, while not willing to compromise on its belief that Jesus Christ is the full and final revelation of God, through whose incarnation, death and resurrection our salvation is made possible, has also been unwilling to say that other faiths and their adherents are outside the scope of God's saving activity.

The 1995 Doctrine Commission report *The Mystery of Salvation* looked at this issue in detail. It suggests that:

> . . . there is a plurality of ways by which people are being made whole in the here and now; these are ways the Spirit of God is working. And there is an expectation in the future, that, while people may have the freedom to reject the salvation that is available to all, through God as Trinity, God will save ultimately those who are willing to be saved, by their penitence and

acceptance of the love which stretches out to them, in the way that it meets them in their lives and within their traditions. There is only one way, but that way is one that is without barbed wire or boundary fences, so that all may join this way. If we think of salvation in the broadest sense as encompassing all that heals and enhances human life, then clearly aspects of salvation are available in many ways, not only explicitly through Jesus Christ. In the ultimate sense, salvation is defined by having Jesus Christ as its source and goal. To use the terms we deliberately put aside earlier, this pluralism and this exclusivism are reconciled, not in some form of exclusivism (in the usual sense) but eschatologically, in the final purposes of God. To recognize the life, death and resurrection of Jesus as 'constitutive' of salvation as well as revelatory, as Christians do, is to anticipate that he will prove to be the definitive focus of salvation in its fully comprehensive form. It may be, too, that our understanding of Christ will itself be enhanced when people of other faiths are gathered in.[1]

The report further declares that although we restrict the fullness of God's love if we deny 'the truth and goodness which Christ as Logos, and God by the Spirit, can also inspire in those of other faiths and of none', nevertheless Christians believe:

> . . . that God has chosen to provide the fullest revelation of his love for all humanity in the cross and resurrection. Hence we naturally pray that God will bring all people, including those of other faiths, to explicit faith in Christ and membership of his Church. This is not because we believe that the God revealed in Christ is unable to save them without this, but because Christ is the truest and fullest expression of his love, and we long for them to share it. In the Lord's words in St John's Gospel, 'I came that they might have life, and have it abundantly.'[2]

The approach taken in the Doctrine Commission's report explains why the Church of England can simultaneously seek to develop good relations with other faiths and to work constructively

---

1 *The Mystery of Salvation*, London: Church House Publishing, 1995, pp. 183–4.
2 Ibid., p. 184.

with them in projects that promote the common good and at the same time be committed, in obedience to the great commission, to bringing all people, including those of other religions, to faith in Jesus Christ, to baptism and to full participation in the life of the Church. This dual approach to interfaith relations is explored in the report *Presence and Engagement – The Church's Task in a Multi-faith Society*, which was produced by the Church of England's Inter Faith Consultative Group in 2005. This report draws on the experiences of churches working in multi-faith contexts and it forms the basis for a continuing programme of work on the matters which it highlights.

MULTI-FAITH WORSHIP AND USE OF CHURCH BUILDINGS

It is because the Church of England takes this dual approach that the issues of multi-faith worship and the use of church property by those of other faiths remain sensitive and difficult issues. On the one hand there is a proper desire to affirm what Anglicans have in common with those of other faiths, to be hospitable to them, and to respect their desire to express their own religious convictions, particularly on major public occasions or occasions in which good relations between the faiths are being celebrated or affirmed. On the other hand there is also the need to avoid a syncretistic blurring of religious beliefs and to avoid compromising the Church of England's witness to the unique significance of Christ.

There has been discussion of these issues and related questions in a number of Church of England reports and documents.

For example, the 1992 report by the Inter Faith Consultative Group *Multi-Faith Worship?* warns that 'there must be no slide into either syncretism (a thoughtless confusion of different faith traditions) or idolatry (giving worship to that which is not God)'.[1] However, it also argues that we should not regard all worship by members of other faiths as being unacceptable to God:

---

1 The Inter Faith Consultative Group, *Multi-Faith Worship?* London: Church House Publishing, 1992, p. 25.

Whilst the Church on earth may join in the worship of the hosts of heaven here and now (Revelation 5:13) its worship looks forward to a greater completion. Similarly, but to deeper and varying degrees, we may regard the worship of those of other faiths as incomplete, but not necessarily wholly misplaced. That is the most natural reading of a verse such as Malachi 1:11, where Malachi claims for God worship that is not explicitly offered in his name, but is sincere and validated by a pure heart.[1]

On this basis the report suggests that there can be a 'limited but positive place for some forms of "multi-faith worship"'[2] and goes on to explore what this might mean in terms of Christians sharing in the worship of other faiths, those of other faiths sharing in Church of England worship, and the holding of different kinds of multi-faith services.

For another example, the 1996 report by the Inter Faith Consultative Group, *Communities and Buildings*, lays down principles for the use of Church of England buildings by members of other faith communities. It recommends that if such use is agreed after appropriate consultation 'such activities should normally be restricted to the church hall or ancillary areas distinct from the area used for Christian worship'[3] and that:

> In cases where a multi-purpose building is used for Christian worship and for other activities, and where the sanctuary can be screened off, this should be done and the sanctuary should remain unused except for Christian worship. Christian symbols, pictures etc. should otherwise remain in place and undisturbed.[4]

It further recommends that:

> . . . some regular contact takes place between members of the Christian congregation and the other faith users of the church

---

1   Ibid., p. 25.
2   Ibid., p. 27.
3   The Inter Faith Consultative Group, *Communities and Buildings*, London: Church House Publishing, 1996, p. 61.
4   Ibid., p. 61.

building. Regular meeting could involve occasions of inter-faith dialogue or the exchange of simple hospitality at the time of festivals. The expectation of regular meetings and lasting friendships should be explained to the other faith users at the time of the original agreement so that the arrangement is not regarded by either side as a purely commercial one.[1]

The 1996 report also considers the question of the disposal of redundant churches. It notes that there is a balance of conflicting arguments concerning whether they should be leased or sold for use by other faiths. Its conclusion is that this should not be ruled out in a situation where no other Christian community is ready or able to take over the building and that: 'The basic consideration should be the responsibility of the local church for promoting the mission of God.'

It argues that: 'A decision of this sort should be taken bearing in mind the feelings of the total local community, the effect upon Christian relations with those of other faiths in this country, and the possible impact on churches overseas'[2] and that 'Where a decision is made not to sell or lease a Church of England church building to another faith community which has asked for it, the reasons should be clearly, sensitively and publicly given.'[3]

The Code of Practice relating to the 1983 Pastoral Measure also discusses the issue of the disposal of redundant church buildings to those of other faiths. The Code declares that:

Central to the Christian faith is the unique revelation of God in Jesus Christ and the restoration of humankind's relation with God through Christ. Any consideration of suitable alternative uses must be placed in this context. Moreover, ecclesiastical buildings and consecrated places bear enduring witness to the faith and values of the Christian community.[4]

---

1 Ibid., p. 61.
2 Ibid., p. 57.
3 Ibid., p. 58.
4 Pastoral Measure 1983, 4th edn, 2006, p. 115. Text at www.cofe.anglican. org/about/churchcommissioners/pastoral/pastadmin/code/ pm1983code.doc.

It states that consideration of disposal of church buildings to those of other faiths 'must be set within the context' of this declaration and that 'use for worship by adherents of non-Christian faith would not tend to be preferred to other types of use'.[1] However, it notes that a refusal to allow such disposal could be contrary to the Human Rights Act unless objective and reasonable justification could be given for such a refusal and concludes that each case must be considered on its own merits.[2]

Like the 1996 report, the Code lays down a number of considerations that need to be taken into account when deciding whether to dispose of church buildings in this way. For example it says that consideration should be given to:

- the views of formally constituted Anglican and Christian bodies in the locality;
- the effect upon the life and mission of the church locally and more widely;
- the beliefs and practices of the community in question which should be considered carefully, particularly where it is not from one of the main world faiths or is of a particular tradition whose practices might not find wider acceptance within society;
- the effect upon relationships with other Christians and between them and other faiths locally and more widely.[3]

FOR FURTHER READING

The Doctrine Comission, *The Mystery of Salvation*, London: Church House Publishing, 1995.

The Inter-Faith Consultative Group, *Communities and Buildings*, London: Church House Publishing, 1996.

The Inter-Faith Consultative Group, *Multi-faith Worship?*, London: Church House Publishing, 1992.

The Inter-Faith Consultative Group, *Presence and Engagement: The Church's Task in a Multi-faith Society*, London: Mission and Public Affairs, 2005.

---

1   Ibid., p. 117.
2   Ibid., p. 118.
3   Ibid., p. 117.

12 The Church of England and Mission

THE NATURE OF MISSION

There is now widespread ecumenical agreement that the mission of the Christian Church is rooted in what has come to be known as the *missio dei*. As Paul Avis explains:

> The Latin term is necessary because it holds a depth and power that English translation cannot capture: the mission of God, the mission that belongs to God, the mission that flows from the heart of God. *Missio dei* speaks of the overflowing of God's being and nature into God's purposeful activity in the world.[1]

Saying that the mission of the Church is rooted in the *missio dei* thus means saying that the Church's mission does not begin with the activity of human beings but the activity of God Himself. The mission of the Church is its participation in this activity.

If we look at two recent Church of England statements about mission we can see that the Church of England shares this ecumenical view of the nature of mission.

The Church of England–Methodist Church of Great Britain joint statement An Anglican–Methodist Covenant declares that:

> Mission is grounded in God: it is always God's mission. Its content and unsurpassable expression is Jesus Christ himself. God purposed in Christ to reconcile the world to himself and was incarnate in Christ to bring this about (Colossians 1:20; 2 Corinthians 5:18).
>
> By the power of the Holy Spirit, God graciously enables us, as

---

1   P. Avis, *A Ministry Shaped by Mission*, London and New York: T&T Clark, 2005, p. 5.

unworthy but forgiven sinners, to participate in the mission of God. Because God's mission is definitively expressed in Christ, our participation is located in the Body of Christ, the Church. 'The Church's task is to participate in God's mission' . . . In mission the Church seeks to reflect Jesus Christ in its life and worship and to proclaim him in word and deed.[1]

The 2004 Church of England report *Mission-shaped Church* gives a more detailed account of the relationship between the activity of God and the mission of the Church, relating mission to the Trinitarian nature of God:

When Christians speak of 'God', it is as shorthand for the Holy Trinity. Two things follow from this. First, God has to be understood relationally and communally: 'Father, Son and Holy Spirit, who mutually indwell one another, exist in one another and for one another, in interdependent giving and receiving.' Second, God is a missionary. We would not know God if the Father had not sent the Son in the power of the Spirit.

In fact the mission of God (*missio dei*) itself expresses God's relational nature.

The communion of the persons of the Trinity is not to be understood as closed in on itself, but rather open in an outgoing movement of generosity. Creation and redemption are the overflow of God's triune life.

The mission of God as creator, through Christ, in the Spirit, is to bring into being, sustain and perfect the whole creation.

The mission of God as redeemer, through Christ, in the spirit, is to restore and reconcile the fallen creation (Colossians 1.20).

God's missionary purposes are cosmic in scope, concerned with the restoration of all things, the establishment of shalom, the renewal of creation and the coming of the Kingdom as well as the redemption of fallen humanity and the building of the Church.

---

1 *An Anglican–Methodist Covenant*, Peterborough & London: Methodist Publishing House and Church House Publishing, 2001, p. 29.

The Church is both the fruit of God's mission – those whom he has redeemed, and the agent of his mission – the community through whom he acts for the world's redemption. 'The mission of the Church is the gift of participating through the Holy Spirit in the Son's mission from the Father to the world.'[1]

As well as seeing mission as something that is rooted in the activity of God, the Church of England also sees mission as something that involves more than simply evangelism.

In a definition that has come to be widely used, the 1918 report of the Archbishops' Committee on the Evangelistic Work of the Church describes evangelism as follows: 'To evangelise is so to present Christ Jesus in the power of the Holy Spirit, that men shall come to put their trust in God through him, to accept him as their Saviour, and serve him as their King in the fellowship of his Church.'[2]

The reason that mission cannot simply be identified with evangelism thus defined is because, in the words of Avis:

> . . . mission is bigger than evangelization. Evangelization is a *part* of which mission is the *whole*. As Moltmann puts it: 'Mission embraces all activities that serve to liberate man from his slavery in the presence of the coming God, slavery which extends from economic necessity to Godforsakenness. Evangelisation is mission, but mission is not merely evangelisation.'[3]

What this means in specific terms is that activities such as feeding the hungry, caring for the sick and working for social justice through involvement in political activity can all be seen as part of mission even though they are not explicitly evangelistic in nature.

The fact that the Church of England sees mission as involving more than simply evangelism can be seen from the endorsement by General Synod in 1996 of the 'Five Marks of Mission', produced by the Anglican Consultative Council in 1990. These are the closest there is to an official Church of England definition of mission and they declare that the mission of the Church is:

---

1 *Mission-shaped Church*, London: Church House Publishing, 2004, p. 85.
2 Quotation in Avis, op. cit., p. 17.
3 Ibid., p. 14, quoting J. Moltmann, *The Church in the Power of the Spirit*, London: SCM, 1977, p. 10.

- to proclaim the Good News of the Kingdom;
- to teach, baptize and nurture new believers;
- to respond to human need by loving service;
- to seek to transform the unjust structures of society;
- to strive to safeguard the integrity of creation and sustain and renew the life of the earth.

The first two marks correspond to the Great Commission in Mt. 28:18–20 and constitute evangelism as defined by the report of the Archbishops' Committee in 1918.

The third mark involves the performance of what have traditionally been known as the 'corporal works of mercy', that is to say, acts of love which meet the physical needs of other people as described by Christ in his parable of the sheep and the goats in Mt. 25:31–46.[1]

The fourth mark highlights the realization which has always been a part of the Christian tradition, but which has come to be particularly emphasized from the nineteenth century onwards, that the Church needs to challenge and seek to change the existence of unjust political structures that prevent people from flourishing in the way that God intends.

Taken together, the first four marks indicate a relatively long-standing agreement that authentic Christian mission has to include not only evangelism but also a commitment to justice and human welfare. As the former Archbishop of Canterbury, George Carey, has put it: 'Mission which does not have evangelism as a focus is not Christian mission; and evangelism which keeps itself aloof from matters of justice and human welfare does not reflect adequately the biblical revelation.'[2]

By contrast, the fifth mark says something distinctively new about the proper content of mission. It reflects the growth in environmental awareness among Christians during the second half of the twentieth century. Theologically, it is based on the teaching in the first two chapters of the book of Genesis that the world is

---

1 Such acts are know as the 'corporal' works of mercy because they care for the body (Latin *corpus*) rather than for the soul. The traditional list of such works is feeding the hungry, giving drink to the thirsty, clothing the naked, receiving the stranger, tending the sick, visiting those in prison and burying the dead.

2 G. Carey, 'The Way Ahead: Preparing the Church of England for the New Millennium', The Ashe Lecture, 1997, p. 7, cited in Avis, op. cit., p. 20.

God's creation and that human beings are called to care for it on his behalf. This teaching is highlighted by the 2005 Church of England report *Sharing God's Planet*, which states:

> God created the universe; human beings can only hope to adapt it. A Christian understanding of the environment has to start with this fundamental premise. The creation belongs to God, not to humans. The human role is defined as a steward of creation, exercising dominion under God, whose rule is sovereign.[1]

The report uses the three biblical roles of prophet, priest and king to explain what this means.

As *prophets*, it says, human beings are called 'to speak of the beauty and goodness of the creation; to make people see things as they really are; and to free the earth (in this context) from the oppression of exploitation, ignorance and plunder'.[2]

As *priests*, human beings are called to receive the things that God has made as gifts from Him, to transform them through their creative activity and then to offer them back to God in worship: 'As priests, human beings have the choice to live sacramentally, receiving all creation as a gift, transforming it and returning it to God, or to live selfishly, separating creation from its source and accruing it to themselves exclusively.'[3]

As *kings*, human beings are called to exercise dominion over the earth and thus help it to flourish:

> How are the children of God to bring this about? Paul provides the answer. Christ, he says in 1 Corinthians 15, is the second Adam. The role to which the first Adam was called and failed to fulfil, the role to which Christ and the children of God that follow him are now called, was to 'till and keep' the garden (Genesis 2.15). This is the kingly role, the exercise of dominion for humanity to fulfil, commanded of Adam before the Fall and prophesied by Isaiah:

---

1 *Sharing God's Planet*, London: Church House Publishing, 2005, p. 16.
2 Ibid., p. 23.
3 Ibid., p. 24.

In days to come Jacob shall take root,
Israel shall blossom and put forth shoots,
and fill the whole world with fruit. Isaiah 27.6

Dominion is an exercise of vice-regency: lordship under God. The biblical term for humanity's relationship with creation is 'steward'. A steward is a servant who relates to God, on whose behalf s/he exercises dominion. S/he is also called to render an account to God of his/her stewardship of tilling and keeping.[1]

By identifying caring for the environment as a fifth mark of mission, the Church of England declares that it is the Church's calling to help human beings to fulfil these three roles.

MISSION IN ENGLAND

(a) The history of mission in England

Taking the five marks of mission as a starting point, it is possible to look back at the history of mission in the Church of England and note developments both in the mission emphasis of the Church of England and in the way that mission has been undertaken.

At the beginning of its history the Church of England faced the challenge of seeking to convert a pagan society and therefore concentrated on the first two aspects of mission, proclaiming the good news and seeking to teach, baptize and nurture new believers. This is evident, for example, in the account given by Bede of the mission undertaken in Northumbria in the seventh century by St Paulinus, Bishop of York and later Rochester. Bede tells us that Paulinus was determined:

> . . . to bring the nation to which he was sent the knowledge of the Christian truth, and to fulfil the Apostle's saying, 'to espouse her to one husband, that he might present her as a chaste virgin to Christ'. Therefore, directly he entered the province he began to toil unceasingly not only by God's help to maintain the faith of his companions unimpaired, but if possible

---

1 Ibid., p. 26.

to bring some of the heathen to grace and faith by his preaching.[1]

Paulinus' missionary efforts were initially unfruitful, but after the baptism of the Northumbrian king, Edwin, his people began to turn to Christianity as well:

Indeed, so great was the fervour of faith and the desire for baptism among the Northumbrian people that Paulinus is said to have accompanied the king and the queen to the royal residence at Ad-Gefrin and remained there thirty six days constantly occupied in instructing and baptizing. During this period, he did nothing from dawn to dusk but proclaim Christ's saving message to the people, who gathered from all the surrounding villages and countryside; and when he had instructed them, he washed them in the cleansing waters of baptism in the nearby River Glen.[2]

What we also see in this account is mission being spearheaded by a bishop, and the evidence that we have from Bede is that this was typical of the mission of the early English church as a whole. It was the bishops assisted by their priests who were the pioneer missionaries who undertook the conversion of England.

The mention of the king and queen in the second quotation is significant in that it points us to the fact that the key to the conversion of England was the conversion of the royal families of the various English kingdoms. As Bede's account makes clear, once the kings and their nobility were converted the conversion of their kingdoms then followed. The conversion of England was a 'top down' event. In the case of Northumbria for example, it was the conversion of King Edwin and his nobles that led to the events described in this quotation.

In his account of the conversion of Northumbria, Bede further tells us that the king's conversion led to the erection of church buildings:

---

1 L. Sherley-Price, *Bede: A History of the English Church and People*, Bk II, Ch. 9, Harmondsworth: Penguin, 1968, p. 115.
2 Ibid., Bk II, Ch. 14, p. 129.

The king's baptism took place at York of Easter Day, the 12 April, in the church of St Peter the Apostle, which the king had hastily built of timber during the time of his instruction and preparation for Baptism, and in this city he established the see of his teacher and bishop Paulinus. Soon after his baptism, at Paulinus' suggestion, he gave orders to build on the same site a larger and more noble basilica of stone, which was to enclose the little oratory he had built before.[1]

What took place in York seems to have been typical of what happened across England as a whole. The acceptance of Christianity by the royal family and the nobility was followed by the erection of a church and associated buildings to act as the seat of the bishop and the centre of further mission in the kingdom concerned.[2]

Once the initial missionary activity just described had taken place and Christianity had become the accepted religion of the English people, the mission priorities of the English church changed. The proclamation of the good news was aimed at reminding people of the truth of their faith rather than converting them to it. The instruction, baptism and nurture of believers continued, but took the form of the instruction and nurture of the children of Christian parents, children who had been baptized as infants.

The importance of undertaking acts of loving service to those in need was emphasized as a key part of Christian discipleship.

The growth of the church led to new church buildings being built to act as centres of mission. As chapter two noted, these new buildings originally took the form of minsters, monastic institutions that acted as centres of mission for the surrounding area. To quote the historian John Blair, if we ask 'by what means were Christian belief and observance transmitted and fostered?' the sources that we have 'permit a fairly confident answer: priests travelled around among rural settlements, and their work was

---

1 Ibid., pp. 128–9.
2 In the case of St Augustine in Canterbury there was an existing church building built in Roman times and this was restored instead of a new building being erected.

supervised by minsters'.[1] We get a glimpse of how this system worked in practice in Bede's account of the way of life of the monastic community on Lindisfarne in the middle years of the seventh century:

> . . . in those days the sole concern of these teachers was to serve God, not the world; to satisfy the soul, not the belly. Accordingly the religious habit at that time was held in high esteem. Wherever any priest or monk paid a visit, he was joyfully welcomed by all as the servant of God. And if people met him on the road, they ran to him and bowed, eager to be signed by his hand or receive a blessing from his lips. Whenever he spoke a word of encouragement, he was given an attentive hearing. On Sundays the people flocked to the churches and monasteries, not to obtain food, but to hear the word of God. When a priest visited a village, the people were quick to gather together to receive the word of life; for priests and clerics always came to a village solely to preach, baptize, visit the sick, and, in short, to care for the souls of its people.[2]

As chapter two also noted, from the tenth century onwards, local churches serving villages or particular areas of towns began to be established by monasteries and landowners. This meant that the primary areas of mission came to be the parishes that these new churches served and the primary agents of mission came to be the local parish priests. What happened was, essentially, that the itinerant ministry described by Bede became fixed and permanent in the work of the parochial clergy. It was they who were primarily responsible for preaching, for the instruction, baptism and nurture of the faithful, and for ensuring that provision was made for those in need.

In the fourteenth century, Geoffrey Chaucer, in his famous account of the Poor Parson in the prologue to the *Canterbury Tales*, describes how the parochial clergy were meant to operate as agents of mission. He tells us that:

---

1 J. Blair, *The Church in Anglo-Saxon Society*, Oxford: Oxford University Press, 2005, pp. 161–2.
2 Bede, op. cit, Bk III, Ch. 26, p. 194.

A holy-minded man of good renown there was, and poor, the Parson to a town, yet he was rich in holy thought and work. He also was a learned man, a clerk, who truly knew Christ's gospel and would preach it devoutly to parishioners, and teach it. Benign and wonderfully diligent, and patient when adversity was sent (for so he proved in great adversity) he much disliked extorting tithe or fee, nay rather he preferred beyond a doubt giving to poor parishioners round about from his own goods and Easter offerings. He found sufficiency in little things. Wide was his parish, with houses far asunder, yet he neglected not in rain or thunder, in sickness or in grief, to pay a call on the remotest whether great or small upon his feet, and in his hand a stave. This noble example to his sheep he gave, first following the word before he taught it, and it was from the gospel that he caught it.[1]

This is an idealized account of the parochial clergy, and from evidence such as bishops' visitation records it is clear that not all clergy lived up to the ideal. However, this does not mean that Chaucer's account is completely fictitious. There is other evidence that indicates that there were those who did approach the ideal. For example the visitation records for Branscombe in Devon in 1301 tell us that the parishioners declared that: 'Thomas their vicar beareth himself well in all things and preacheth willingly, and visiteth the sick, and doth diligently all that pertaineth to his priestly office.'[2]

Although the picture of mission being undertaken in the Middle Ages through the network of parish churches and by the parochial clergy is generally true it also has to be qualified in two respects.

First, the parish churches were not the sole centres of mission. Preaching, pastoral care and the relief of those in need was also provided by the monasteries, chapels of ease (additional church buildings erected in large parishes in which travel to the parish church would be difficult) and private chapels in palaces, castles, hospitals, colleges and so forth.

Secondly (and consequent upon this), the parochial clergy were

---

1   G. Chaucer, *The Canterbury Tales*, Harmondsworth: Penguin Books, 1951, p. 38.
2   Quoted in J. R. H. Moorman, *A History of the Church in England*, Harrisburg, PA: Morehouse Publishing, 1980, p. 99.

not the sole agents of mission. A significant role was also played by the members of monastic communities, by the chaplains of private chapels and, in the later Middle Ages, by the friars. The friars, who began their work in England in 1221, were members of two religious orders, the Dominicans and the Franciscans. They were like monks in that they followed a rule of life, but unlike members of the existing monastic communities their vocation was to an itinerant preaching ministry. In the words of Moorman, a friar was 'free to go among men wherever he could find an opportunity of witnessing by word and by example to the faith that was in him'.[1]

The itinerant nature of the ministry of the friars brought them into conflict with the parochial clergy and by the end of the Middle Ages their skill in fund raising had given them a reputation for avarice. However, to quote Moorman again:

> . . . in their great days they did much to regenerate the life of the Church. They brought new life into the parishes and new hope to the people, they stirred up the clergy to greater efforts and efficiency, they captured the universities by their knowledge and sincerity, they set up a whole network of schools from which all could benefit, and they provided a way of life, simple, austere and holy, in which those who were prepared to forsake all for Christ's sake could find a spiritual home.[2]

At the Reformation the religious orders were abolished and so both the monasteries and the friars vanished from the scene. The parochial system, however, remained intact and the vast majority of the parochial clergy stayed in post, playing the same fundamental role in the mission of Church of England as they always had done, albeit within a new theological and liturgical framework. As the Prayer Book Ordinal put it in the service for the ordering of priests, it was still their task to:

> . . . be messengers, watchmen and stewards of the Lord; to teach and to premonish, to feed and provide for the Lord's family; to seek abroad for Christ's sheep that are dispersed

---

1 Moorman, ibid., p. 103.
2 Ibid., p. 106.

abroad, and for his children who are in the midst of this naughty world that they may be saved through Christ for ever.

From 1560 onwards provision was made for 'sober, honest and grave' laymen to exercise a limited form of ministry[1] as readers in place of a parish priest when a parish was without one. However, this experiment never really took off and from the Reformation until the nineteenth century it was the clergy who were virtually the sole recognized agents of mission in the Church of England.

In his book *A Priest to the Temple*, which was published after his death in 1633, the seventeenth-century clergyman George Herbert provided what came to be seen as the classic account of how this role should ideally be exercised. An examination of this work, the full title of which was *A Priest to the Temple, or, The Country Parson his Character and Rule of Holy Life*, reveals that what is being described is fundamentally the same form of mission in which Chaucer's Poor Parson was engaged some three hundred years before. This can be seen, for instance, in Chapter VIII, 'The Parson on Sundays', which gives a flavour of the work as a whole:

> The Country Parson, as soon as he awakes on Sunday morning, presently falls to work and seems to himself so as a Market-man is, when the Market day, comes, or a shopkeeper, when customers use to come in. His thoughts are full of making the best of the day, and contriving it to his best gains. To this end, besides his ordinary prayers, he makes a peculiar one for a blessing on the exercises[2] of the day. That nothing befall him unworthy of that Majesty before which he is to present himself, but that all may be done with reverence to his glory, and with edification to his flock, humbly beseeching his Master, that how or whenever he punish him, it be not in his ministry: then he turns to request for his people, that the Lord would be pleased to sanctify them all, that they may come with holy hearts, and

---

1   Readers were permitted to:
   - read whatever was appointed by authority and to conduct service in church;
   - bury the dead;
   - church women;
   - keep registers.
2   Or, as we should say, 'those things that have to be done'.

awful minds into the Congregation, and that the good God would pardon all those, who come with less prepared hearts than they ought. This done, he sets himself to the Consideration of the duties of the day, and if there be any extraordinary addition to the customary exercises, either from the time of the year, or from the state, or from God by a child born, or dead, or any other accident, he contrives how and in what manner to induce it to the best advantage. Afterwards, when the hour calls, with his family attending him, he goes to Church, at his first entrance *humbly adoring, and worshipping the invisible majesty, and presence of Almighty God*, and blessing the people either openly, or to himself. Then having read divine service twice fully, and preached in the morning, and catechized in the afternoon, he thinks he hath in some measure, according to poor, and frail man, discharged the public duties of the Congregation. The rest of the day he spends either reconciling neighbours that are at variance, or in visiting the sick, or in exhortations to some of his flock by themselves, whom his Sermons cannot, or do not reach. And every one is more awaked, when we come, and say, *Thou are the man*. This way he finds exceeding useful, and winning: and these exhortations he calls his privy purse, even as Princes have theirs besides their public disbursements. At night he thinks it a very fit time, both suitable to the joy of the day, and without hindrance to public duties, either to entertain some of his neighbours, or to be entertained of them, when he takes occasion to discourse *of such things as are both profitable and pleasant, and to raise up their minds to apprehend God's good blessing to our Church, and State, that order is kept in the one and peace in the other, without its disturbance, or interruption of public divine offices.* As he opened the day with prayer, so he closeth it, humbly beseeching the Almighty to pardon and accept our poor services, and to improve them, that we may grow therein, and that our feet may be like hind's feet ever climbing up higher, and higher unto him.[1]

A Priest to the Temple and the way that Herbert exercised his own ministry as rector of Bemerton in Wiltshire came to be seen as

---

1 G. Herbert, *A Priest to the Temple*, Ch. VIII. Text at www.ccel.org/ccel/herbert/temple2.xi.html, italics in the original, but spelling updated.

exemplifying the way in which the clergy of the Church of England should undertake their duties, and his pastoral and parochial approach to mission continued to be followed in general outline by many Church of England clergy, particularly in rural parishes, until well into the twentieth century. Indeed, it can be argued that Canon C24, 'Of Priests having a cure of souls', which outlines the basic responsibilities of a parish priest, continues to describe an approach to mission that would be recognized by Herbert and by Chaucer's Poor Parson before him.

A portrait of George Herbert by Robert White, engraving, 1674 (National Portrait Gallery, London)

However, from the eighteenth century onwards changing circumstances made this approach to mission less effective.

First, it was only suitable in a relatively small rural parish in which it was possible for the parson to know all his parishioners personally. With rapid population growth and urbanization from the eighteenth century onwards, this situation ceased to apply in many parishes.

Secondly, it was based on the premise that all those living in the parish were part of the church and that, except for very young children, they all had at least a working knowledge of the content of the Christian faith. Mission thus meant not the conversion of those who were not Christians, but helping those that were to lead more godly lives. From the eighteenth century this premise became increasingly questionable as an ever-growing segment of the population ceased to have any connection with the life of the church or any real knowledge or acceptance of the Christian faith.

Thirdly, it was based on the premise that the Church of England was the only church in the parish. The rise of Non-Conformity and the revival of Roman Catholicism meant that this too ceased to be the case in many places and this posed the question as to how mission should be undertaken in areas where there were Christian communities from other traditions. In such circumstances should mission take the form of competition or cooperation?

Fourthly, as Herbert's choice of appropriate dinner table conversation indicates, this approach was based on a belief that the existing social order reflected the providence of God. As a result of the increasingly desperate social conditions resulting from industrialization and urbanization and the influence of the French Revolution, this approach came to be challenged as an increasing number of Christians came to believe that for human beings to flourish in the way intended by God there had to be fundamental changes to the existing social order. In terms of the five marks of mission, awareness of the fourth mark – 'to seek to transform the unjust structures of society' – began to grow.

From the eighteenth century onwards, the Church of England reacted to these changing circumstances in three ways.

The first way was to seek to strengthen the existing parochial system. For example, under Acts of Parliament passed in 1818 and 1821–22 new parishes were established and church buildings erected in places in which the existing parishes had too many people living in them to operate effectively. As Nick Spencer explains, the result of this was that: 'The following thirty years saw

612 new parishes defined and nearly 2000 new churches built, with the emphasis being on the areas of greatest need in Yorkshire, Lancashire and the suburbs of London.'[1]

A good example of what this meant in a particular locality is what took place in Leeds. After Walter Hook became vicar of Leeds in 1837 he addressed the issue of ministering to its rapidly growing population by both rebuilding Leeds Parish Church so that it could seat 1,600 people, and by dividing the old Leeds parish into 21 new parishes, each with its own member of the clergy and its own church building.

This process of creating new parishes and erecting new church buildings in areas of population growth has continued, albeit at a slower rate, to this day.

For example, the Parish of St Barnabas, St Paul's Cray in the diocese of Rochester was created in the 1950s in order to meet the needs of people who had been relocated from the East End of London to an area of new housing in the southeastern suburbs and consideration is now being given to how to adapt the existing parochial system to respond to the huge new housing developments planned for the southeast of England.

Daughter churches and mission halls were established in parishes which remained intact, but in which there was nonetheless a large population.

An attempt was made to ensure that as far as possible each parish had its own parish priest, and additional clergy were recruited in order to allow this to happen. In addition, in many parishes (particularly in urban and suburban areas with a high population) lay workers, including members of the religious communities that were re-established in the nineteenth century, were appointed to assist the clergy.

Systematic attempts were made to reach out to those in the parishes who were on the fringe of the church, or outside it altogether, through holding more attractive and accessible services, through the distribution of literature in the form of pamphlets and leaflets that were short in length and popular in content, through the holding of special evangelistic meetings and through the development of a range of social activities that would help to attract people and retain them within the life of the church.

---

1 N. Spencer, *Parochial Vision: The Future of the English Parish*, Carlisle: Paternoster, 2004, p. 34.

Systematic attempts were also made to provide for the education of the children in the parishes and to update the traditional forms of catechesis through the establishment of a network of church schools[1] and Sunday Schools, with the idea being that these would provide an integrated pattern of Christian education.

Concerted efforts were made to address the social needs of those in the parishes, with clergy and lay workers seeking to address issues of poverty, disease, poor housing and drunkenness that were endemic in many areas, both in the cities and in the countryside. These efforts were particularly important before Britain began to develop a state welfare system in the twentieth century.

The second way was to develop new approaches that operated outside the traditional framework of parochial ministry. For instance:

- Church of England clergymen such as John Wesley and George Whitefield undertook an itinerant nationwide ministry in the second half of the eighteenth century.
- Large-scale evangelistic events were held that were aimed at whole towns or cities rather than particular parishes, as in the case of the Missions to London in 1858 and 1949 that were led by the then Bishops of London, Tait and Wand.
- The Church Army was established by Wilson Carlile in 1882 as a Church of England mission agency undertaking evangelistic and social work within the Church of England, but alongside its existing parochial framework.
- Missions were developed to work with particular parts of the population rather than the inhabitants of particular parishes. Thus in the nineteenth century, missions were founded to address the spiritual needs of, among others, cab drivers, navvies, railway workers and seamen. A twentieth-century development of this tradition was the emergence of industrial mission, in which members of the clergy and lay workers sought to engage in mission in people's places of work and to engage from a Christian perspective with the issues raised by working life and wealth creation.

In line with the fourth mark of mission, political action began to

1 See the explanation of the work of the National Society in chapter two.

be taken at the national level to combat particular evils in the life of society as a whole and members of the Church began to address the question whether the life of the nation as a whole needed to be organized in a different way in order to accord better with Christian principles. For example, in the mid-nineteenth century the Earl of Shaftesbury, who was a Church of England layman, introduced a number of Acts of Parliament that improved the working conditions and limited the working hours of children and was also involved with legislation to combat disease through the introduction of improved sanitation. In the same period other members of the Church of England, such as John Ludlow, Frederick Denison Maurice and Charles Kingsley, were developing the idea of addressing the evils of society through the development of a Christian socialism that would lead to a more just society through the application of Christian principles in all areas of the nation's social and economic life.

The tradition of applying a Christian critique to the ills of contemporary society that originated with the Christian socialists continued in the twentieth century. It can be seen for example in the influential 1942 work by Archbishop William Temple, *Towards a Christian Social Order*[1] and in the 1984 report *Faith in the City*[2] which drew attention to the extent of the poverty in Britain's urban areas and which led to the creation of the Church Urban Fund to support the mission of the church in these areas.

The same tradition also continues in the twenty-first century, as can be seen from the publication in 2006 of the report *Faithful Cities*,[3] which was the follow-up to *Faith in the City*, produced by a Commission on Urban Life and Faith set up by the Church of England. This report explores the question of what makes a 'good city' and looks at the ways in which Christians and those of other faiths can contribute towards helping city life to flourish.

The third way was to work with Christians from other churches. As time has gone on, members of the Church of England have increasingly cooperated in mission with Christians from other churches, both at the parochial level and in extra-parochial activity.

---

1 W. Temple, *Towards a Christian Social Order*, Harmondsworth: Penguin, 1942.
2 *Faith in the City*, London: Church House Publishing, 1984.
3 *Faithful Cities*, London and Peterborough: Church House Publishing/ Methodist Publishing House, 2006.

At the parochial level there are numerous stories from the eighteenth century onwards of Anglicans and those from other churches holding joint services, running joint outreach events and working together to help those in need.

In terms of extra-parochial activity the stories are similar. For example, Christians from the Church of England and a range of other churches supported both the Sankey and Moody and the Billy Graham missions, the London City Mission was (and is) supported by both Anglicans and Christians from other churches, and Anglicans have worked together with those from across the churches to try to achieve social reforms.

Initially, this type of cooperation in mission took place informally or through the auspices of pan-denominational groups such as the Bible Society or the Evangelical Alliance, but such cooperation was one of the factors that led to the development of the ecumenical movement and, once this had begun to affect the life of the churches, cooperation began to take place on a more formal basis, either in the context of bilateral relations between Christians of different traditions or in the context of the local or national ecumenical structures.

Finally, as we have already noted, in the second half of the twentieth century growing awareness of a looming ecological crisis led to the realization that care for the environment ought to be one of the central aspects of responsible Christian activity in today's world, and hence to the development of the fifth mark of mission.

(b) Mission in England today

The result of this history is that the Church of England's mission is now based on an adapted and updated version of the traditional parochial system.

On the one hand, parochial ministry remains the backbone of the Church of England's mission work. This is partly because the parish system is the way that the Church of England has been organized for over a thousand years and as a result it is so embedded in the life of the church that it would not be practical simply to abolish it and try to substitute some other way of operating in its place. More fundamentally, however, it is because the parish system still provides the most effective framework for the Church of England to carry out its mission to the nation.

As Avis explains:

What the parochial system ultimately means is that every person who does not opt out is assigned to the pastoral care of a parish priest. Everyone is fully entitled (by law in the last resort) to the ministry of the clergy and to attend their parish church. Either they know who their vicar is or, by taking a little trouble, they can find out. Conversely, the clergy are not freelance spiritual consultants, waiting for their clients to approach them, but are commissioned to offer, in a proactive way, the ministry of word, sacrament and pastoral care, to all who are willing to receive it. In the abstract, this is a daunting, perhaps an impossible task. But the responsibilities of the clergy are delimited by geographic and demographic boundaries. It is not that they are uninterested in anyone outside the parish or that they will turn away a person who is not a parishioner. It is rather that these given factors constrain the task and make it bearable. The work of the clergy and those lay ministers who assist them is earthed and rooted in a specific community (one that often coincides with spheres of civic responsibility). Their work receives shape and focus by being linked to a defined cure.

. . . Even where parish boundaries are blurred in the minds of parishioners and churchgoers, the defined area of a parish represents a specific quantum of pastoral responsibility – and the limits of responsibility – for the Church, its clergy and its local councils. Looking in from the outside, as it were, the parish structure looks outmoded; looking out from its heart it makes sense. With its legal reinforcement of the clergy's primarily moral obligations to baptize, marry and conduct the funerals of parishioners, the parochial structure still provides a framework for mission that has not been superseded and a salutary pastoral discipline for those engaged in it.[1]

On the other hand the parochially based pattern of mission has also undergone significant changes.

First, parishes were traditionally independent units of mission that determined their own mission strategies and cooperated with each other on an occasional basis. This is frequently no longer the case. Parishes are now often part of multi-parish benefices, and team or group ministries, and undertake their missions as part of

---

1 P. Avis, *A Church Drawing Near*, London and New York: T&T Clark/ Continuum, 2004, p. 195.

these larger units. In addition, the way that parishes undertake mission is increasingly shaped by deanery and diocesan mission strategies.

Secondly, the responsibility for mission was traditionally seen as lying with the parish priest and his assistant curates (if he had any). Today, although the role of the ordained ministers as agents of mission remains crucially important, there has been a switch of emphasis that means that responsibility for mission is seen as something that lies with all the Christians of the parish and not just with the clergy. To quote An Anglican–Methodist Covenant:

> Mission is entrusted to the whole Church, not merely part of it. As the task of the whole Church, mission is the vocation and responsibility of all baptised believers, the laos, the redeemed and sanctified 'people of his own' (Titus 2:14; cf. 1 Peter 2:9), without distinction between ordained and lay Christians.[1]

There is also growing agreement that the life of the local Christian congregation is crucial in giving credibility to the gospel message. In a phrase that has become famous, the mission theologian Leslie Newbigin made this point by declaring that it is the local Christian congregation that is the 'hermeneutic of the gospel':

> How is it possible that the gospel should be credible, that people should come to believe that the power which has the last word in human affairs is represented by a man hanging on a cross? I am suggesting that the only answer, the only hermeneutic of the gospel, is a congregation of men and women who believe it and live by it.[2]

If we ask in more detail what the characteristics of such a church would be like, the Bishop of Rochester, Michael Nazir-Ali, provides a picture that would elicit widespread assent in his book *Shapes of the Church to Come*. Drawing on Newbigin's teaching about the key role of the local congregation in providing a plausible

---

1 *An Anglican–Methodist Covenant*, p. 29.
2 L. Newbigin, *The Gospel in a Pluralist Society*, London: SPCK, 1980, p. 227.

interpretation of the gospel to the surrounding community, he writes that:

> As the Christian congregation rehearses the word and works of Jesus, exhibits his risen life in the sacraments, renews itself again and again in these ways, it draws others into this life. In doing so, it provides them also with the 'lenses' needed to interpret an ambiguous world.

A congregation will be an effective 'hermeneutic' of the gospel if it is a community of praise and thanksgiving. As another bishop, Stephen Sykes, has said, those who praise God in the congregation are led to praise him in the world. It will be a community of truth, living by that true story which reveals the purpose of this world and tells us something of our destiny. In doing this, it will have to battle with other accounts of our existence that deny purpose or belittle human dignity. It will be deeply involved in all that promotes the common good in the neighbourhood. Its members will be trained, supported and nourished in their task of being a royal priesthood. That is to say, they will be enabled to bring God to the world and the world to God. It is the task of the ministerial priesthood to make sure that this enabling is happening. They exercise their specific ministry so that all of the baptized can exercise theirs. Such a community will be an example of mutual support and responsibility, setting its face against individualism even when it is about spiritual fulfilment. Above all, it will be a community of hope: hope in making things better in this life (as the Christian Aid slogan has it 'We believe in life before death') but also hope in the fulfilment of our deepest spiritual longings for fellowship with God, the source of all that exists. These communities of praise, truth and hope will make a difference to the world and, in doing so, will most effectively communicate the good news of Jesus Christ.[1]

It should be noted, however, that although the existence of a Christian community such as the one just described is what will make the gospel message credible, there is still the need for the

---

1   M. Nazir-Ali, *Shapes of the Church to Come*, Eastbourne: Kingsway, 2001, p. 111.

message itself to be explained. In recent years it has been found that one of the most effective ways of doing this is by exploring the meaning of the Christian faith through discussion in a small group of people who meet together on a regular basis for this purpose over an extended period of time. The best-known set of resources for this sort of discussion group is provided by the Alpha Course, pioneered by Holy Trinity Brompton ('HTB'), a large Charismatic Evangelical church in Central London. However, other resources have been developed for this purpose such as Emmaus, which takes a more Catholic approach and Christianity Explored, which reflects the Conservative Evangelical tradition within the Church of England.[1]

Thirdly, while there have always been other forms of mission alongside mission in the parishes, these have become increasingly important. There are two forms that this sort of extra-parochial mission takes. The first is sector ministry, in which clergy or lay ministers undertake mission in a variety of specific settings such as hospitals, prisons, schools, airports or shopping centres. The second is mission to particular groups in society. For example, the Church Army runs a project called The Bridge that works with homeless women at the Marylebone women's hostel in London. This project aims at 'building trust through developing authentic and personal Christian presence and support for homeless women' and 'creating opportunities to move women from temporary hostel accommodation to settled independent living within existing or developing Christian communities'.[2]

Fourthly, as has already been noted, while parish churches retain responsibility for mission to everyone living in the parish, it has become increasingly accepted that this responsibility is something that is shared with other Christian communities in the area and should be discharged in cooperation with them. Often this cooperation in mission takes place on an informal basis, but it is also expressed more formally through the signing of covenants between local churches or the establishment of Local Ecumenical Partnerships.

Fifthly, in recent years there has been the growth of what is

---

1   For details of these courses see http://ukalpha.org, www.e-mmaus.org.uk and www.christianityexplored.com.
2   For details of The Bridge see www.churcharmy.org.uk/ChurchArmy/web/site/MaryleboneProject/The Bridge_m.asp.

known as 'church planting'. This is a mission strategy that involves the establishment of new Church of England churches that are additional to existing parish churches. There are two types of church plant. The first is a 'neighbourhood' church that seeks to serve a particular neighbourhood within an existing parish. The second is a 'network' church that aims to serve, not a particular geographical area, but a particular social or cultural group. This second type of church plant can be seen as a development of the long-established idea of mission to particular groups in society.

Alongside the recognition that church plants create new opportunities for mission there has also been a concern about the potential for church plants to undermine the existing parochial system, particularly when such plants cross parochial boundaries. There have been two Church of England reports that have considered the issue of church plants, *Breaking New Ground*,[1] published in 1994 and *Mission-shaped Church*. Both these reports have concluded that properly regulated church plants supplement rather than threaten the parochial system and that they have an important part to play in reaching out to groups of people that existing forms of church do not currently reach, thus enabling the Church of England better to fulfil its mission to the nation.

At the time of writing, the Church of England's Dioceses, Pastoral and Mission Measure is going through Parliament. This will provide a legal framework within which what will be known as 'mission initiatives' can be established and regulated by means of Bishops' Mission Orders. This will open up the possibility for all kinds of non-traditional communities of Christian disciples being established to minister to particular sections of society within the overall framework of the Church of England.

(c) Structures for mission in England

At the national level mission and evangelism are the responsibility of the Mission and Public Affairs Division of the Archbishops' Council. Within this division there are two specialist officers with particular mission responsibilities: the National Mission and Evangelism Adviser and the Mission Theology Adviser. In addition the Council for Christian Unity has a National Adviser for

---

1 *Breaking New Ground*, London: Church House Publishing, 1994.

Unity-in-Mission who is responsible for overseeing the links between mission and ecumenism.

The mission theology adviser services the Mission Theological Advisory Group (MTAG), which is an ecumenical partnership between the Mission and Public Affairs Division and the Churches' Commission on Mission of Churches Together in Britain and Ireland and brings together people from churches in England, Wales, Scotland and Ireland. The function of MTAG is to offer advice to the churches 'on matters affecting the mission of the whole Church. Its particular interest is in the relationship between the gospel we are called to proclaim and the western culture where we are called to proclaim it.'[1]

An important new initiative in mission at the national level is Fresh Expressions, a new initiative by the Church of England and the Methodist Church that began in 2004. The aim of Fresh Expressions is to encourage and resource those 'hoping to establish "new and different forms of church for our changing culture"'. The term 'fresh expressions' is taken from *Mission-shaped Church* and is used to refer to a 'form of church for our changing culture, established primarily for the benefit of people who are not yet members of any church'.

The Fresh Expressions website (www.freshexpressions.org.uk) explains the rationale of the initiative in the following terms:

> According to the best available research approximately 60 per cent of the British population are probably beyond the reach of existing churches. This proportion is much higher in urban areas and among the under forties. It is increasing year by year.
>
> Many people in this group have a belief in God; many are interested in spiritual things and in Christian spirituality. But the gap between where they are now and church is too wide to be easily crossed.
>
> The challenge for the churches in the next decade is therefore to develop a both–and strategy:
>
> **Both** to continue our mission of sharing faith to this 40 per cent of the population who have some church background and connection.
>
> **And** to develop new ways of sharing faith with the 60 per cent

---

1   www.cofe.anglican.org/faith/mission/mtage.html.

of the population who are beyond the reach of the churches. This part of the strategy means developing fresh expressions of church life in a range of different ways.

The church of the future will be a mixed economy. There will be traditional churches sharing faith with those on the edge and fresh expressions of church reaching out to those who know little or nothing of Christian faith.

The website also gives more information about the concept of fresh expressions and has a list of examples of what it means in practice. This list exemplifies the notion of a 'mixed economy' in that it contains both church plants and existing parish churches pioneering forms of outreach to the un-churched.

At the diocesan level all dioceses have a board or council that has responsibility for supporting the mission work of the diocese. The Diocese of Canterbury, for instance, has a Board of Mission and according to the diocesan website:

> The Board of Mission is responsible for the Home and Overseas mission activity of the Diocese working through its two committees, Diocesan Evangelism Working Group (DEWG) and the Canterbury World Awareness Group (CWAG). DEWG concentrates with the Diocesan and Children's missioners, on Home Mission at all levels within the Diocese. CWAG deals with the Overseas Mission activity of the diocese, in particular the coordination of the overseas mission agencies and their impact at parish and deanery level.[1]

In addition, most dioceses have appointed diocesan officers with specific responsibility for mission. As indicated above, the Diocese of Canterbury, for example, has a Diocesan Missioner and a Children's Missioner who offer help with preaching, mission weekends, children's holiday clubs, days away, Archbishop's teaching missions, mission events, diocesan missioners and initiatives.[2]

1   http://canterbury.anglican.org/vision/index.htm.
2   http://canterbury.anglican.org/mission/mis.htm.

(d) Mission to children

The reference to the Children's Missioner in the diocese of Canterbury is a pointer to the fact that work with children is a very important part of mission. Traditionally, work with children has taken the form either of special services for children or families or of Sunday School classes held either alongside or separately from the normal church services.

In its heyday, the Sunday School system was an extremely successful form of outreach. It has been calculated that at one stage some 55 per cent of children attended Sunday School. However, changing social patterns, particularly the way in which Sunday has become a day in which children play sport and families go shopping or take part in leisure activities, has meant that the numbers attending Sunday School have suffered an immense decline, and for the same reason it can be difficult to attract non-church children or their families to family or child-oriented services that are held on Sunday.

However, as the 2006 report *Mission-shaped Children* explains, successful mission work with children is still taking place in a whole variety of different ways. In spite of the challenges posed by changed patterns of family life, special Sunday services for children and families still have their place, as does the work of Sunday Schools, but they are being supplemented by a variety of other ways of bringing children into the life of the Church, including worship in church schools, midweek and home groups, toddler groups and buggy services for very young children and their parents or carers, and children's pilgrimages and Christian holidays.

In many ways the biggest challenge in terms of mission to children is getting adult Christians to accept that mission to children is a responsibility of the whole of the church community rather than something that can be devolved to a few children's work leaders or Sunday School teachers.

The conclusion reached by *Mission-shaped Children*, for example, is that:

The number of children and their parents who know the Christian story is still frighteningly low. There is, however, goodwill towards children hearing that story and experiencing worship that was not there ten years ago. Statistics show that churches are reaching large numbers of children through ways apart from Sunday. We must maximize these opportunities and be prepared for changes and surprises along the way. At the same time, those involved in education and liturgical reform need to develop as a matter of urgency forms of worship, including eucharistic worship, for when children are present.

The real battle for children being part of the Church, however, is not about finding workers to lead children's groups or establishing worship that is more accessible, much though they are needed. It is about changing the hearts and minds of adult Christians so that they can share responsibility for the Church's mission among the youngest and most vulnerable generation.[1]

The Church of England has a national strategy for children that provides an overall framework for its mission to them. This strategy is set out in the document *Sharing the Good News with Children*, which was endorsed by General Synod in 2003. This strategy has four key areas:

- Worship and the Nurture of Children
- Children and Evangelism
- Supporting Ministry among Children
- Training for Ministry among Children.

According to this strategy: 'The Church's primary aim for children is their spiritual development: that they should come to worship, know and love God in Word and sacrament and through personal prayer with other Christians, in ways suitable to their age, culture and stage of faith', and the purpose of evangelism among children is to enable them 'to hear the Christian story and discover the Gospel in a way that is appropriate to their age and culture. It will be sowing seeds in neglected ground and entrusting the results to the Lord of the harvest.'[2]

In order to achieve these two objectives the Church of England is committed to developing appropriate forms of support and training for those working with children, whether in a voluntary or a paid capacity.

Implementation of this strategy at the national level is the

---

1   M. Withers, *Mission-shaped Children*, London: Church House Publishing, 2006, pp. 120–1.
2   *Sharing the Good News with Children*, pp. 3, 4.

responsibility of the National Children's Officer, who works within the Division of Education. In addition to the work undertaken at the national level by the National Children's Officer and by the Archbishop's Officer for Evangelism among children, there is also a network of diocesan children's work advisers/children's missioners who support work with children at the diocesan level.

MISSION WORLDWIDE

(a) The history of the Church of England's involvement in worldwide mission

During the Anglo-Saxon period missionaries from the English church were engaged in mission among the peoples of Frisia, what is now northwestern Germany. The earliest of these missionaries was St Wilfrid of Ripon, who spent some months evangelizing in Frisia in 678, but the most important was St Boniface, who began work in Frisia in 718, was made Archbishop of Mainz in 745, and was eventually martyred by hostile pagans in 754. As Moorman comments: 'Boniface left behind him a Church well taught and well led, independent yet orthodox, abounding in monasteries and schools. It was one of the greatest achievements of which the Anglo-Saxon Church could boast.'[1]

It is important to note that the mission undertaken by St Boniface was not a solo effort. It was a missionary outreach supported by the English church. To quote Moorman again:

> Boniface, throughout, kept in close touch with England, writing constant letters to his friends at home who supplied him with books, vestments, ornaments, and, above all, recruits. The close contact between the missionaries in Germany and the Church in England was one of the strongest elements in this great enterprise.[2]

What made the missionary work of St Boniface and others in Germany possible was the fact that there were communication links between England and Frisia across the North Sea. With the

---

1 Moorman, op. cit, p. 36.
2 Ibid., p. 35.

conversion of the peoples of Germany and subsequently Scandinavia to Christianity by the end of the Anglo-Saxon period, missionary areas in which the English church could operate effectively ceased to exist. Asia and North Africa were too far away and America and Australasia were, of course, unknown.

With the opening up of global communications from the end of the fifteenth century onwards this situation changed and the Church of England began to engage in overseas missionary activity once again.

This began to happen once English colonies were established in North America and the West Indies. From the time these colonies were founded there was an awareness of a responsibility to seek to convert the native populations to Christianity. Thus, as W. M. Jacob explains:

> The charter granted by James I in 1606 to the Virginia Company to exploit and develop a new colony on the east coast of North America, included an evangelistic purpose. The hope was expressed that '. . . so noble work may by the Providence of Almighty God hereafter tend to the glory of his Divine Majesty, in propagating of Christian Religion to such people as yet live in darkness and miserable ignorance of the true knowledge and worship of God and may in time bring the infidels and savages (living in those parts) to human civility, and to a settled and quiet government.' For the furtherance of this purpose, a chaplain, chosen on the advice of the Archbishop of Canterbury, accompanied the first group of settlers to Virginia.[1]

A similar awareness of missionary responsibility can be seen in the revisions made to the Book of Common Prayer in 1662. Among these revisions was the provision of service for adult baptism. This was partly intended for those in England who had not been baptized during the period of the Commonwealth, but it was also stated that the service 'may be always useful for the baptising of Natives of our plantations[2] and others converted to the faith'.

Although there was thus a missionary awareness in the Church of England during the seventeenth century it was not until the very

---

1 W. M. Jacob, *The Making of the Anglican Church Worldwide*, London: SPCK, 1997, p. 38.
2 'Plantations' in this context means what we would now call 'colonies'.

end of the century that a systematic attempt was made to support missionary work. In England at the end of the seventeenth century there was a tendency towards forming voluntary societies for religious and social purposes and in 1699 a group of concerned members of the Church of England led by a clergyman called Thomas Bray founded a voluntary society called the Society for the Propagation of Christian Knowledge (SPCK). Their statement of purpose was as follows:

> Whereas the growth of vice and immorality is greatly owing to gross ignorance of the Christian religion, we whose names are underwritten do agree to meet together, as often as we can conveniently, to consult (under the conduct of the Divine Providence and assistance) how we may be able by due and lawful methods to promote Christian knowledge.[1]

The due and lawful methods they decided upon were the provision of missionaries for the English colonies, the publication and circulation of Bibles and other books and the foundation and running of schools.

Soon after the foundation of the SPCK the responsibility for providing missionaries for the colonies was handed over to another society, the Society for the Propagation of the Gospel (SPG). This society, too, was the result of the work of Thomas Bray. In 1701 he persuaded King William III to issue a charter for the foundation of a 'Body Politic and Corporate for the Propagation of the Gospel in Foreign Parts'. Its purpose was to be twofold: to provide for the spiritual needs of the colonists and to evangelize 'the heathen'. The first annual sermon of the Society made its aims clear:

> The design is, in the first place, to settle the state of Religion as well as may be among our own People there, which by all accounts we have, very much wants their pious care; and then to proceed in the best methods they can towards the *Conversion* of the *Natives* . . . This may be a great Charity to the souls of many of those poor Natives who may by this be converted from that state of Barbarism and Idolatry in which they now live, and be brought into the Sheepfold of our blessed Saviour.[2]

---

1 Quoted in S. C. Neill, *Anglicanism*, London: Mowbray, 1977, p. 197.
2 Ibid., p. 198.

In the eighteenth century the SPG worked in the English colonies in North America (until these became independent) and in the West Indies. The plight of the slaves who were being taken to the North American and West Indian colonies also led one of the SPG chaplains, Thomas Thompson, to visit the west coast of Africa. This visit led to three African boys being sent to England for education and one of these, Philip Quaque, was ordained as the first non-European Anglican priest in 1765 and then sent back as a missionary to his own people.

As Stephen Neill records:

> There were difficulties. In England Quaque had entirely forgotten his own language – an early warning of the dangers inherent in Westernization of the leaders in the younger Churches. He had to contend with indifference on the part of the Africans and opposition from the Europeans. But he held on faithfully for more than fifty years until his death in 1816, a solitary light in what was then a very dark land.[1]

The other sphere of overseas mission work in the eighteenth century was India.

The SPG felt that it was the responsibility of the chaplains of the East India Company to undertake work in India and the East India Company in turn discouraged its chaplains from undertaking missionary activity lest this offend the Indians and thus damage trade. As a result it was the SPCK that began Church of England missionary work in India.

Initially, the SPCK supported the work of the Danish Lutheran missionaries in the Danish colony of Tranquebar. Subsequently, it also undertook work in other parts of India, but an inability to recruit clergy from the Church of England meant that it had to employ missionaries in Lutheran orders, the majority of whom were from Germany, although they also employed two Danes and one Swede.

The nineteenth century saw both the SPCK and the SPG continuing their work, with the SPG taking over the SPCK's Indian work in 1829 and beginning to employ Church of England clergy for this purpose. From the end of the eighteenth century

---

1 Ibid., p. 221.

other Church of England missionary societies also came into existence, all of which were voluntary societies along the lines of the SPCK. In order of their foundation, these other societies were:

- The Church Missionary Society (CMS) (1799) (now the Church Mission Society). This was the first Evangelical missionary society. It undertook, and continues to undertake, missionary work around the world. In 1922 theological disagreements within the CMS led to the foundation of the Bible Churchmen's Missionary Society, now known as Crosslinks.

  As well as undertaking missionary work among those who were not Christians, the CMS also sought to provide help to the existing Syrian Malabar Church in the 1820s and 1830s, and the BCMS similarly sought to give assistance to the Coptic Church in Ethiopia from the 1930s onwards.
- The London Society for Promoting Christianity Among the Jews (1809) (now the Church's Mission Among Jewish People (CMJ)). As its name indicates, this Evangelical society was founded to undertake evangelistic work among Jewish people and it still continues this work today.
- The Newfoundland Society for the Education of the Poor (1823) (now the Intercontinental Church Society (ICS)). An Evangelical society founded originally to undertake educational work in Newfoundland, but later expanding its activities to include first educational work and then other forms of missionary activity around the world. Today its focus is on mission in Continental Europe and it works closely with the Diocese in Europe.
- The South American Missionary Society (now the South American Mission Society (SAMS)) (1844). An Evangelical missionary society originally founded to evangelize the native peoples of Patagonia, it now works across South America and also in Spain and Portugal.
- The Universities' Mission to Central Africa (UMCA) (1857). Inspired by the exploits of the explorer David Livingstone, this was a missionary society in the High Church tradition that drew its recruits from the Universities of Oxford and Cambridge and worked in Southern and Central Africa. It merged with the SPG in 1965 to form the United Society for the Propagation of the Gospel (USPG).
- The Cambridge Mission to Delhi (1877). This was another

High Church missionary society. As its name suggests, it recruited from the University of Cambridge and worked in Delhi and the surrounding areas. It worked in partnership with the SPG and subsequently merged with it.

- The Church of England Zenana Missionary Society (1880). This was an Evangelical missionary society for women that undertook mission in India through educational work in the Zenana, the area of an Indian house reserved for women. This society later merged with the CMS.

During the course of the nineteenth century, the work of the missionaries sent out by these societies, together with the work undertaken by the SPG and the SPCK, the worldwide growth of the British Empire and the work of American missionaries sent out by the Episcopal Church of the United States eventually led to the spread of the Anglican version of Christianity across the globe and the emergence of a network of self-governing Anglican churches, each with their own bishops. The missionaries initially led these churches, but the vision of Church of England thinkers such as Henry Venn (the honorary secretary of CMS from 1841–72) was always that this situation would be temporary and that eventually these churches would be 'self-supporting, self-governing and self-extending'.

Although Samuel Crowther became the first African Anglican bishop when he was ordained as Bishop on the Niger in 1864 and Vedanayakam Samuel Azariah became the first native Indian bishop in 1912, it took a long time for this vision to become a reality. In many parts of the world it was not until well after the Second World War that fully indigenous Anglican churches led by local people became a reality.

With the eventual emergence of fully indigenous Anglican churches, the traditional understanding of mission as the Church of England sending out missionaries to other parts of the world began to change. Mission came to be viewed instead as a partnership involving interdependence and mutual responsibility in which churches around the world assisted each other in the task of making Christ known to the whole world.

Thus Resolution 58 of the Lambeth Conference of 1958 called on:

A portrait of Bishop Samuel Adjai Crowther by Ernest Edwards, circa 1864
(National Portrait Gallery, London)

. . . every Church member, clergy and laity alike, to take an active part in the Mission of the Church. It is a Mission to the whole world, not only in area but in all the concerns of mankind. It has no frontiers between 'Home' and 'Foreign' but is concerned to present Christ to people everywhere.

Each generation needs to be evangelised and to this all-important task we summon the people of God in every land.[1]

Thus also Archbishop Michael Ramsey told the Anglican Congress held in Toronto in 1963:

We must plan our mission together and use our resources in the service of a single task. The word 'missionary' will not mean colonialism of any kind but going to one another to help one

1 *The Lambeth Conference 1958*, London: SPCK, 1958, p. 143.

another. Let African and Asian missionaries come to England to help convert the post-Christian heathenism in our country and convert our English church to a closer following of Christ.[1]

The understanding of mission reflected in these two quotations is the view of world mission held by the Church of England today. What it means in practice is that Christians from the Church of England who have particular skills to offer still go to other parts of the world to work as 'mission partners' alongside the local church; Christians from other parts of the world are engaged in mission in this country; Anglican dioceses in different parts of the world are linked together for mutual support, and the Church of England's Partnership for World Mission involves 'Mission Agencies' that work both in England and overseas.

PARTNERSHIP FOR WORLD MISSION

The Partnership for World Mission (PWM), which was established in 1979, is a committee of the Church of England's Mission and Public Affairs Division. It has four main roles:

- to assist the Church of England in furthering partnership in mission within the Anglican Communion;
- to help to coordinate the policies and selected tasks of the Mission Agencies (what were formerly known as the Missionary Societies);
- to support the work of the Diocesan Companion links;
- to help both the dioceses and the General Synod of the Church of England to see more clearly how they can participate in world mission both as part of the Anglican Communion and ecumenically.

The Partnership for World Mission is governed by the PWM panel, which consists of members of the General Synod, representatives of the full PWM Mission Agencies and its Associate

---

1 Archbishop Michael Ramsey, quoted in T. Yates, 'Anglicans and Mission', in S. Sykes and J. Booty (eds), *The Study of Anglicanism*, London and Minneapolis: SPCK/Fortress Press, 1988, pp. 438–9.

Members, representatives of the Diocesan Companion Links and representatives of the Church of England's ecumenical partners.

There are 11 full PWM Mission Agencies. Eight of these have been mentioned already. These are the Church Army, the Church's Ministry Among Jewish People, the Church Mission Society, Crosslinks, the Intercontinental Church Society, the South American Mission Society, the Society for Promoting Christian Knowledge, and the United Society for the Propagation of the Gospel. The other three are the Church Pastoral Aid Society (an Evangelical society founded in 1836 which supports and resources the mission of the Church in England), the Mission to Seafarers (a society founded in 1835 which aims to meet the practical and spiritual needs of seafarers and which has a network of chaplains, lay staff and volunteers in 300 ports around the world) and the Mothers Union (a society founded in 1876 which aims to 'support and preserve family life through Christianity' and which now has more than a million members in Mothers Union branches in 70 countries across the globe).

There are also over twenty Associate Members of the Partnership for World Mission. Examples of Associate Members are the Borneo Mission Association, which supports the work of the Anglican dioceses of Kuching and Sabah, the Fellowship of the Maple Leaf, which promotes links between the Churches in Canada and Great Britain, and Sharing of Ministries Abroad (SOMA), which seeks 'to assist in the renewal of the Anglican Communion world-wide through the renewing power of the Holy Spirit by sending teams of clergy and lay people on short term mission in the developing world'.[1]

DIOCESAN COMPANION LINKS

According to the Partnership for World Mission website:

> Diocesan Companion Links began in the mid 1950s. Dioceses in the United States began to form Links with dioceses in other parts of the Anglican Communion as a means of providing personal connections and human faces to a rapidly growing

---

1 www.pwm-web.org.uk/associates. This link also gives a full list of the PWM Associate Members.

communion of Christians. It was a time when Churches founded by the mission boards and agencies of the Church of England and the American Episcopal Church were becoming independent.

Diocesan Links expanded rapidly from the 1960s. A particular impetus was the 1963 Anglican Communion Congress in Toronto, which called for greater mutual responsibility and interdependence (MRI) within the Communion. It encouraged Churches across the Communion to identify their needs and resources and for Churches elsewhere in the Communion both to offer and to ask for help. Dioceses identified projects to which other dioceses initially contributed financial help and connections began to be made.

It was soon discovered that just giving to projects was not enough. If true mutuality in mission was to develop then there needed to be face-to-face contact and sharing. Focusing on money distorted the relationship. It did not allow the sharing of other gifts from God – hospitality, work for justice, generosity, evangelism, experience of poverty, spirituality and much more. So the Partners in Mission (PiM) programme developed to encourage genuine two-way partnership and sharing in the gospel.[1]

The first diocesan companion link was founded in 1963. Today all the dioceses of the Church of England have some form of links with churches, provinces or dioceses around the world.[2] The nature of these links varies in each case and, although the majority of links are within the Anglican Communion, there are an increasing number of ecumenical links with churches from other Christian traditions, indicating the way in which partnership in mission is increasingly being seen in a wider ecumenical perspective.

Three examples illustrate the links that exist today:

- The Diocese of Carlisle has links with the dioceses of Madras in the Church of South India, Zululand in the Church of the Province of South Africa, Northern Argentina in the Anglican

---

1   www.pwm-web.org.uk/guidelines.
2   In the case of the Diocese in Europe it is the North West Europe Archdeaconry that has the link.

Church of the Southern Cone of America, and Stavanger in the Church of Norway.

● The Diocese of Salisbury has links with the Episcopal Church of the Sudan, the Roman Catholic Diocese of Evreux in France and the Evangelical Lutheran Church of Latvia.

● The Diocese of Winchester has links with the Provinces of Uganda, Rwanda, Burundi, Congo and Myanmar.

FOR FURTHER READING

Avis, P., *A Ministry Shaped by Mission*, London: T&T Clark, 2005.

Jacob, W. M., *The Making of the Anglican Church Worldwide*, London: SPCK, 1997

'Mission and Evangelism', www.cofe.anglican.org/faith/mission/mission and evangelism.

Mission-shaped Church, London: Church House Publishing, 2004.

Neill, S. C., *Anglicanism*, 4th edn, London: Mowbray, 1993.

Osmaston, A. and A. White, 'Sharing our Faith in the World', in I. Bunting (ed.), *Celebrating the Anglican Way*, London: Hodder & Stoughton, 1996.

Withers, M., *Mission-shaped Children*, London: Church House Publishing, 2006.

Yates, T., 'Anglicans and Mission', in S. Sykes and J. Booty (eds), *The Study of Anglicanism*, London and Minneapolis: SPCK/Fortress Press, 1998.

Index

Pictures and diagrams are given in *italics*.